BLACKSTONE'S
LAW
QUESTIONS
& ANSWERS

CONSTITUTIONAL AND ADMINISTRATIVE LAW

D1823792

Questions and Answers Series

Series Editors   Margaret Wilkie and Rosalind Malcolm

Titles in the Series

Other titles in preparation

BLACKSTONE'S LAW QUESTIONS & ANSWERS

CONSTITUTIONAL & ADMINISTRATIVE LAW

RICHARD CLEMENTS
LLB (University of Sheffield), LLM (University of London)

JANE KAY
LLB, LLM (University of Birmingham), MA (Brunel University)

BLACKSTONE
PRESS LIMITED

First published in Great Britain 1997 by Blackstone Press Limited, 9-15 Aldine Street, London W12 8AW. Telephone: 0181-740 2277

ISBN: 1 85431 539 0

British Library Cataloguing in Publication Data
A CIP catalogue record for this book is available from the British Library

Typeset by Montage Studios Limited, Tonbridge, Kent
Printed by Bell & Bain Limited, Glasgow

Contents

Preface

The ideas on which the questions and answers in this book are based have been accumulated over many years of teaching and lecturing. Our thanks are due to many colleagues and students with whom we have shared ideas, and especially to those students whose errors have revealed the kind of assistance students need when grappling with this subject.

We would be grateful to receive any comments about this book and even more grateful for notification of any errors.

Richard Clements
Jane Kay
April 1997

Table of Cases

Table of Statutes

1 Introduction

The two authors have a long and varied experience of teaching constitutional and administrative law and related subjects at different universities and colleges. We think that this enables us to give some guidance and advice on how to approach this subject and tackle typical questions. What we do not claim to do is to give you the answer to every possible question that might be asked.

Constitutional law is different from the other compulsory law subjects in that it is very wide ranging. Much of it is not really law at all and therefore calls for different skills in the student. To understand constitutional law properly it helps to have some knowledge, or at least an interest in current affairs and politics. Students often think that it is unfair to expect them to know things that are not in the text book or were not in the lecture but there is no point in complaining. The reason that constitutional law is a compulsory subject is because you should know about what is happening in the world around you. So take an interest even if it is only for the period of study of constitutional law.

With this subject there is often no right answer: all there might be is a difference of opinion. So you need to read a lot to see those different views. There is also no written constitution so the syllabus is very wide ranging. Lecturers will differ on what they want students to study. We have tried to take the most typical subjects for this book. Be warned, however, your lecturer may have a slightly different syllabus in mind. If you go to lectures and, particularly, seminars you can normally get a good idea of what are the most important topics. If you study past examination papers at your institution you should be able to work out the most likely topics, the usual style of questions and, if you are fortunate, you may be able to identify questions that come up often, albeit in slightly different forms.

Essays in this subject often cause students problems. It is possible to ask the same question in many different ways. Often the same sort of basic material of cases, opinions and examples can be 'recycled' to answer several different questions. You need to combine the use of this material with powers of organisation and argument. These can be practised. Plan in advance roughly what you would do when faced with several varieties of the same sort of question. The examples we give in the book are meant to help here. You do not have to agree with our arguments or conclusions and indeed we would not want you to copy them word for word. Try to look at the material used and how the argument is structured and then you should be able to do it for yourself.

Read essay questions carefully, they can often be misunderstood. Identify the main topic first. Do not, as one author once did, mistake a question on Crown privilege for one on the royal prerogative! They are not at all the same thing. Often rather dense and obscure quotations are used, followed by 'Discuss'. Do not worry if you have never seen the quotation before, never heard of the author and do not understand it. Once you have identified the area, try to work out the main ideas involved and then try to talk about them. A question like the following might seem intimidating, but in reality it is not hard.

> The short explanation of the constitutional conventions is that they provide the flesh which clothes the dry bones of the law; they make the legal constitution work; they keep it in touch with the growth of ideas.

> Sir Ivor Jennings.

Discuss

It is obviously about constitutional conventions! It indicates that only a small part of the constitution is law, 'the dry bones', much of it is convention. They are 'dry bones', because if we only looked at the law we would get a very misleading impression of the constitution. Without conventions the constitution would be unworkable. The student could give examples. 'The growth of ideas' bit indicates that conventions are flexible and change as politics and society change. Again, give examples!

Many students find problem questions in constitutional and administrative law a bit easier. Again the first thing to do is to identify the main topics that the problem focuses upon. Be warned: it is possible to 'disguise' areas quite easily in this subject. Then you identify the main legal points raised. They should often trigger cases in your memory. Do not worry if you cannot remember the exact name, still include them in your answer.

Whether you are writing an essay or a problem answer it is always best to do a rough plan first, listing the main points that you intend to cover. For a problem you might also include a list of the main cases. For an essay you would need not just cases, but authors' opinions and examples.

If you have done some work and have some basic knowledge there is nothing of which to be frightened. It does not matter if you are not sure that you have the right answer. In this subject there usually is no right answer.

Some students are concerned about whether they can express strong political views. Two points can be made. First it depends upon whether the question is asking for a fairly factual account or is asking for a view. A public order problem on the Criminal Justice and Public Order Act 1994 is asking you to apply the law to the facts supplied. An essay on the same area might ask you to express an opinion on whether this is a good or bad piece of legislation. Secondly, when putting forward a point of view you must have a proper argument supported by evidence. If you are asked about reform of the House of Lords you should not say that they are a lot of senile old fools who should be shot. You could instead argue that it is an unelected body, unrepresentative, has an elderly membership, has a permanent Conservative majority, lacks any real power and would be better abolished.

As in all legal subjects there are not any real short cuts to success but we hope that this book can convince you that constitutional and administrative law is not quite as intimidating as you thought.

2   The Nature and Sources of Constitutional Law

INTRODUCTION

For many this is the most difficult area of the whole subject. It is rather
theoretical and seems to have no beginning and no end. Different lecturers have
very different approaches in this area. Some like to include a lot of political
theory and others do not.

There is a fairly traditional set of issues that have been considered relevant to
'the nature of the British constitution'. For reasons of space this book has
restricted itself to them. We hope, though, that the techniques indicated in the
Suggested Answers could be applied to other constitutional questions. These
questions might be general, such as, what is democracy?, is Britain democratic?, what is the nature of the state?, explain limited government and the
concept of legitimacy? More specific issues such as federation or the Citizens'
Charter might also be investigated. In some respects these are just more modern
ways of asking the old questions like, what is the rule of law?, does a separation
of powers control the executive? Often the same sort of material, e.g., cases,
past political incidents, academic opinion crops up whatever the question being
asked. For example, a famous case like *Council of Civil Service Unions* v
Minister for the Civil Service [1985] AC 374 could be used to illustrate
arguments relating to convention, the rule of law, the separation of powers, the
lack of a written Bill of Rights as well as the attitudes of the courts to the state
and the unlimited power of the government.

A good starting point is, why do we or any country have a constitution at all?
The obvious answers are: first, to limit the power of the government so that it

cannot do whatever it likes; secondly, to protect the rights or liberties of the individual not just from the government, but also from other powerful groups; and a third less obvious reason is legitimacy. Why do we, the people, accept that this particular group of people is entitled to govern us and make laws? This is often a function of a written constitution: such documents often say that the people of the country have decided upon these particular constitutional arrangements. For example, 'We the People of the United States ... do ordain and establish this constitution for the United States of America.'

Britain is different: it is one of the few countries in the world without a written constitution. Most British constitutional writing would claim that, despite this, Britain does have a constitution. Some critics, however, dating back to Thomas Paine in the eighteenth century (*The Rights of Man*) and continuing into modern times (e.g., F. F. Ridley, 'There is no British Constitution: A Dangerous Case of the Emperor's Clothes,' 41 *Parliamentary Affairs* (1988)) claim that Britain's arrangements are so defective that there is no constitution at all as none of the three aims listed in the previous paragraph has been achieved.

The traditional view is that Britain does have a constitution, but it can be found elsewhere than a single written document (e.g., A. V. Dicey; *The Law and the Constitution*, Sir Ivor Jennings). It can be found in Acts of Parliament and cases, but unlike a written constitution, both can be changed and have no special protection. This flexibility and evolution is supposed to be the advantage of the British constitution.

Much of the constitution does not exist in any legal form at all. Conventions, in other words, customs, habits or understandings, are said to fill the gaps. Vitally important matters like the existence of the Prime Minister and the real powers of the Queen are governed by convention.

This is still not enough, so it has been argued that there are sets of beliefs upheld by people like politicians, judges and sometimes even the people, which restrain the government from doing exactly what it pleases. Traditional examples would be the rule of law and the separation of powers. More modern equivalents would be constitutionalism and legitimacy. The problem with beliefs is that it is hard to pin down exactly what they are. Each person has their own ideas.

We hope that the questions and suggested answers in this chapter will help you to a better understanding of these issues.

QUESTION 1

'In so far as Dicey's general statement of the rule of law may be taken to involve the existence in the English constitution of certain principles almost amounting to fundamental laws, his doctrine is logically inconsistent with the legislative supremacy of Parliament.' O. Hood Phillips, *Constitutional and Administrative Law*.

Discuss.

Commentary

Students often dislike answering questions on the rule of law because it seems too vague. Lots of different ideas and theories are identified as the rule of law, which is what causes the confusion. The student must be familiar with at least some of these theories, be able to criticise them and compare them. A good starting point is Dicey's version of the rule of law. It should be mentioned in any question on the rule of law even if, unlike in our question, it is not specifically mentioned. Students should also be able to discuss at least one other theory of the rule of law.

Suggested Answer

The idea of the rule of law was not invented by Dicey, but he popularised it in the late nineteenth century. His book, *Introduction to the Study of the Law of the Constitution* (1885) can be seen as a strong defence of the English constitution when compared with the constitutions of other countries, particularly those with written constitutions. De Smith states that, 'His ideas ... were very influential for two generations; today they no longer warrant detailed analysis' (*Constitutional and Administrative Law*, 1994). It is true that Dicey's ideas went out of fashion for a time, but they have now come back into favour, particularly with senior members of the judiciary. So, once again, they require detailed analysis.

It is often said that Britain has an 'unwritten constitution', meaning that it is not contained in one document and much of it has no formal legal status. Dicey argued that not only did this not matter, but in fact it was a positive advantage. In Britain there was a long tradition of respect for individual liberty and democracy. This tradition was upheld in our constitutional arrangements. For short it could be called the rule of law. Dicey summarised it under three main principles.

His first principle concerned the rule of law and discretionary powers. No person could be punished or interfered with by the authorities unless the law authorised it. Put another way, all government actions must be authorised by the law. This contrasted the situation in England with a country where there were no rules. In the latter, the government could do as it pleased and there would be no legal controls over its activities. Examples would be imprisonment when someone had broken no law, or the lack of any trial before punishment.

Dicey also felt that governments should not possess wide discretionary powers. The classic example of these ideas was *Entick* v *Carrington* (1765) 19 St Tr 1030 where the courts declared that the Secretary of State could not order the search of Entick's house, because there was no law that authorised such searches. The court would not accept arguments of 'state necessity' or that there was one law for government activities and another for ordinary people.

Dicey's second principle has the resounding title of 'equality before the law'. This held that the government and its officials should not have any special exemptions or protections from the law. He did not like the French system where government activities were dealt with by separate administrative courts. These he considered to be too partial to the government and inferior to ordinary courts of law.

The final principle concerns individual rights. The English constitution respects personal liberty. There is no need for a Bill of Rights because civil liberties are respected anyway. The courts protect them in their decisions by developing the common law in a way that respects individual liberty. Parliament legislates on particular problems. In contrast, Bills of Rights are documents which promise all sorts of rights. These promises are so general and capable of so many meanings that they are meaningless. Again the Bill of Rights might not be respected by the government and might be unenforceable.

Dicey's theory is open to many objections. Some might say that these ideas are so vague and wide ranging that they have no real meaning. As de Smith states: 'The concept is one of open texture; it lends itself to an extremely wide range of interpretations.' He also said: '... everyone who tries to redefine it begins with the assumption that it is a good thing, like justice or courage'. Some might say that his theory is so obvious that it is not worth stating it. Of course the government must obey the law and the courts enforce it in a modern constitutional system. R. F. V. Heuston ('The Rule of Law' from *Essays in Constitutional Law*, 1964) claims that Dicey misunderstood French administrative courts. They are not biased in favour of the government and they do at least as well, if not better, in controlling the government as the English courts. Separate 'public law' or 'constitutional' courts are the normal arrangement in continental Europe. E. Barendt ([1985] *Public Law* 596) argues that Dicey also misunderstood the nature of written constitutions. Although in 1885 Bills of Rights might just have been pious declarations that no one could enforce, nowadays most countries that have them possess sophisticated enforcement mechanisms.

The main criticism of the rule of law is that it fails to deal with the supremacy of Parliament. If Parliament legislates in a way that is contrary to the rule of law, it is still the law and there is nothing that the courts can do about it. Statutes can annul inconvenient court decisions. For instance, the War Damage Act 1965 reversed *Burmah Oil* v *Lord Advocate* [1965] AC 75, where the House of Lords ordered the government to pay compensation to Burmah Oil for the wartime destruction of its oil installations. Statutes also grant government officials some immunities from legal action, e.g., the Crown Proceedings Act 1947. Some Acts of Parliament grant the government wide and uncontrolled discretionary powers, e.g., the Deregulation and Contracting Out Act 1994. Dicey claimed that Parliament would protect our liberties and restrain the government. Perhaps that was true in 1885, but nowadays the government of the day controls Parliament through its majority and can nearly always get its own way.

The key element of Dicey's rule of law was that the government must possess clearly defined legal powers to authorise its actions. Under the unwritten English constitution it is in fact difficult to be precise about the legal powers that the government possesses. Prerogative powers still exist and it can be difficult to identify those powers accurately. For instance in *R* v *Home Secretary ex parte Northumbria Police Authority* [1988] 1 All ER 556 the court accepted the existence of a prerogative power, to maintain peace in the realm, which had not previously been identified. Again much of the constitution is convention, not law, for example, the powers of the Prime Minister. As they are not law, the courts cannot control these powers. Indeed there must be some doubts about whether the courts are always keen to ensure that the government keeps within its legal powers. In *Malone* v *Metropolitan Police Commissioner* [1979] Ch 344, Malone's telephone had been tapped by the police. He claimed that there was no law that authorised telephone tapping. These facts have strong similarities to the classic rule of law case, *Entick* v *Carrington* (1765). However, in *Malone* the judge came to the opposite conclusion. No law forbade telephone tapping by the police, therefore it must be legal.

Despite these criticisms, the rule of law still has its defenders. T. R. S. Allan ([1985] *Cambridge Law Journal* 111) stressed that Parliament still has a controlling effect on the government, particularly as it is elected by the people. The government does not always get its way in Parliament and although Parliament can be persuaded to change the law in a way favourable to the government, until that has happened the government must obey the existing law. Judges will ensure that they do. Judges can also minimise the effects of 'unjust' laws by using techniques of statutory interpretation.

Perhaps Dicey never intended his rule of law as an accurate description of the 'English Constitution'. Perhaps he was just trying to say that this is the way it should be, not the way it actually was. These were the ideals that government, administrators and judges should endeavour to uphold.

The rule of law has recently attracted the attention of many senior judges. In *M v Home Office* [1994] 1 AC 377 the House of Lords confirmed the rule of law in its basic meaning. The government must obey the law. It had no immunity from court orders and government ministers were liable for contempt.

More significantly the courts are now showing a keen interest in the rule of law in its wider sense. In *Bennett v Horseferry Road Magistrates* [1993] 3 All ER 138, the defendant had been illegally abducted from South Africa to stand trial in England. Despite the fact that no English laws had been broken, the House of Lords threw the case out on the grounds that it would be an abuse of fair procedure to try Bennett. The courts would not turn a blind eye to the authorities' involvement in law-breaking.

In a series of articles, senior judges have insisted that they should enforce respect for fundamental principles of human rights, which, as Dicey said, are part of our 'unwritten constitution', although Dicey would have called them civil liberties. The principles of human rights could be drawn from the European Convention on Human Rights. Lord Woolf ([1995] *Public Law* 57) stated that judicial review went far beyond merely confining the government to the words of a statute. The courts could often insist that the government did not use its powers unfairly and unreasonably. He suggested that if Parliament tried to prevent judges judicially reviewing in this way, the courts might ignore that Act of Parliament. An independent judiciary was an essential part of the rule of law. Laws J has further suggested ([1993] *Public Law* 59 and [1995] *Public Law* 72) that judicial review should be used to protect fundamental rights and freedoms and to ensure respect for fundamental principles of democracy. He hints that parliamentary supremacy should not stand in the courts' way. Several judges are willing to question government actions if they do not conform to fundamental principles of human rights, e.g., Sedley J in *R v Secretary of State ex parte McQuillan* [1995] 4 All ER 400 and Simon Brown LJ in *R v Ministry of Defence ex parte Smith* [1995] 4 All ER 427.

The greatest problem with the rule of law, as defined by Dicey, is that it gives no protection if Parliament legislates in an unfair or unjust way. He would probably have said that it was most unlikely that Parliament would do this. Our legislators respect the rule of law and would rarely, if ever, enact laws that contradicted basic standards of justice. What some judges are saying now is that if Parliament was to do such a thing they might be willing to disregard an Act of Parliament. This would truly be a revolution in our constitution.

QUESTION 2

In a variety of important ways, ideas of the separation of powers have shaped constitutional arrangements and influenced our constitutional thinking, and continue to do so. The separation in the British constitution, although not absolute, ought not to be lightly dismissed. Colin Munro, *Studies in Constitutional Law*.

Commentary

Questions on the separation of powers are somewhat easier to approach than questions on other constitutional theories like the rule of law. At least the separation of powers has a clearly defined meaning.

Our example is a pretty typical question on this subject. To answer the candidate must be able to explain the theory of the separation of powers and perhaps give an example of a constitution based on those principles, such as the USA or France. Then it is necessary to show how the UK's constitution does not conform to the theory. The difficulty in questions on separation is in what the question asks you to do next. You might be asked to criticise the UK constitution for its lack of separation. Alternatively, you might be asked to do the opposite and argue that there is a type of separation of powers in the UK constitution.

Our question is of the second kind. Students should, however, realise that the same basic material can be deployed to answer either type of question.

Suggested Answer

Munro is suggesting that the separation of powers in its classic form does not exist in the UK constitution and yet it still has an importance. It is best to start by exploring the classic definition of the separation of powers and then seeing how it applies to the UK constitution.

In 1748 a French author, Montesquieu, who had been in exile in England, wrote his book, *De L'Esprit des Lois*. In it he put forward his theory of the separation of powers, which was influenced by what he had seen of the British system of government. It was not merely a description of the British system though, but an idealised picture of a government system. The idea of the separation of powers was not novel to Montesquieu, but is an ancient idea traceable back to Aristotle. Very simply, to prevent the abuse of power, government power should not be left completely in the hands of one person or body. It should be divided or separated in some way. It could be said that the ancient composition of Parliament, consisting of the King, Lords and Commons reflects these ideas. Montesquieu went further and identified three major functions of government. These were the legislative or law- making function: the executive, or law-applying function and the judicial, or law-enforcing function. 'There would be an end to everything if the same man, or the same body ... were to exercise those three powers', as Montesquieu put it. The three functions should be kept separate in two ways. Different persons or bodies should exercise each power. One branch of government should not exercise the power of another, e.g., the executive should not legislate.

Complete separation would probably be unworkable as a system of government. Montesquieu realised this and accepted some overlapping: 'neither should exercise the *whole* power of the other branch of government'. For instance the executive should be able to veto legislation and decide when a new legislature should be elected. In fact Montesquieu's theory was derived from his observation of Britain's constitution: the executive was the King and his ministers, who in those days were separate from Parliament.

Montesquieu's theories were popular and were incorporated into several written constitutions such as those of France and the United States of America. The clearest example is the US Constitution. Article 1 of the constitution (1787) states that the legislative power shall belong to Congress. Congress is elected separately from the President and may turn out not to be of the same political persuasion. Article 2 states that the executive power belongs to the President. The President and his advisers are not permitted to be members of the Congress.

Lastly, Article 3 declares that the judicial power belongs to the Supreme Court and such inferior courts as may be created. Much of US constitutional law revolves around keeping the three powers separate. In *Myers* v *US* 272 US 52 (1926) the Supreme Court held that only the President, as Chief Executive, could remove a Postmaster, another member of the executive, from office. The Senate, part of the legislature, could not be involved.

Another feature of the US constitution is an intricate set of 'checks and balances' between the three branches of government, much as Montesquieu described. The President may veto legislation, but he needs the support of a third of either House of Congress to do this. The President may also negotiate treaties, but two thirds of the Senate must ratify them. The President appoints the judges of the Supreme Court, but the Senate must approve the appointment. Even in a system like this, conventions and judicial decisions may modify the constitution, as in Britain. The President may make 'executive agreements' instead of treaties to avoid the need for Senate ratification. The Supreme Court has ruled that it has the power to compare legislation with the written constitution and declare it void: *Marbury* v *Madison* 1 Cranch (5 US) 137 (1803).

The United Kingdom has not recently had a revolution and its constitutional arrangements have a very different history. The medieval King's 'Curia Regis' controlled all three functions, so it is hardly surprising that the British constitution tends to mingle the three powers. In particular, as Bagehot said, the 'efficient secret' of the constitution was 'the close union, the nearly complete fusion, of the legislative and executive powers'. The executive can be identified as, nowadays, the Prime Minister, the Cabinet and other ministers. By convention, they must be members of either the House of Commons or the House of Lords. Therefore the executive are members of the legislature as well. This is a complete contradiction of the separation of powers. Critics of the UK constitution would say that this is the main problem. The government has a majority and therefore its executive dominates the legislature. Lord Hailsham described this as an 'elective dictatorship' (*The Dilemma of Democracy*).

The judges, by and large, form a separate body, but even here there is incomplete separation. The Lords of Appeal in Ordinary, the Lord Chief Justice and the Master of the Rolls all sit in the House of Lords when it acts as a legislature. The executive, in the form of the Lord Chancellor and Prime Minister, appoints the judges. The Lord Chancellor spans all three government functions. He acts as Speaker of the House of Lords, when it sits as a legislature: he is a member of the Cabinet, controlling an important government department and he also sits as a judge in the House of Lords.

Traditionally it has been pointed out that these constitutional arrangements do not in fact, lead to tyranny. There are 'checks and balances'. The executive is accountable to the legislature, government ministers must explain and justify their actions to the Commons and to a lesser extent the Lords. The independence of the judiciary is fiercely protected, not least by the judiciary themselves. The executive may appoint judges, but by convention party politics does not influence the choice. Even J. A. G. Griffith in his book, *The Politics of the Judiciary* could find no evidence, in recent times, of party influencing selection. Once appointed, judges can decide a case in any way that they want. The executive cannot dismiss them. It takes an address of both Houses of Parliament to do this (originally the Act of Settlement 1700, now s. 11(3), Supreme Court Act 1981). Writers such as Munro have tried to explain these types of restraint as a distinctively British version of the separation of powers. Many judges have explored such views.

If we examine the relationship between the executive and the legislature it can be seen that the executive does not always completely dominate. The government may only have a small majority or it may be uncertain of the loyalty of its own MPs. In 1995 and 1996, both factors limited the freedom of action of the executive of which John Major was the Prime Minister. Parliament, the legislature, has a whole series of mechanisms to obtain information from the executive and hold it to account. They include the annual Finance Bill, the Estimates and the Public Accounts Committee which all look at vital government finance. Questions, both oral and written, Select Committees and debates all try to obtain information and criticise the executive. The executive is always heavily outnumbered in the legislature. Out of 651 MPs, the House of Commons Disqualification Act 1975 only allows 95 to receive a ministerial salary.

The relationship between the legislature and the judiciary is fairly clear. Ever since the Glorious Revolution of 1689 and the Bill of Rights, the judiciary have accepted the supremacy of Parliament. They cannot question the validity of an Act of Parliament. To do so meant drawing the judges into political controversy, for they would be seen as 'taking sides' on a political matter. This would compromise their independence. For example, in *Duport Steel v Sirs* [1980] 1 All ER 529 at 541, Lord Diplock upheld the immunity of trade unions from being sued in tort:

> At a time when more and more cases involve the application of legislation which gives effect to policies that are the subject of bitter public and parliamentary controversy, it cannot be too strongly emphasised that the

British Constitution though largely unwritten, is firmly based on the separation of powers: Parliament makes the laws, the judiciary interpret them.

The judiciary have taken their views further than just refusing to question Acts of Parliament. They, generally, will not intervene in any matter before Parliament, particularly if Parliament has voted to approve it. In *R* v *Environment Secretary ex parte Notts CC* [1986] AC 240 the House of Lords declined a judicial review of the Secretary of State's decision on rate support grants, as it had been approved by Parliament. In Lord Scarman's view it was a matter of 'political judgment' by the executive, which was accountable to the legislature. The separation of powers meant that the courts should be slow to intervene in such matters. Probably what Lords Diplock and Scarman meant was that there were some issues best left to Parliament and some best left to the courts.

This judicial thinking can also be seen in the relationship between the executive and the judiciary. The courts may use their powers of judicial review if they consider that the executive has gone beyond the powers granted to it by the legislature. In recent years the courts have been more adventurous in controlling the executive. In *M* v *Home Office* [1994] 1 AC 377, the House of Lords held that a government minister could be in contempt of court. In *CCSU* v *Minister for the Civil Service* [1985] AC 374 it was held that the courts could also question the use of prerogative powers. Yet again, though, a kind of separation of powers is maintained: some matters are for the judge, some for the minister. Senior judges, e.g., Bingham LCJ in 1997, are quick to condemn what they see as 'interference' by the Home Secretary in their sentencing function. In contrast matters of defence and national security are generally left to the executive. In *Chandler* v *DPP* [1964] AC 763, the House of Lords decided that the disposition of the armed forces was a matter for the executive and could not be questioned. Similarly, in the infamous *Liversidge* v *Anderson* [1942] AC 206 the House of Lords declined to question the Home Secretary's decision to detain a man whom he had 'reasonable cause to believe' had hostile associations. Viscount Maughan revealed his understanding of the subtle constitutional relationships in the UK, when he noted that the Home Secretary was accountable to the Commons for his decision.

Recently, the relationship has changed. Perhaps because the judges are concerned about excessive executive power, or maybe because they feel that sometimes the label has been abused, they have begun to question claims that 'national security' is threatened. This can be seen in both *CCSU* v *Minister for*

Civil Service (1985) and in cases like *R* v *Judith Ward* [1993] 2 All ER 577. Defenders of the 'unwritten constitution' would say that therein lies its strength: the executive, the legislature and the judiciary are constantly adjusting their positions relative to each other as the political background changes.

Munro is correct, up to a point. There is a separation of powers in the British constitution or at least judges believe that there is. Unfortunately it does not conform to the classic Montesquieu theory. The executive is fused with the legislature and has too much power over it. Although the judiciary can control the executive they cannot control the legislature. They cannot question an Act of Parliament.

QUESTION 3

The main purpose of constitutional conventions is to ensure that the legal framework of the Constitution will be operated in accordance with the prevailing constitutional values or principles of the period. *Re Amendment of the Constitution of Canada* [1982] 125 DLR (3d)1.

Discuss

Commentary

Nineteenth century writers like A. V. Dicey and early twentieth century ones like Sir Ivor Jennings stressed the importance of conventions in the UK constitution. Probably they over-stressed their importance and constitutional writers looked for conventions which did not really exist, e.g., in the area of ministerial responsibility. There was a reaction in the 1960s and some writers asserted that there were no such things as conventions. Opinion has now swung back again, as in *Re Canada* (1982). Conventions definitely exist and are important. Their limitations must be understood though. That is what the essay title is about. Other quotations could be used but all questions tend to call for the same basic response: what are conventions, how do they differ from the law, how do they change and how can they be enforced? The student is usually expected to be critical and to give examples.

Suggested Answer

In all constitutions, even those that are written, like that of Canada, various practices or ways of doing things that are not strictly provided for in the constitution grow up over the years. These practices can harden and become the accepted way of doing things. Then they can be called conventions. In *Re Canada* (1982), although the written Canadian constitution did not require it, it was the convention that the consent of the Canadian provinces had to be obtained before changes were made to the constitution. In the UK, a country without a written constitution, conventions are particularly important.

In the late nineteenth century the famous constitutional writer, A. V. Dicey, drew attention to the role of conventions in the UK. He believed that most of the UK constitution and many of its most important parts consisted of conventions. This did not mean that there were no rules, merely that a lot of the rules were not legal ones. As he put it in, *An Introduction to the Study of the Law of the Constitution*:

> The other set of rules consist of conventions, understandings, habits or practices which, though they may regulate the conduct of several members of the sovereign power, of the Ministers, or of other officials, are not in reality laws at all since they are not enforced by the courts. This portion of constitutional law may, for the sake of distinction, be termed 'the conventions of the constitution', or constitutional morality.

If we only look at the legal rules of the constitution we gain a seriously misleading impression. Legally, the Queen may refuse the Royal Assent to a parliamentary Bill. By convention she always agrees, taking the advice of Her Majesty's government. Legally, the Queen chooses the Prime Minister, but by convention it is always the person who can command a majority in the House of Commons. Legally the Queen chooses her own ministers, but by convention they are chosen by the Prime Minister.

Conventions are clearly not the law because, as in the above examples, they sometimes contradict the strict legal position. The courts take judicial notice of the existence of conventions and sometimes they can even influence their decisions, but the courts cannot enforce conventions because they are not law. In *Attorney-General* v *Jonathan Cape* [1976] QB 752 there is an interesting discussion of the various conventions relating to Cabinet secrecy, but the court cannot enforce them, only the law, which was breach of confidence in that case. In *Madzimbamuto* v *Lardner-Burke* [1969] AC 645 the court observed that there was a convention that the UK would not legislate for Rhodesia without that colony's consent. This could not stop the UK Parliament from legislating in breach of the convention if it chose.

There are many examples of convention. It is probably impossible to make a complete list. The office of Prime Minister and the existence of the Cabinet are conventional only. Ministers are accountable to Parliament and responsible for the actions of their civil servants. There are detailed 'rules' governing things like gifts to ministers and their financial interests, which have been written down in a booklet, *Code of Conduct for Ministers*. Parliament meets every year, but the Bill of Rights 1689 only says that it should meet 'frequently'.

The problem with all these conventions is that it is hard to decide which ones definitely exist and which are just everyday politics. Sir Ivor Jennings recommended a three stage test in, *The Law and the Constitution*. First, we must look for the precedents, how often and how consistently has this practice been observed before? Secondly, did the actors in the precedent believe that they were bound by the rule? In other words, did they believe that they had some sort of obligation to follow the precedent? Thirdly, there must be a reason for the rule. In other words, the convention must fit in with our general ideas of the constitution like democracy, accountability etc. This test works well with some of the major conventions. We know that the Queen always gives the Royal Assent because there are thousands of examples of her doing so. A Monarch has not refused since 1708 to give the Royal Assent. It seems clear that she feels that she has no choice in the matter. The reason is that a hereditary Monarch should abide by the wishes of the democratic government. With other proposed conventions such as when a minister should resign this test does not work so well. This gives rise to many doubts about conventions generally.

Conventions are continually changing. Up until 1902 a Prime Minister could come from the House of Lords. Since then they have always come from the Commons. Up until 1992 a new Speaker came from the governing party. In that year Labour's Betty Boothroyd was elected. This evolution leads to uncertainty. Although we can say what happened last time a situation occurred, we cannot be absolutely certain that the precedent will be followed next time. As an editorial in *Public Law* in 1963, pp. 401–2, put it: 'so let us delete those pages in constitutional text books headed conventions, and talk about what happens and why what happened yesterday may not happen tomorrow'.

Conventions are called rules but they do not look much like rules. They are often vague and imprecise. No body deliberately creates them, unlike an Act of Parliament. It is not necessary for a court to rule upon whether they exist or not. In many cases, despite the efforts of writers like Jennings, it is hard to say whether conventions exist or not.

A major problem with convention is that there seems to be no sanction if a convention is broken. If they are rules of a constitution it seems strange that there can be no enforcement. A government minister might lie to Parliament, in clear breach of convention, but it does not necessarily mean that he has to resign. The major apologists for conventions had their solutions. Dicey states that if a convention was broken legal problems would eventually arise. His example was that if Parliament did not meet every year the Budget could not be authorised nor could a standing army, both legal necessities. It is hard to see how this could apply to some conventions like, for instance, ministerial responsibility. Jennings believed that conventions had to be obeyed because the 'system' would break down if it did not, 'political difficulties' would occur. If the Queen refused her Assent there would be a crisis as indeed there would if the Prime Minister tried to govern without a majority. Again this can only apply to some conventions. When Mrs Thatcher refused opposition nominations for life peerages hardly anyone noticed.

Re Canada (1982) considered the sanctions available. In extreme cases of unconventional behaviour a constitutional superior can dismiss the guilty person. In 1975 the Prime Minister of Australia was dismissed by the Governor-General for trying to govern without an approved Budget. Prime Ministers frequently dismiss erring ministers. The real enforcement though is reflected in the quotation in the question. Conventions merely reflect 'the prevailing constitutional values or principles of the period'. This recognises that conventions are constantly changing. It is now unacceptable to us for the Queen to actively rule the country or an unelected lord to lead the government. It also means that constitutional 'rules' are not like 'legal rules'. As Dicey suggested years ago they are more like moral rules. People refrain from breaking constitutional rules because they feel that it is wrong or they fear the disapproval of fellow politicians or the public. As with any moral rule, there are genuine disagreements as to what the rules are and some rules are considered more important than others. There are strong or normative conventions such as those that surround the role of the Queen. These will seldom if ever be broken. In contrast there are weak or simple conventions, such as that judges must abstain from party politics, more honoured in the breach than the observance.

The UK system which is based on conventions can accommodate enormous constitutional change without the need for a revolution or new constitution. The Queen no longer governs, we have party politics, the Lords now has little power, are just some examples. The weakness is that the evolution of the constitution cannot be halted and government may be tempted by the lack of legal restraint to take more power for itself. For example, local government was considered a counterbalance to central government but since the Second World War central government has removed most of its powers. This may or may not be 'unconventional' but it is not illegal.

QUESTION 4

The term 'British constitution' is near meaningless even as used by British writers. It is impossible to isolate parts of the system of government to which the label may authoritatively be attached. There is no test to discriminate between constitutional and less than constitutional elements . . . .

F. F. Ridley, *There is No British Constitution.*

Discuss

Commentary

General essay questions, asking the student what they think about the whole British constitution, are quite commonly used. Quotations from practically any constitutional writer can be used so it is impossible to question spot! The quotations usually have one thing in common, they are asking the student to be critical. It is not enough for the student just to describe the elements of the constitution, he or she must know enough to be able to highlight the weak points such as the vagueness of British arrangements, their changeability and the lack of any ultimate legal control over government. Poorly prepared students may be tempted to choose such questions in the hope that they can get away with 'waffle'. Unfortunately it soon becomes evident if the student knows nothing. Constitutional sources and theories must be supported by examples. Our quotation stresses the lack of any clear definition of what is part of the constitution and what is not. The implication is that this means that we do not have a constitution at all. Other quotations might highlight the lack of a written constitution. That would in fact be asking much the same question.

Suggested Answer

All modern states have a constitution. Its main purpose is to restrain the government: that is to ensure that government is not arbitrary. Government must be carried out according to established rules. Those rules are the constitution. The existence of a constitution also protects the individual, not just from the power of the government but also from other powerful bodies or individuals. It is also thought that a constitution grants the government the right to rule: it legitimates its authority. There is also the idea that somehow the people have at least consented to these arrangements. In the words of Thomas Paine, from *The Rights of Man.*

> A constitution is not the act of a government, but of a people constituting a government, and a government without a constitution is a power without right ... A constitution is a thing antecedent to a government, and the government is only the creature of a constitution.

The word 'constitution', though, can be misleading. It is used in at least two senses. 'First of all, it is used to describe the whole system of government, the collection of rules which establish and regulate it.' (K. C. Wheare, *Modern Constitutions.*) In this sense it is usually thought that the United Kingdom has a constitution, but it is one of the purposes of this essay to examine whether this is really so.

The second sense is better known. As Bradley and Ewing put it: '... a constitution means a document having a special legal sanctity'. Nearly all modern states have such a document. Britain is one of the very few exceptions that does not. Another purpose of this essay is to examine whether this really matters. Before going on to examine the British constitution it is worth noting that the presence or absence of a written constitution can be seriously misleading. No written constitution can contain all the constitution. For instance a world famous written constitution, that of the USA, is a very brief document. Much of the US constitution is, as in Britain, found elsewhere in cases, legislation and convention. Although Britain does not have a special constitutional document, much of the constitution is written down in legislation, cases and even in documents of constitutional importance such as Magna Carta 1215 and the Bill of Rights 1689. Before concluding whether the UK's constitution is better or worse than that of a state with a written constitution, it would be best to examine where the British constitution can be found, usually known as the sources of the constitution.

Many important provisions of the constitution are contained within Acts of Parliament. The Act of Settlement 1700 lays down the royal succession; the Acts of Union 1707 created the United Kingdom of England and Scotland and the Parliament Acts 1911 and 1949 reduced the powers of the House of Lords and stipulated that general elections should be held at least every five years. These are fundamental parts of the constitution, but they are no different from any other Act of Parliament. There is nothing to distinguish them as Acts of Parliament of constitutional significance and there is no special procedure to enact or repeal them. An ordinary Act of Parliament, passed by a simple majority, will do.

Case law also establishes many important constitutional principles. The House of Lords upheld the supremacy of Parliament in *Pickin* v *BRB* [1974] AC 756 but then modified it to take account of European Community membership in *R* v *Secretary of State for Transport ex parte Factortame* (No. 2) [1991] 1 AC 603. Again this means that there is nothing fixed about the UK constitution. As in the previous example there is nothing to stop the courts changing their minds. There is also no fixed procedure: not all constitutional cases need go to the House of Lords. The magistrates' courts daily make decisions of constitutional significance in areas of civil liberties like police powers and public order.

The royal prerogative is an important source of government power which includes the right to declare war, conclude peace treaties, appoint and dismiss ministers, award honours and much more. It is the remains of the power of the Monarch and is laid down by common law rather than by legislation or a written constitution. Case law ultimately decides which prerogatives remain and even in recent times significant decisions are still being made. In *R* v *Home Secretary ex parte Northumbria Police Authority* [1987] 2 WLR 998 the Crown's power to maintain the peace of the realm finally received recognition.

Some of the most important parts of the constitution are not legal at all. Conventions, which are the understandings, habits and practices that have evolved over the centuries, regulate many vital areas. Legally the Queen still has many powers, but by convention they are exercised in her name by Her Majesty's government. The very existence and powers of the Prime Minister and the Cabinet are conventional only. The problem with conventions is that they are constantly evolving, so that at any one time it is not possible to say what precisely the convention requires. Accountability to Parliament and ministerial responsibility are thought to be key conventions. For example a minister is not supposed to mislead Parliament and resignation has followed in the past, e.g., Profumo and Brittan. Yet there have been many examples where a minister misled Parliament and did not resign, e.g., Waldegrave over arms to Iraq. This brings us to another problem with a constitution that depends upon conventions, namely the lack of enforcement. There is no sanction if a minister refuses to resign or indeed any other convention is broken. The only penalty is the disapproval of other politicians or the public.

Partly because of the lack of a written constitutional document, defenders of Britain's constitution like A. V. Dicey have tried to argue that certain principles are adhered to which are better than more formal arrangements. The rule of law means that the government must obey the law just as an ordinary citizen must. It cannot act without legal authorisation and this protects the citizen. This forms the basis of British civil liberties in cases like *Entick* v *Carrington* (1765) 19 St Tr 1030: officials of the state cannot enter a citizen's home and search it simply because it is in the interest of the state. There must be a specific law which allows such actions. The limits to this idea are fairly obvious. Nowadays the government usually controls Parliament through its majority and can legislate to provide itself with any power that it lacks. In *Burmah Oil* v *Lord Advocate* [1965] AC 75 the government was ordered to pay compensation for wartime damage. The War Damage Act 1965 swiftly followed so that the government did not have to pay.

Writers such as Munro (*Studies in Constitutional Law*) have tried to revive the old idea of the separation of powers as an important controlling force in the constitution. The legislature and the judiciary control the executive. Unfortunately the executive, again through its majority, can usually get its way in the legislature. The judiciary can control the executive, if it acts beyond its legal powers, by means of judicial review, but they cannot challenge the supremacy of an Act of Parliament. As there is no written constitution, ideas like the rule of law and the separation of powers have no recognised status in the UK constitution. Other constitutional writers, such as de Smith (*Constitutional and Administrative Law*) consider them to be of no importance and unworthy of discussion in a modern constitutional text book.

In answer to F. F. Ridley's question it can be agreed that there is considerable disagreement as to the contents of the UK constitution. Some might argue that the Criminal Justice and Public Order Act 1994 is an Act of major constitutional importance because of its restriction of key civil liberties such as the right to silence and freedom of assembly. Others might regard it as simply some very necessary improvements to the criminal law. The Matrix Churchill trial and the whole Scott report about 'arms to Iraq' might be regarded by some as important constitutional sources on public interest immunity and accountability to Parliament. Others might regard the whole affair as an impenetrable political squabble which will soon be forgotten.

The implication of F. F. Ridley's quotation is that the UK constitution is profoundly unsatisfactory. There is insufficient control over what a government can do. It can change anything it wants with an Act of Parliament including overturning unsatisfactory court decisions. Conventions can be manipulated to the government's advantage. For instance, it is extremely unclear when a minister must resign and it usually occurs when the Prime Minister or the minister's own party wants them to go, as in the cases of David Mellor and Edwina Currie. Constitutional theories are all very well but there is no means of enforcing them because, unlike Acts of Parliament, they are not the law.

Yet in contrast there must be something there when we talk about the constitution. Government runs pretty smoothly and we do not live in a dictatorship. Governments could, legally, do all sorts of outrageous things but generally they do not. They restrain themselves. Perhaps Dicey was right when he referred to 'political morality'. Politicians do not do certain things, through a combination of feeling that it would be wrong, fear of what other politicians would think and fear of public opinion.

3 Parliamentary Supremacy

INTRODUCTION

This chapter covers the most important and controversial aspect of the present UK constitution, and one which is very likely to appear on any examination paper. Although it is possible for a question to be set which concentrates on the traditional doctrine, and an example of such a question is given here, most examiners will set a question on the effect of membership of the European Union on parliamentary supremacy. Two examples are given, in the form of an essay and a problem question. The principal difficulty which students experience in answering such questions lies in distinguishing between the attitude of European Community law, as laid down by the European Court of Justice, and the attitude of English law, as shown by the English courts. Only precedents from the English courts should be cited as authority for what English law actually is. Whether this complies with European Community law is a separate issue, and may not always be relevant, depending on the terms of the question asked.

QUESTION 1

What is meant by the term parliamentary supremacy? What are its implications in matters other than those raised by Britain's membership of the European Union?

Commentary

This question requires the student to demonstrate a general understanding of the theoretical basis of parliamentary supremacy and its effects. Because it specifically excludes the problems arising from membership of the EU, which are dealt with in a subsequent question, the student can concentrate on some of the other issues which have attracted attention, such as the ability of Parliament to impose special procedures for the passage of later legislation. In many examination papers, this type of question will include discussion of the EU; the student should assume that the EU is meant to be discussed if it is not, as here, expressly excluded.

Suggested Answer

In most states, the validity of any law can be traced back to a written constitution, which forms the basis of the organisation of the state. But in the UK, once the origin of a legal rule is traced back to an Act of Parliament, there is no further document by which the validity of that Act can be determined. Instead, the lawyer is forced simply to assert the proposition that an Act of Parliament is law, because Parliament has the power to enact laws. Why Parliament has that power is an interesting historical and political question, but the lawyer is generally happy to accept the existence of Parliament's power as unquestioned and unquestionable.

The historical origins of parliamentary supremacy lie in the gradual development of the understanding that changes to the law required not merely the personal decision of the Monarch, but the 'advice and consent' of the representatives of Lords and Commons, formally assembled in the two Houses of Parliament. This understanding was challenged in the seventeenth century, but was confirmed once and for all by the Bill of Rights 1689, Art 1:

> That the pretended power of suspending of laws, or the execution of laws by regal authority without consent of Parliament is illegal.

From this point, the creation of new law has been a power possessed by Parliament alone.

But what was not clear was whether there were any restrictions or limits on that power. During the seventeenth century there were suggestions that any Act of Parliament which was unreasonable, repugnant or impossible would be declared invalid by the courts. These suggestions were heavily influenced by the philosophy of natural law, by which human law is judged against the standards set by an ideal, God-given law. With the decline of this philosophy and the growth of positivism, such sentiments were no longer expressed, and, as Parliament was not in any case interested in enacting unreasonable legislation, the courts were happy to accept the validity of any Act passed by traditional parliamentary procedure. Parliament was to be treated as the supreme law-maker.

The most celebrated statement of parliamentary supremacy is that of Dicey;

> that Parliament has the right to make or unmake any law whatever; and further that no person or body is recognised by the law of England as having a right to override or set aside the legislation of Parliament.

It received judicial confirmation in *Madzimbamuto* v *Lardner-Burke* [1969] 1 AC 645, where Lord Reid said:

> It is often said that it would be unconstitutional for the UK Parliament to do certain things, meaning that the moral, political and other reasons against doing them are so strong that most people would regard it as highly improper if Parliament did these things. But that does not mean that it is beyond the power of Parliament to do such things. If Parliament chose to do any of them, the courts could not hold the Act of Parliament invalid.

It is clear that Parliament can do, and has done, many things which in other countries might be regarded as unconstitutional. It may break international law; see *Mortensen* v *Peters* (1906) 8F(J) 93. It may legislate retrospectively; see War Damage Act 1965. In *Manuel* v *Attorney-General* [1983] Ch 77, 95, the courts refused to entertain a claim by native Canadian chiefs that the Canada Act 1982, which repatriated the Canadian Constitution, was invalid because it infringed the rights of the native peoples. As the Act had been passed and was legally valid, it could not be challenged whatever it did.

It is virtually impossible to imagine any circumstances (other than a breach of EC law) where the UK courts would refuse to accept the validity of an Act of Parliament properly passed. Further, the courts will not involve themselves in questions relating to the way in which the legislation was passed. In *British Railways Board* v *Pickin* [1974] AC 765, the respondent alleged that a private Act of Parliament had been passed only after Parliament had been misled by the appellants. But the court upheld the validity of the Act, stating that it would be for Parliament itself to investigate any defects in the procedure.

There remains, however, one disputed area. Can Parliament bind its successors? The orthodox view is that it cannot. The Parliament which is supreme is the current Parliament, so it has the power to repeal the legislation of any previous Parliament. Normally such repeal is expressed in the later Act. But if, through inadvertence or caution, Parliament simply enacts something inconsistent with an earlier Act, the courts will treat this as an implied repeal of the earlier Act by the later. In *Ellen St Estates Ltd* v *Minister of Health* [1934] 1 KB 590, the Court of Appeal rejected an attempt to argue that the Housing Act 1925 should be read subject to inconsistent provisions in the Acquisition of Land Act 1919. The 1925 Act impliedly repealed those provisions.

What is the origin of this rule that Parliament cannot bind its successors? If it is regarded as a rule of common law, then logic would suggest that, like all other rules of common law, it would be subject to alteration by Act of Parliament. But, as Wade argued in his 1955 article, 'The Basis of Legal Sovereignty', if the rule is regarded as the rule of recognition, on which the whole basis of constitutional legality rests, it is not like other common law rules, and nothing short of a legal revolution could change it. Any attempt by an Act of Parliament to change the basis on which Acts of Parliament are treated as law is doomed to failure. But, in various contexts, the issue of Parliament's ability to bind its successors has arisen and given rise to legal and academic debate.

The first concerns grants of independence to former colonies, which are given legal effect by an Act of Parliament stating that Parliament will no longer legislate for the country in question. Could such an Act be repealed? Legal theory suggests that it could, but, as was pointed out in *British Coal Corporation* v *R* [1935] AC 500, that has no relation to realities. The independent state would take no notice of any attempt to revoke its independence without its consent. It appears though that the UK courts would feel themselves bound to obey the express terms of the UK statute. But no such issue is ever likely to arise in practice, so this remains a theoretical problem only.

There have been some differences of opinion between Scottish and English lawyers over the status of the Acts of Union 1707, various provisions of which were stated to be unalterable. It is argued that as the Acts were the work of the then separate English and Scottish Parliaments, they could not be repealed by the UK Parliament which replaced them and which owes its very existence to those Acts. In fact some of the 'unalterable' provisions have been altered, without successful legal challenge in Scotland or England. It is conceivable that any attempt to alter such fundamental matters as the status of Scots law or the nature of the Church of Scotland would be rejected, at least by the Scottish courts. But again, no such change could ever be imagined, so no legal ruling will ever be needed.

The question which has given rise to most debate is whether Parliament could prescribe special procedures for the passing of future legislation which could be made binding on future Parliaments. There is nothing to prevent Parliament creating special procedures; for example, the Northern Ireland Constitution Act 1973 requires the holding of a referendum before any legislation to remove Northern Ireland from the UK. But this so-called constitutional guarantee derives its validity from the 1973 Act, which could itself be repealed without a referendum. Would it be possible to prevent this by stating in an Act that the Act itself could not be repealed without a referendum?

There is a school of thought that Parliament would in fact be bound by such a provision regulating the manner and form of future legislation. This would enable the partial entrenchment of legislation, by requiring referenda or special majorities before laws, for example protecting civil rights, could be repealed. The contention is supported by reference to various Commonwealth cases, such as *Attorney-General for New South Wales* v *Trethowan* [1932] AC 526, *Harris* v *Minister of the Interior* 1952 (2) SA 428, and *Bribery Commissioner* v *Ranasinghe* [1965] AC 172. But in all these cases, the requirements as to the manner and form of future legislation were contained in the original UK statutes by which independence was granted, and it logically followed that these requirements could not be changed by the actions of a non-sovereign legislature. The problem in applying these precedents to the UK Parliament is that it would have to limit itself, rather than being subjected to external constitutional constraints.

Although the current orthodoxy is that Parliament could not bind itself to obey any special procedures, it is possible to imagine the development of a new orthodoxy under which the repeal of such constitutional guarantees as a Bill of Rights would require the observance of the special procedures laid down when it was first enacted. Such a development would follow the growth of a public opinion and a consensus lasting over several Parliaments that such a law should not lightly be repealed. The process might be similar to that which has seen the courts adjusting to the implications of membership of the EU. It might perhaps be predicted that, as with some of the other issues relating to the supremacy of Parliament, the theoretical powers of Parliament will not be tested in the courts because no Parliament will wish to avoid the restrictions imposed on it.

QUESTION 2

What impact has British membership of the European Communities had on the doctrine of parliamentary supremacy?

Commentary

The issues raised by this question are likely to be central to any constitutional law course. Students must be careful to discuss this question in the light of case law, not the often ill-informed pronouncements of politicians. There have now been enough cases to enable definite answers to be given to most issues, but the exact boundaries to the courts' obedience to EC rather than UK law remain uncertain and therefore debatable. The student will need to explain the general doctrine of parliamentary supremacy, but there is no need to go into detail about the other complex issues which would arise in a more general question.

Suggested Answer

When Britain joined the EC, concerns were expressed in many quarters about the constitutional implications. In particular, how could EC membership be reconciled with the traditional doctrine of parliamentary supremacy? In states with a written constitution, it was generally possible to spell out the implications of EC membership by an appropriate constitutional amendment. But because the British constitution is unwritten, no such process was available. All that Britain could do was to pass the European Communities Act 1972, by the same procedure as for all other statutes and with, prima facie, the same legal force as all other statutes, leaving many unanswered questions.

According to Dicey, 'no person is recognised by the law of England as having a right to over-ride or set aside the legislation of Parliament'. This doctrine forms the very basis of the British constitution with the effect that the current Parliament can pass any legislation it wishes, including legislation to amend or repeal, expressly or by implication, legislation passed by an earlier Parliament.

Although there has been considerable academic debate about possible exceptions to this power, and possible methods of entrenching legislation, the orthodox view accepted no limits on Parliament's authority.

But, before Britain ever joined the EC, the European Court of Justice had established, in *Costa* v *ENEL*, Case 6/64, [1964] CMLR 425, that Community law was to prevail over incompatible national law. The doctrine of direct effect obliged national courts to give effect to rights arising under Community law, regardless of any national law to the contrary. No doubt, in an ideal world, no national law inconsistent with the state's EC obligations would ever be enacted. But in the real world, it was all too likely that a state would enact such legislation, whether by inadvertence, or in the hope that the inconsistency would not be noticed or challenged. The particular problem faced by the British legislators was to find some way to instruct the courts to give effect to Community law in preference to Acts of Parliament whenever passed.

It was straightforward to provide, in s. 2(1) of the European Communities Act 1972, that all rights arising under the EC Treaties were to be given effect in preference to pre-existing UK law. The orthodox doctrines of express and implied repeal authorised that. But the real problem concerned legislation passed after 1972 which was inconsistent with EC law. This was dealt with in s. 2(4) of the 1972 Act, which provides that legislation passed, or to be passed in the future, should be construed and have effect subject to the rule laid down in s. 2(1), that is, that effect must be given to EC rights. This was reinforced by s. 3(1), which instructed the courts to decide any issues of Community law 'in accordance with the principles laid down by, and any relevant decisions of, the European Court of Justice'. This would include the principle of the supremacy of EC law laid down in *Costa* v *ENEL* (1964).

The 1972 Act therefore appeared to provide the courts with an instruction that they should obey Community law, but left unresolved the question of what would happen if different instructions were provided in a later Act of Parliament. Leaving aside for the moment the issue of an express instruction to breach Community law, what if an Act passed after 1972 contained provisions inconsistent with Community law? By the traditional methods of interpretation, where provisions in an earlier Act are inconsistent with a later Act, the earlier Act is impliedly repealed; see *Ellen St Estates Ltd* v *Minister of Health* [1934] 1 KB 590. It could therefore be argued that any Act passed after 1972 could impliedly repeal the European Communities Act, so that the phrase 'legislation passed or to be passed' would be read with the proviso 'except this new Act'. This would leave the UK in breach of its obligations under the EC Treaties. How could the courts avoid this?

The solution, for many cases, was found in the long-standing rule of statutory interpretation that, where legislation is passed to implement the UK's international obligations, any ambiguity should be construed so as to comply with those obligations rather than conflict with them. This rule, taken with the express wording of s. 2(4) of the 1972 Act, has been treated by the courts as a clear instruction to interpret any UK legislation passed to implement EC law in such a way to ensure that there is no discrepancy between them. In *Garland* v *British Rail Engineering* [1983] 2 AC 751, the court preferred the interpretation of the Sex Discrimination Act 1975 which was consistent with Article 119, EC Treaty, to the interpretation which created conflict between them. The courts have been willing to use purposive methods of interpretation rather than traditional literal methods to ensure compliance with EC law. In *Pickstone* v *Freemans plc* [1989] AC 66, and *Lister* v *Forth Dry Dock* [1990] 1 AC 546, the courts went far beyond literal interpretation, even implying extra words into a regulation in order to ensure that EC law was complied with. This approach has proved to deal satisfactorily with all cases where UK legislation is passed in order to incorporate EC directives and Treaty provisions into UK law.

A different problem was posed by the decision of the European Court of Justice in *Marleasing*, C-106/89, [1992] 1 CMLR 305, that all national legislation, whenever passed, should be interpreted in the light of EC law, in order to give effect to rights even if they did not have direct effect. The UK courts had earlier refused, in *Duke* v *GEC Reliance Ltd* [1988] AC 618, to interpret UK statutes passed in 1970 and 1975 in the light of a 1976 directive, on the grounds that that could not possibly have been Parliament's intention; the rules stated in the statutes were unambiguously in conflict with the directive. But in *Webb* v *EMO Air Cargo (No. 2)* [1995] 4 All ER 577, the House of Lords without debate interpreted an ambiguous 1975 Act to give effect to a 1976 directive, just as the European Court of Justice decision required. There remains considerable uncertainty in both UK and EC law as to just how far a national court is supposed to go in rewriting its existing laws under the guise of interpretation, but the UK courts seem willing to follow the instruction given by the 1972 Act.

The above cases, being treated as issues of statutory interpretation and the reconciling of apparently contradictory rules, managed to avoid the fundamental problem of a direct clash between EC law and a statute passed after 1972. In *Macarthys Ltd* v *Smith* [1979] 3 All ER 325, Lord Denning expressed the view that, in such a situation, it would be the court's duty to give effect to EC law. But the issue did not arise in an unavoidable form until the *Factortame* cases, C-213/89, [1990] 3 CMLR 375 and C-221/89, [1991] 3 CMLR 589.

These concerned an apparent clash between the EC laws forbidding discrimination on grounds of nationality and the Merchant Shipping Act 1988 which
imposed discriminatory rules on fishing boats. When Factortame challenged
the application to them of the 1988 Act, they asked for an interim injunction
suspending the Act, pending a reference to the European Court of Justice.
English law would not permit such a suspension as it would clearly breach
Dicey's formulation of parliamentary supremacy, but the European Court of
Justice held that EC law could require it. The House of Lords were therefore
faced with the ultimate choice: to obey the 1988 Act, as the newest statement
of Parliament's intentions, or to obey the 1972 Act and enforce EC law. The
House of Lords chose to obey the 1972 Act and awarded the injunction. In
effect, the 1972 Act was held not to be subject to the doctrine of implied repeal.
All legislation passed after 1972 has a proviso implicitly contained within it —
'unless EC law provides otherwise'. The European Communities Act 1972 is
treated by the courts as a uniquely significant Act which, by incorporating into
UK law a new body of law including the concept of supremacy for EC law,
changed the assumptions underlying all subsequent legislation.

All EC law, however, obtains its effect in UK law only by virtue of its
incorporation through s. 2 of the European Communities Act 1972. Were that
Act to be expressly repealed, EC law would, in the eyes of the UK courts, lose
its force. Such a repeal would appear to be a breach of the EC Treaty, which
was concluded for an indefinite period, unless preceded by an amending Treaty
agreed by all other member states, but there would be no option but to accept
a decision by Britain to withdraw. Parliament's supremacy would be restored
to its Diceyan form by the repeal.

It is interesting to consider the effect of an express enactment, short
of a complete repeal of the European Communities Act 1972, stating that
some particular provision was to prevail over any EC rule to the contrary.
Given that the 1972 Act would still be in force, would the courts follow that
or the later Act? In *Macarthys Ltd* v *Smith* (1979) Lord Denning suggested
that in such a case, unlikely though it was, the courts would have to obey
the new statute as the expression of the current will of Parliament. Any
such legislation would provoke a political crisis as between Britain and the
EC, and no doubt applications would be made to both British and European
courts. But it would be most uncomfortable for the British courts to do anything other than follow the expressed wishes of Parliament and government,
leaving it to those political institutions to solve what would be in essence a
political problem.

In conclusion, it can be argued that the UK Parliament, through its power to repeal the 1972 Act, or legislate expressly contrary to it, does retain its ultimate supremacy, in spite of the fact that, in its daily operation, it is now constrained by Community law. The courts have in effect taken Parliament at its word as expressed in 1972, and will continue to do so until expressly instructed to the contrary. Any other decision would have led to the courts provoking clashes with Community law. It is right that the ultimate decision as to whether Community law should continue to have force in the UK should rest with the UK Parliament.

QUESTION 3

In January 1992 the EC Commission issued Directive 1/1992 which provided, inter alia, that:

> In the event of property of an EC citizen being compulsorily acquired into public ownership that citizen shall be entitled to prompt, adequate and effective compensation from the nationalising government.

In February 1995 a Conservative government of the UK enacted the Electricity Act which had the effect of privatising the UK electricity supply industry. Section 113 of the Act provided that 'compensation at the level of the full market value must be paid to all affected shareholders' should the industry or any part of it be compulsorily returned to public ownership.

In March 1997 a Labour government is returned on a mandate to re-nationalise the electricity supply industry. It proposes in clause 123 of its Electricity Nationalisation Bill that 'No compensation shall be payable to shareholders in the aforesaid electricity companies'. The Bill has passed all its stages in the Commons and its Third Reading in the Lords.

Joan, a UK citizen, and shareholder in one of the private electricity companies to be re-nationalised, wishes to challenge the legality of the Bill. Advise her.

Commentary

The most usual question on parliamentary supremacy nowadays is the effect that joining the EC has had upon the traditional doctrines. This lends itself to problem questions, as here, but the same basic question could equally well be asked in an essay. The commonest mistake that students make in answering such a question is to dive straight in, cite *R v Secretary of State for Transport, ex parte Factortame Ltd* [1991] 1 AC 603 and say very little more. Examiners expect a discussion of the case law that led up to *Factortame*. A really good answer would also consider what came after *Factortame*.

Sometimes it is best to tackle problem questions line by line to ensure that nothing is missed out. In complex questions, such as this one, it is probably easiest to pick out the main issues and tackle them one by one. There is no preset order in which one should do this; it is a matter of personal preference. Personally we always favour tackling the easiest issues first. This creates a favourable impression with the examiners and allows the candidate to build up their confidence before tackling the more difficult areas.

The same basic question could be asked in a number of different ways. You would be unfortunate if you were asked one as long and as complex as this. It has been used because it gives an excellent opportunity to tackle the major issues and rehearse the relevant points.

Such questions would not usually contain the element of the ability of Parliament to repeal earlier legislation, here the 1997 Bill repealing the 1995 Act. Such an issue could be a question in its own right.

Again the type of EC law specified might not be a directive. If it is a regulation then it is directly aplicable and there is no need to go into all the problems caused by whether directives have direct effect or not. Similarly Treaty Articles do not cause many problems. They usually have direct effect and there is no problem about the difference between horizontal and vertical direct effect; see *Van Gend en Loos* v *Nederlandse* [1963] CMLR 105.

Whatever the form and style of the question asked, the core of the answer remains the same. How have the UK courts adapted to the Supremacy of EC law?

Suggested Answer

According to A. V. Dicey, 'Parliament ... has ... the right to make or unmake any law whatever'. Therefore, no wording in an Act of Parliament can prevent a later Act from repealing it. Parliament can repeal an Act either by explicitly referring to the previous Act, which is known as express repeal, or if two Acts conflict the latter is taken to be the law, which is known as implied repeal. Under these traditional theories of parliamentary supremacy, the 1997 Parliament is perfectly at liberty to repeal a 1995 Act of Parliament. No wording in the 1995 Act can prevent this, particularly as here it is an express repeal; see *Vauxhall Estates Ltd* v *Liverpool Corporation* [1932] 1 KB 733 and *Ellen Street Estates Ltd* v *Minister of Health* [1934] KB 590.

Again, traditionally, the courts have always rejected any attempt to challenge an Act of Parliament. This was confirmed in 1974 by the House of Lords in *Pickin* v *BRB* [1974] AC 765. Once a Bill has been passed by both the Commons and the Lords and has received Royal Assent, it cannot be questioned. Joan might well argue that she does not wish to challenge an Act, but stop a Bill from becoming an Act. *Pickin* does not offer her any more hope. The court stated that they did not have the power to investigate what went on in Parliamentary proceedings. Other cases, though on delegated legislation, support the idea that the courts will not make any rulings on Parliamentary proceedings; see, for example, *R* v *Secretary of State for the Environment ex parte Notts CC* [1986] AC 240. Indeed Article 9 of the Bill of Rights 1689 states that '... proceedings in Parliament ought not to be ... questioned in any court...'. So, in conclusion, under the traditional theories, Joan has no case at all.

EC membership has changed this traditional view, though, at first, this was not clear. Section 2(1), European Communities Act 1972 stated that all EC law was now part of the law of the UK. Section 3(1) stated that the UK courts now had to abide by the decisions of the European Court of Justice. The Act did not clearly state what would happen if EC law conflicted with a UK Act of Parliament. Under the traditional theories of implied repeal, EC law would take priority over any Act of Parliament enacted *before* the European Communities Act 1972; see *Vauxhall Estates Ltd* (1932). Under the traditional theories any Act of Parliament *after* 1972 would take priority over EC law. Section 2(4) has attracted a lot of attention although its exact meaning is obscure. It states that:

> ... any enactment passed or to be passed ... shall be construed and have effect subject to the foregoing provisions of this section ...

This could mean that EC law has supremacy over Acts of Parliament passed after 1972, or it could just mean that such Acts should be interpreted ('construed') so as to try to avoid any conflict with EC law. Both interpretations seem to have found favour with the judiciary, as we shall see.

It is clear that some time before the UK joined the EC the EC's own court, the European Court of Justice, had decided that there had been 'a partial transfer of sovereignty from Member States to the Community'. For the EC's 'legal order' to function it was necessary for EC law to override incompatible national laws; see *Costa* v *ENEL* [1964] ECR 585 at 593. For Joan to succeed in a UK court in overturning the 1997 Electricity Nationalisation Bill, she would need to show that the UK courts had accepted the principle of EC supremacy laid down by the European Court of Justice.

One problem that Joan has is that she needs to rely on a directive. These do not normally have any direct effect in a member state until they are enacted by that state. Therefore, until they are enacted by that member state, here the UK, they cannot be used in that state's courts as they form no part of the law; see *Duke* v *GEC Reliance* [1988] AC 618. This principle has been modified by the European Court of Justice, so that in certain circumstances a directive can have direct effect; see *Van Duyn* v *Home Office* [1975] Ch 358 and *Marshall* v *Southampton and SW Hants AHA* [1986] QB 402.

The wording of the directive must be clear and precise and preferably grant some sort of right to the person bringing the case. Directive 1/1992 would seem to satisfy that test as it states: 'that citizen shall be entitled to prompt, adequate and effective compensation'. If there is a time limit for implementing the directive that must have expired. In the question, no indication of a time limit is given, so we will assume that it has expired. Lastly, the directive can only be enforced against the government that has failed to implement it. This is known as vertical effect. In *Duke* v *GEC Reliance Ltd*, Reliance were a private employer so that a directive could not be enforced against them. In *Foster* v *British Gas* [1991] 1 AC 306, British Gas were held to be part of the government so in contrast the directive could be enforced against them. So here Joan must make sure that she brings her case against an 'organ of the state'. The government minister responsible for introducing the Bill would be the most suitable defendant. Bringing the case against the privatised electricity company might not be possible, as it may no longer be 'an organ of the State'; but see *Foster* v *British Gas* (1991).

As the directive is part of UK law it can be contrasted with the 1997 Bill. Lord Denning said in *Macarthys* v *Smith* [1979] 3 All ER 325 that UK legislation should, if possible, be interpreted to agree with EC law. The House of Lords has endorsed this approach in cases such as *Garland* v *BREL* [1983] 2 AC 751 and *Pickstone* v *Freemans* [1988] 2 All ER 803. Indeed, in *Lister* v *Forth Dry Dock* [1990] 1 AC 546 the court said that, if necessary, words could be implied into the UK legislation to avoid conflict.

On the facts given, it also seems arguable that the Electricity Act 1995 was passed to give effect to the Directive 1/1992. The UK courts have agreed that in those circumstances the Act must be interpreted to give effect to the directive; see *Duke v GEC Reliance* and *Pickstone v Freemans*. Unfortunately, this does not help Joan a great deal as her problem is the 1997 Bill. This seems clearly designed to take away her right to compensation granted in the directive and 1995 Act. It would seem very hard, if not impossible, to interpret the 1997 Bill to conform with the wording of the 1995 directive.

In that case we have a clear case of conflict between a UK Act and EC Law. Lord Denning was brave enough to say, in *Macarthys Ltd v Smith*, that the UK courts should accord supremacy to EC law in such a case of conflict. His fellow Court of Appeal judges were not willing to go that far and endorse such a radical break with the traditional theories. It was not until *R v Secretary of State for Transport, ex parte Factortame* [1991] 1 AC 603 that the House of Lords were willing to accept that EC law now had supremacy. Significantly, the House of Lords did not discuss this in any great detail, as they would not want to be seen to be questioning traditional theories too openly. Lord Bridge (at 659) merely said that:

> Under the terms of the Act of 1972, it has always been clear that it was the duty of a United Kingdom court, when delivering final judgment, to override any rule of national law found to be in conflict with any directly enforceable rule of Community law.

This is what s. 2(4) required.

Joan would therefore be well advised to follow *Factortame* and ask the court for an interim injunction asserting the supremacy of EC law. In *Factortame* the injunction ordered a government minister not to enforce the offending UK legislation. Joan's case is a little different. She is trying to challenge a Bill which is not yet an Act. In the light of my earlier comments, about the traditional theories on parliamentary supremacy in *Pickin v BRB* etc., it seems unlikely that the courts would order Parliament not to legislate. Joan might well be obliged to wait until the Bill becomes law as an Act. Maybe she could then ask the courts to follow *Factortame* and issue an injunction forbidding the enforcement of the Act and the confiscation of her shares. Alternatively, Joan could ask the courts merely to state that the 1997 Act was in conflict with EC law, as the House of Lords was willing to do by issuing a declaration in *R v Employment Secretary ex parte Equal Opportunities Commission* [1994] 1 All ER 910.

If Joan brings legal proceedings they have to commence in a UK court and the final order or ruling must come from a UK court, as indicated in *Factortame* and *Equal Opportunities Commission*. It is very likely, though, that at some stage in the proceedings, the UK court would seek the guidance of the European Court of Justice by a reference under Article 177 of the Treaty of Rome. This occurred, for example, in *R v Secretary of State for Transport ex parte Factortame (No. 1)* [1990] 2 AC 85. If Joan did not want to enforce EC law on her own behalf she could ask the Commission of the EC to bring proceedings before the European Court of Justice. This, too, occurred in *Factortame*: see *Re Nationality of Fishermen* [1991] 3 CMLR 706.

There is one final possibility that is not favourable to Joan's case. Lord Denning observed in *Macarthys* that EC law only had supremacy in the UK because an Act of Parliament said so. Parliament could always change its mind about this. The European Communities Act 1972 could always be repealed or parts of EC law could be contradicted by another and more recent Act of Parliament. Lord Bridge appears to agree with these propositions in *Factortame*. For Parliament to do this though it must make its intention clear or 'express' as Lord Denning put it in *Macarthys*. Presumably it means clear wording in the Act. The Electricity Nationalisation Bill 1997 clearly indicates that: 'No compensation shall be payable . . .'. I do not think that this would be enough to indicate to the courts that EC law should here be disregarded. Following *Factortame*, I think that the Act would have to say specifically that it overrode EC law. If in doubt the courts could always refer to Hansard to discover the intention of Parliament. This was allowed in *Pickstone v Freemans*.

Apart from the problems of express repeal, Joan has an excellent chance of success. Whether the UK courts could award compensation for her lost shares remains to be decided. *Francovich v Italy* [1993] 2 CMLR 66 is a ruling by the European Court of Justice that a government must pay compensation for failure to implement a directive to those damaged by that failure. There are as yet no UK cases upon whether the UK courts will implement this principle, although *Kirklees Council v Wickes Building Supplies Ltd* [1992] 3 WLR 170 suggests, obiter dicta, that they would. We await developments, perhaps in the *Factortame* litigation.

4 The Royal Prerogative

INTRODUCTION

The title 'royal prerogative' seems rather quaint, ancient and irrelevant to the modern constitution. If the ordinary person has heard of it at all it summons up images of the Queen, ceremonials and obscure customs like the Queen's right to whales, sturgeons and swans on the river Thames. This gives an extremely misleading impression. The royal prerogative in fact contains some of the most important powers of government: foreign affairs, defence and justice. Munro defined it as: 'those attributes peculiar to the Crown which are derived from common law, not statute and which still survive' (*Studies in Constitutional Law*, 159).

Despite the 'royal' the Queen is not in fact the person who takes the decisions. Although, legally, powers under the prerogative belong to the Queen, by convention they are actually exercised by Her Majesty's government, often by the Prime Minister personally. The main issue that has concerned constitutional lawyers is how this power can be controlled. Questions on the subject, which would usually be essays, generally reflect this concern.

Often the questions concern judicial control, or more specifically judicial review of the prerogative. The most important case here is *Council of Civil Service Unions* v *Minister for the Civil Service* [1985] AC 374. Students often make the mistake of just learning this one case and then are stumped for anything else to talk about. There are other cases! There are not many of them but it is important to know them well in order to answer questions on this area. They would include *Attorney-General* v *De Keyser* [1920] AC 508, *Burmah*

Oil v *Lord Advocate* [1965] AC 75, *R* v *Home Secretary ex parte Northumbria Police Authority* [1987] 2 WLR 998, *Blackburn* v *Attorney-General* [1971] 2 All ER 1380 and *R* v *Home Secretary ex parte Bentley* [1993] 4 All ER 442.

Sometimes questions also concern parliamentary control over prerogative acts. For this the student also needs some knowledge of how parliamentary accountability works (see **Chapter 5**).

The most interesting constitutional question is, in what circumstances might the Queen resume her legal powers and take prerogative decisions once again? This can also be seen as an issue of control. It is thought that the Queen could, in certain circumstances, dismiss a government which was behaving 'unconstitutionally' by abusing her prerogative powers. Questions on this area overlap with conventions in **Chapter 2** and the position of the Prime Minister in **Chapter 6**.

One of the widest prerogatives that exists is the Crown's power to conduct foreign affairs. The Crown's decisions in this area are unchallengeable as are some of its actions.

QUESTION 1

'As De Keyser's case shows, the courts will inquire into whether a particular prerogative power exists or not, and, if it does exist, into its extent. But once the existence and the extent of a power are established to the satisfaction of the court, the court cannot inquire into the propriety of its exercise.'

Lord Fraser in *Council of Civil Service Unions* v *Minister for the Civil Service* [1985] AC 374.

Commentary

This is the commonest question on the royal prerogative and a quite well-used quotation. Note, in particular, that the answer does not confine itself to *Council of Civil Service Unions*, i.e., the *GCHQ* case. The only disconcerting feature of this quotation is that it says the opposite of what the law is generally supposed to be. Some students find this more than off-putting! The key to it is that Lord Fraser is explaining what the law used to be *before* the *GCHQ* case. A student with a good knowledge of the case might know that. Otherwise just be confident and discuss judicial review of the prerogative.

Suggested Answer

The royal prerogative is the remains of royal power. Munro describes it as: 'those attributes peculiar to the crown which are derived from common law, not statute, and which still survive ...' (*Studies in Constitutional Law*, 159). Because they are the powers of the Crown it was thought for a long time that they enjoyed the same legal immunities as the Queen and could not be reviewed by the courts. The House of Lords had made this clear in cases like *Chandler* v *DPP* [1964] AC 763 and *Gouriet* v *UPW* [1978] AC 435. This was despite trailblazing dissents by Lord Denning, notably in *Laker Airways* v *Department of Trade* [1977] QB 643 and even Lord Devlin in *Chandler* had expressed some doubt. To Lord Denning prerogative powers were government powers just like statutory powers and if they were abused they should be controlled.

Despite this the courts had always been able to exercise some sort of control over prerogative. Since as early as the *Case of Proclamations* (1611) 12 Co Rep 74, they have claimed the right to decide whether there was adequate precedent for the prerogative claimed to exist. This gives the courts more power than is commonly realised because the precedents are often unclear. For instance in both *A-G* v *De Keyser's Hotel* [1920] AC 508 and *Burmah Oil* v *Lord Advocate* [1965] AC 75 the court decided that, although the government could seize and even destroy, a person's property in order to defend the realm, compensation must be paid. The right to compensation was not clearly established in the older cases but the court thought it appropriate. The prerogative, of maintaining the peace of the realm, could even be recognised by the courts, for the first time as late as 1987 in *R* v *Home Secretary ex parte Northumbria Police Authority* [1987] 1 WLR 998. What is certain though is that the courts will not recognise a 'new' prerogative for which there is no historic precedent. As Diplock LJ said in *BBC* v *Johns* [1965] Ch 32 at 79: 'It is 350 years and a civil war too late for the Queen's courts to broaden the prerogative.'

De Keyser (1920) had, however, made clear that the courts could not go beyond deciding whether prerogative still existed or not. Judicial review of the prerogative was finally allowed in *Council for Civil Service Unions* v *Minister for the Civil Service* [1985] AC 374. Lord Fraser gave a number of reasons for the change of heart in his judgment. The chief one was that the Queen was not personally involved in the use of the prerogative so that the court would not be questioning her legal immunity. He also noted that the courts had already judicially reviewed the decisions of a tribunal created under the royal prerogative in *R* v *Criminal Injuries Compensation Board ex parte Lain* [1967] 2 QB 864 and a prerogative court in *A-G of Duchy of Lancaster* v *Overton Farms Ltd* [1982] Ch 277. With the development of judicial review in the last 30 years there was no reason nowadays to distinguish between statutory and prerogative powers.

All five House of Lords judges agreed that *some* prerogative powers could be judicially reviewed. It is unclear though *which* prerogative powers would be subject to judicial review. All their lordships agreed that a minor use of the prerogative such as, in this case, the conditions of service of civil servants could be reviewed. Lords Fraser and Brightman thought that this was possible because it was only a delegated use of the prerogative. An Order in Council gave the minister for the Civil Service power to alter civil servants' conditions of service. The Order in Council itself could not be reviewed but the minister's decision under it could. Prerogatives like control of the armed forces and foreign policy 'were unsuitable for discussion or review in the law courts' (Lord Fraser, 398).

The other three judges, Lords Scarman, Diplock and Roskill felt that only some prerogatives could be reviewed. It depended upon its 'subject matter'. Only the lower level, non-political uses of the prerogative could be considered by the courts. Decisions on matters like national security, also involved in this case, had to be left to the executive government. Only they had the information upon which to make a decision. Lord Roskill supplied a handy list of prerogatives that had to be left to government and were unreviewable: treaties, defence, mercy, honours, the dissolution of Parliament and the appointment of government ministers. Lord Diplock thought that they should also consider the effect that the prerogative act had on the private rights and expectations of citizens.

Lord Diplock also took the opportunity to restate the three main grounds for judicial review: illegality, irrationality, and procedural impropriety. These could now be applied to both statutory and prerogative powers. Lord Diplock did, however, mention that it would be rare for a prerogative act to be found irrational. The prerogative relies on policy choices and it would be hard for a court to say that a minister's policy decision was so strange that it was irrational and therefore illegal.

Bearing this in mind it is perhaps not very surprising that, even after the *GCHQ* case, successful judicial reviews of the prerogative have been rare. *R* v *Foreign Secretary ex parte Everett* [1989] AC 1014 concerned the refusal to renew Everett's passport. The court followed the reasoning of Scarman, Diplock and Roskill in *GCHQ* and stated that they could not review the prerogative when it concerned matters of 'high policy'. This case did not concern weighty questions of foreign policy and also affected the rights of the individual. It was therefore susceptible to judicial review, but on the facts the court concluded that there had not been a breach of natural justice.

In *R* v *Home Secretary ex parte Bentley* [1993] 4 All ER 442 the court was prepared to ignore the previous case law, including the obiter dicta of Lord Roskill in *GCHQ*, and permit judicial review of the prerogative of mercy. The Home Secretary had misunderstood his legal powers when taking his decision and was asked to reconsider. In contrast the Privy Council declined to follow *Bentley* in *Reckley* v *Minister of Public Safety (No. 2)* [1996] 1 All ER 562.

The most recent case appears to be *R* v *Home Secretary ex parte Fire Brigades Union* [1995] 2 All ER 244. There the Home Secretary wanted to alter the prerogative based Criminal Injuries Compensation Scheme. He was not permitted to do so, because a statute based scheme had replaced it under the Criminal Justice Act 1988. Successive Home Secretaries had failed to bring these provisions into force. The House of Lords ruled that the Home Secretary had failed to consider bringing the statutory scheme into force and had therefore defied the will of Parliament. This case is therefore not really a review of the prerogative but of a statutory power.

Lord Fraser was stating the law as it existed before the *GCHQ* case. The judgment in that case purported to change this law. In reality little has changed. Many areas of the prerogative are still regarded as non-justiciable and successful cases, like *Bentley*, look likely to remain rare.

QUESTION 2

The principal convention of the British Constitution is that the Queen shall exercise her formal legal powers only upon and in accordance with the advice of her Ministers, save in a few exceptional situations.

De Smith and Brazier, *Constitutional and Administrative Law*.

Discuss.

Commentary

This is the sort of question that many students of constitutional law dislike! At first glance it is unclear what area of the syllabus it concerns. The student who looks a little longer might think that it is about convention. It is, in a way, but only about a very specific group of conventions: those that surround the role of the Queen. The point about the question is that the Queen nearly always acts on the advice of her ministers. The student would need to give examples of the situations where this happens. Even more importantly the student would need to be aware of the situations in which it is thought that the Queen could say 'No' to her ministers. A knowledge of actual incidents where this had happened would be essential for this question. Lastly, the question raises the issue of constitutional control. Should the Queen take a more active role in controlling the excesses of government?

Suggested Answer

Old cases like *The Case of Proclamations* (1611) made a distinction between the ordinary and absolute prerogatives. The ordinary prerogatives were areas in which the Queen had no personal discretion. Nowadays she would merely act on the advice of her ministers. The absolute prerogative covers areas where the Queen has a choice. Usually this is thought to involve only the award of some honours such as the Order of the Garter. It is possible, though, that in some other situations the Queen still might have a choice.

It is accepted that the Queen does have the right to express a view to her ministers upon how her prerogatives are used. Bagehot put it that the Queen has 'the right to be consulted, the right to encourage, the right to warn.' (*The Law of the Constitution*, 1867)). Somewhat more recently, these principles were restated in a letter to *The Times* on 27 July 1986 by the Queen's Press Secretary, Sir William Heseltine. There had been some press coverage claiming that the Queen disapproved of some of the policies of the Prime Minister, Margaret Thatcher. The letter said that the Queen 'was entitled to have opinions on Government policy and to express them to her chief Minister.' However, the Queen was 'bound to accept and act on the advice of her Ministers'. Importantly the letter concluded by reminding us that discussions between the Queen and her ministers are confidential. It is difficult therefore to know for certain whether the Queen, or any previous Monarch, has ever gone beyond expressing a forceful opinion. That is allowed as long as the government has the final say.

Some examples are clear. The Sovereign has not refused assent to an Act of Parliament since 1708. Even that was on the advice of her ministers who did not like what Parliament was proposing. George V expressed the view that he could refuse assent to an Irish Home Rule Bill in 1914. He would do this to 'avert a national disaster' but there was 'no such evidence'.

Conventionally the Prime Minister chooses his or her government. George VI is recorded as having expressed a preference for certain ministerial appointments such as Ernest Bevin as Foreign Secretary. There is nothing particularly remarkable about this. As we saw above the sovereign is entitled to express an opinion in such matters. George VI also expressed opinion on matters such as whether the prerogative of mercy should be extended to persons sentenced to death. Again there is nothing unconstitutional about 'advice'.

If the Queen actually made a personal choice as to who should become Prime Minister it would be very controversial. She would be accused of political favouritism. Usually there is no decision for the Queen to make. There is a clear result from a general election and the leader of the majority party is called upon to form a government. If there is a 'hung Parliament', as was quite common earlier this century, matters are by no means so clear.

In 1916 the country was ruled by a coalition led by the Liberal leader, Asquith. The war was going badly and he resigned. The King sent for Bonar Law, leader of the second largest party, the Conservatives. Bonar Law could not form a government. This put the King in a difficult position. Would he have to make a personal choice? Instead George V hosted a conference of the party leaders and Lloyd George, another Liberal, emerged as the Prime Minister.

A somewhat similar process used to occur when the Conservative party were in office and their Prime Minister resigned. Before 1965 that party had no system for electing a leader. The King or Queen would consult party notables and a new Prime Minister would 'emerge'. This last occurred in 1963 with the selection of Sir Alec Douglas-Home. It is thought that the Monarch would sometimes express an opinion on the merits of a particular candidate, e.g., Lord Halifax instead of Winston Churchill in 1940, but there is no suggestion that the Monarch took the final decision.

The most controversial incident of this type occurred in 1931. Ramsay Macdonald was Prime Minister in the first Labour government. He was convinced that it was in the national interest to reduce public expenditure, in particular unemployment benefit. His own party would not accept this. The leaders of the other parties agreed with Macdonald. Macdonald offered to resign but the King did not accept his resignation. Instead George V consulted the leaders of the other parties. They advised that Macdonald should stay and form a 'national government'. Macdonald took this advice and won a resounding victory at a general election later in the year. Ironically he ended up as the Labour Prime Minister of a largely Conservative government. Subsequently George V has been criticised for playing too active a part in the choice of Prime Minister. Presumably the King did what he did on the advice of the other party leaders and because he thought that it was in the national interest. The electorate seems to have approved.

It is similarly thought that the sovereign could refuse the Prime Minister's request for a general election. In a letter to *The Times* on 2 May 1950 the King's Private Secretary said that refusal could be justified if three conditions are satisfied. First the existing Parliament was able to carry on, secondly a general election would be detrimental to the national economy and thirdly another Prime Minister with a working majority could be found. Although there are Commonwealth examples, in South Africa in 1939 and Canada in 1926, there are no modern British examples. The crucial element justifying the Monarch's refusal would seem, again, to be the national interest.

The most spectacular example of the sovereign resuming an active role would be the dismissal of the Prime Minister. This last occurred in 1834 when William IV dismissed Lord Melbourne. In 1975, however, the Governor-General dismissed the Prime Minister of Australia, Gough Whitlam. The Senate was refusing to agree to his budget because of illegal ministerial misbehaviour in procuring overseas loans. The Prime Minister recommended that there should be an election of the Senate only. The Governor-General refused and dismissed him from office. A Governor-General acts in the name of the Queen and exercises her powers. It is not thought that the Governor-General consulted the Queen in this incident. The Gough Whitlam affair shows that the Queen has the power to dismiss a Prime Minister if he or she is behaving 'unconstitutionally'. The problem in Britain, with its unwritten constitution is, what is unconstitutional? Trying to evade the correct parliamentary procedure and to continue governing without a majority to pass legislation seem to be the 'crimes' of Whitlam.

So what we have is a rather varied series of incidents, both in Britain and the Commonwealth. It does seem that the King or Queen claims the right to protect the 'national interest' even if it is against the wishes of the majority party. The big problem is that opinion upon what is in the national interest can vary. The rarity of incidents of royal interference indicates that Kings and Queens have, rightly, been very cautious about when it is appropriate to interfere.

QUESTION 3

The United Kingdom and Fantasia are in dispute about possession of an island called Lackland which has been ruled by the UK for the last 200 years. Fantasian troops occupy the island and a British force is sent to remove them. No formal declaration of war is made, but the British Crown takes a number of actions. The Crown withdraws the passports of some British citizens resident in Fantasia who, in the opinion of the Crown, are helping the Fantasian invasion forces. Further, Fantasian citizens resident in the UK are arrested and expelled. A number of British owned and registered ships are requisitioned, without compensation, for military use. In Fantasia the British forces occupy and also destroy properties belonging to both Fantasian and British citizens.

The British action is successful and a peace treaty is concluded between the UK and Fantasia. Among other provisions, it stipulates that neither country accepts any liability for loss or damage inflicted during the hostilities. No British legislation is enacted to give effect to the treaty within the UK, as it is not thought necessary.

A number of British and Fantasian citizens are aggrieved by the actions taken against them during the hostilities and seek a legal remedy.

Advise them.

Commentary

The royal prerogative also extends to foreign affairs. The Crown has wide powers at its disposal, which in the older cases were largely unchallenged by the courts. In more modern cases, the courts have been more sceptical and more inclined to protect the rights of the individual.

If we examine the question closely it should give a number of clues as to the prerogatives involved and the cases that need to be considered. War and the deployment of troops, the issue of passports, the expulsion of aliens and the confiscation of property at home and abroad should all ring bells in your memory. The effect of treaties should be easy enough following the rows in 1993 concerning Maastricht. Act of state is lurking in there somewhere. To most students it is a nightmare, but it is important to realise that it is not at all clear from the cases what it is. Cleverer people than you have tried in vain to define it!

It is usually easiest with problem questions to consider each event as it arises by going through the problem line by line. This tactic is certainly best in this example.

Suggested Answer

The declaration and conduct of war is one of the established royal prerogatives. It is most unlikely that a court would entertain any challenge as to whether the war was justified or troops should be sent: *Chandler* v *DPP* [1964] AC 763. This was confirmed by *CCSU* v *Minister for the Civil Service* [1985] AC 374 (the *GCHQ* case) where in particular Lord Roskill listed war as one of the prerogatives that was beyond the control of judicial review. This does not, however, mean the Crown can do as it pleases, as we shall see.

It was once thought that the prerogative to grant, replace or withdraw passports was unchallengeable. After the *GCHQ* case this changed. In *R* v *Foreign Secretary ex parte Everett* [1989] AC 1014 the Court of Appeal held that the Foreign Secretary's refusal to renew a passport was subject to judicial review. Everett had a right to natural justice. In this situation though, this case might be distinguished. Taylor LJ stated that matters of 'high policy' were not justiciable. War is one of those matters of high policy so it is possible that the courts might refuse to intervene here. In *GCHQ* itself, a similar matter of high policy, namely national security, overrode the requirement of natural justice. Also, as in *Everett*, applicants might be thought to be unworthy and in its discretion the court might refuse a remedy.

The expulsion of enemy aliens has been held to be an unchallengeable prerogative matter; *Netz* v *Chuter Ede* [1946] Ch 224. In the famous case of *R* v *Bottrill ex parte Kuechenmeister* [1947] KB 41 it was held that the Home Secretary could intern an enemy alien. What is more, only the Home Secretary could decide when the war was over! That too was a matter of royal prerogative. It is just possible that nowadays the courts might come to a different decision. No war is formally declared and the Home Secretary would probably act under immigration legislation rather than the royal prerogative. At the time of the Gulf war some Iraqi nationals were threatened with deportation. The courts were at least willing to look at their cases, although they decided that they could not investigate an issue of national security; *R* v *Home Secretary ex parte Cheblak* [1991] 2 All ER 319.

The requisitioning of a British subject's property is certainly allowed in wartime. Compensation, however, must be paid; *Attorney-General* v *De Keyser's Royal Hotel* [1920] AC 508.

According to *Burmah Oil* v *Lord Advocate* [1965] AC 75, when British owned property abroad is destroyed for wartime purposes compensation must also be paid. This seems to be confirmed by *Nissan* v *Attorney-General* [1970] AC 179, when British forces requisitioned and damaged a hotel in Cyprus. The House of Lords confirmed that this action did not qualify as an act of state and therefore Nissan might have a remedy. Act of state was here defined as an action of government policy which should not be considered by the courts. To use the American phrase, it is non-justiciable. The case law seems to make a distinction based upon the nationality of the victim. Act of state cannot be committed against a British citizen. Nissan was a British citizen and so had his remedy in a British court. Actions in Fantasia that harm Fantasian citizens are almost certainly an act of the state as held in the old case, *Buron* v *Denman* [1848] 2 Ex 167 where the Royal Navy destroyed Spanish property in Africa, acting upon clear government policy to stamp out the slave trade. This can be contrasted with *Johnstone* v *Pedlar* [1921] 2 AC 262 where the property of a US citizen was confiscated within the UK. This was not an act of state. The true ratio of this case is hard to define. Can an act of state be committed in the UK?

It seems that it cannot be committed against the citizen of a friendly country, here the USA. However *Johnstone* is interpreted, it certainly does not apply to the citizens of a country with which the UK is at war and acts committed in that foreign country.

It is clear that the conclusion of a treaty is an unchallengeable act in the British courts; *Blackburn* v *Attorney-General* [1971] 2 All ER 1780 confirmed in *R* v *Foreign Secretary ex parte Rees-Mogg* [1994] 1 All ER 457. It is also clear, though, that the treaty cannot affect legal rights within the UK unless it is given statutory force. Statutory rights are unaffected; *Laker Airways* v *Department of Trade* [1977] QB 643. So too are rights derived from common law such as trespass and negligence; *The Parlement Belge* [1879] 4 PD 129. The latter point was recently confirmed in *Littrell* v *USA No. 2* [1994] 3 All ER 203.

In conclusion, the British citizen affected by these 'wartime actions' has a fairly good chance of some kind of legal remedy. The removal of passports may, however, be more difficult to challenge. The Fantasian citizens do not have much hope. They are likely to be defeated by the old argument of act of state or the modern one of national security.

QUESTION 4

Behind the phrase 'royal prerogative' lie hidden some issues of great constitutional importance, which are insufficiently recognised.

Munro, *Studies in Constitutional Law*.

Consider whether you agree with this statement.

Commentary

This sort of question is often disliked by students, which is why we included it! It is obviously about the royal prerogative but to answer it properly requires knowledge of other areas of the syllabus. These would include elements of **Chapter 2** on the nature of the constitution and **Chapter 5** on accountability to Parliament. Be warned, it is extremely dangerous to revise for a constitutional examination just by looking at, say, four topics and hoping that they will come up. Many constitutional questions spread across several areas.

This particular question draws upon elements of questions 1 and 2 in this chapter and is really about the large amount of government power hidden behind the prerogative and the lack of adequate controls over it. The answer is an example of a fairly one-sided argument.

Suggested Answer

The phrase 'royal prerogative' makes many people think of the Queen, but that would be highly misleading. It is true that the royal prerogative is the remaining legal powers of the Crown. As De Smith put it 'those inherent legal attributes which are unique to the Crown.' (*Constitutional and Administrative Law*). In reality, though, the Queen has very little to do with the matter. By convention these powers are exercised in the Queen's name by Her Majesty's government. It is true that, by convention again, the Queen must be consulted and, as Bagehot put it, has 'the right to be consulted, the right to encourage, the right to warn' (*The Law of the Constitution*). In fact, though, the royal prerogative is today merely the power of the government.

Many of the central and most important government powers lie within the royal prerogative. They include the conduct of foreign affairs, defence and national security, claims to territory, maintaining the peace, the running of the civil service, mercy and pardon, some aspects of immigration and the honours system.

A problem with these ancient powers is that it is often unclear what exactly they allow the government to do. Occasional legal challenges require the courts to attempt to clarify which powers still exist. For instance, in *Attorney-General v De Keyser* [1920] AC 508 historical research was needed to discover the circumstances in which the Crown could requisition property in wartime. No really clear answer was obtained, so that when a similar point came up again in *Burmah Oil* v *Lord Advocate* [1965] AC 75 there was still doubt. As late as 1987 a 'new' prerogative power could emerge in *R* v *Home Secretary ex parte Northumbria Police Authority* [1987] 2 All ER 282 which stated that the government has the power to maintain peace in the kingdom. This is a prerogative in addition to all the government's statutory powers. The problem with it is, that it is very wide and vague. Could the government imprison people without trial if it claimed that it was keeping the peace of the realm? To take a roughly similar example, the government has the responsibility of protecting national security as recognised in the *GCHQ* case [1985] AC 374. What exactly is national security and what exactly is the government allowed to do to protect it? There are no clear answers to these two questions particularly as it seems from the *GCHQ* case that the courts will be satisfied, on very little evidence, that the government is protecting national security.

In the *GCHQ* case the House of Lords at last said that they could control how the royal prerogative was used by means of judicial review. Control on the basis of illegality, irrationality and procedural impropriety is anyway quite limited but, leaving that aside, all their lordships agreed that some government prerogative powers lay outside the control of the courts. Lords Fraser and Brightman felt that they could only consider delegated use of the prerogative. They could look at the minister's decision but not the Order in Council itself. The politically controversial prerogatives had to be left to the government and Lord Roskill provided a list of these: treaties, defence, mercy, honours, the dissolution of Parliament and the appointment of government ministers.

If we consider cases both before and after *GCHQ* we can see that the courts are in fact very reluctant to interfere with government prerogative decisions. In *Chandler* v *DPP* [1964] AC 763 the deployment and armament of troops was outside the control of the courts. A decision by the Attorney-General to take legal action or not was unchallengeable; *Gouriet* v *UPW* [1977] 2 WLR 310. The decision not to renew a passport was, in theory, reviewable; *R* v *Foreign Secretary ex parte Everett* [1989] AC 1014, but in reality the courts agreed with the government's policy not to renew the passports of wanted criminals. A more successful case is *R* v *Home Secretary ex parte Bentley* [1994] 4 All ER 442. The court disagreed with the Home Secretary's decision not to grant Bentley a posthumous pardon. As Bentley had been dead for over 40 years the decision is of little practical significance, particularly as the courts have declined to follow it in subsequent cases; (*Reckley* v *Minister of Public Safety (No. 2)* [1996] 1 All ER 562).

The courts have often justified their approach by saying, in cases like *Chandler* and *Gouriet* that the proper body to control the use of these highly political powers is Parliament. It is true that Parliament can remove prerogatives as in the Bill of Rights 1689 and the Treasure Act 1996. Acts of Parliament also supersede equivalent prerogative powers and the government must use the statutory power rather than the prerogative one; *De Keyser*. The courts have also held that the government must not ignore the will of Parliament when statutory powers have replaced a prerogative, but have not yet been brought into force; *R* v *Home Secretary ex parte Fire Brigade Union* [1995] 2 All ER 244. However the government usually controls what Parliament does and it is inconceivable that the legislature would be allowed to remove or restrict an important prerogative power against the government's wishes.

By the conventions of our constitution, ministers are accountable for their actions to Parliament. This would include actions under the prerogative. By long standing practices many prerogative areas are hidden from the view of Parliament. Since 1955 successive governments have refused to answer MPs' questions on the Prime Minister's advice to the Queen, the grant of honours, mercy in death sentences and the appointment of bishops, judges and Privy Councillors. Similarly, governments may refuse to answer questions on many defence issues such as arms sales, issues of national security and confidential relations with foreign states. The Parliamentary Commissioner for Administration is also prevented from investigating many of the same areas and also personnel matters in the civil service.

It is clear that the phrase 'royal prerogative' is misleading. In reality we are looking at government power accountable to no one and controlled by no one. This is an issue of great constitutional importance.

5 Parliament

INTRODUCTION

In any constitutional law course, the subject of Parliament is likely to be central. But courses vary greatly in the balance struck between the political and legal aspects. In a course where political issues are given prominence, one would expect to find examination questions about the defects of the electoral system, the powers of back-bench MPs or the reform of the House of Lords. More strictly legal topics would include parliamentary privilege or the legislative process. This chapter includes questions of both types.

Questions addressing possible reforms will be popular with examiners. To answer such questions well, the student who has already formed strong opinions must be careful to marshal the arguments in favour of their opinion and counter the arguments against, not just deliver a vehement oration more suitable for a party manifesto! The student who has no such opinion will need to adopt one for the purpose of answering the question. It is excellent practice for would-be lawyers to develop arguments for or against a proposition, disguising the fact that they are indifferent to it.

QUESTION 1

What do you consider to be the principal requirements for a satisfactory electoral system? To what extent does the present UK electoral system fulfil those requirements?

Commentary

This question covers a large topic, but the student can take comfort from its limitation to 'principal requirements'. This enables the student to choose which issues to concentrate on, before judging the UK system against the chosen criteria. Because there are such great differences between parliamentary and presidential systems, it is reasonable to concentrate, as this answer does, on parliamentary systems only, though in a course which covers presidential systems as well, such an answer would not be satisfactory.

Some students may have strong personal views on this topic, and there is nothing wrong with reflecting these in one's answer. But they must be careful to back up their assertions with evidence and logically constructed arguments.

Suggested Answer

In a parliamentary democracy, elections can be said to serve two purposes which are not easily reconciled: electing a representative Parliament and choosing a government. States have adopted different electoral systems according to which purpose is considered the more important. Some electoral systems are designed above all to identify and legitimate a single party which can then form a government. Other systems are more concerned to ensure that all shades of opinion are represented in Parliament, even if this creates problems in the formation of stable governments.

If the election of Members of Parliament is seen as a means towards the end of choosing a government, it is desirable for the electoral system to facilitate a clear choice by identifying the most popular party and ensuring that it is able to form a stable government. Even if that party does not have an absolute majority in the popular vote, its status as the most popular party could be said to justify its claim to have 'won' the election, particularly if no other party approaches it in popularity. An electoral system may convert a lead into a majority. This may be criticised, but may be regarded as preferable to a system which, by fragmenting representation among a large number of parties, prevents the formation of anything but unstable and short-lived coalition governments. In the worst case, this may discredit the whole democratic regime, as happened in Germany after the First World War.

The UK electoral system does ensure in most circumstances that the leading party has a clear majority in the House of Commons. No party has won more than 50 per cent of the popular vote since 1935, but there is usually a clear winner of the election. The greater the lead enjoyed by the leading party over its nearest rival, the proportionately greater will be the government's majority. However, where the difference between the two leading parties is small, there is no guarantee that the distribution of seats will reflect the distribution of votes. In both 1951 and February 1974, the party which won the largest share of the vote won fewer seats and therefore 'lost' an election which it should have won. The legitimacy of a government formed on this basis is questionable.

Looking at the electoral system in terms of the election of a Parliament only, the obvious requirement is that the distribution of seats should be proportionate to the popular vote, though other factors will be material in deciding whether exact proportionality is considered essential. The opinions of the people should be accurately reflected in Parliament.

The UK electoral system is not and does not purport to be proportionate. It favours those parties whose support is geographically concentrated, whether on a class basis or through particular regional loyalties. It penalises those parties whose support, though widespread, is scattered. The Liberal Democrats and their predecessors have in recent years enjoyed the support of up to 25 per cent of the electorate, but have won only two or three per cent of the seats. If the overwhelming majority of the electorate supports one or other of the two main parties, the UK system is not offensively disproportionate, but where three or more parties are in contention, there is virtually no relationship between the votes cast and the seats awarded. In recent elections, the Liberal Democrats and their predecessors would have won over 100 seats had a proportional representation system been in use.

A powerful argument against exact proportionality is the danger of legitimising extremist opinions by allocating seats in Parliament to parties with very limited support. This may cause particular problems if such parties hold the balance of power in a hung Parliament, enabling them to exercise a political strength far greater than their popular support can justify. The UK electoral system prevents extremist parties from winning any seats. Only in the unlikely event of a concentration of such views in a constituency would such an MP be elected.

No representative of the extreme left or right has been elected in the UK for many years.

A further requirement of an electoral system is that it should give all votes equal value; all should contribute equally to the final result. This is most simply achieved in a party list system, where seats are allocated to parties in proportion to their overall vote, though other systems may also achieve this result. In the UK system, however, various factors operate to make votes unequal in value. The country is divided into single-member constituencies which, in spite of periodic reviews by the Boundary Commissions, are unequal in population size. Reviews take place every eight to ten years, but shifts in population can mean that constituencies become grossly unequal before a review is held. There is a further inequality in that constituencies in England have generally higher populations than those in Scotland and Wales. To some extent this can be justified. The sparsity of population in the remote mountainous areas would make the constituencies too large for one MP to keep in touch with. But there is no justification for the discrepancy in urban constituencies.

Further inequalities in the value of the individual vote arise from the fact that, because of the class-based nature of British politics, many constituencies are safe seats, where the success of one party can be predicted with complete confidence. As a consequence, many votes can be said to be wasted. In the safest seats, many more votes are cast for the winning candidate than are necessary even to secure an absolute majority, and these surplus votes do not contribute to the national result. Votes for the candidates who are bound to lose could also be described as wasted. It could even be argued that all votes for third and other parties are wasted as they are unlikely to contribute to the election of an MP, and have absolutely no chance of affecting the choice of government. It could be suggested that turnout at elections could be even lower than the present 70–80 per cent if more electors realised how unlikely their vote is to matter. Electoral systems such as the single transferable vote go to great lengths to ensure that all votes help in some way to determine the ultimate result, which must encourage participation in the democratic process.

Any electoral system should ensure that the contest is as fair as possible. The secret ballot and universal franchise are clearly essential for this, and the UK system is satisfactory in these respects. It can also be argued that fairness requires equal access to publicity for all parties, regardless of their financial position. The UK system does have strict controls on electoral expenditure, but only at the level of the individual constituency. National expenditure is limited only by the financial resources of the parties, and estimates indicate that the

Conservative Party is able to spend far more on its campaigns than any other party. One significant restraint is imposed by the law forbidding political advertising on commercial television. Party election broadcasts are distributed on an agreed basis, and the broadcasting authorities observe an obligation of impartiality. No such obligation exists in the case of newspapers, which commonly adopt an overt political stance. The majority of the British press is known to be sympathetic to the Conservative Party; indeed some newspapers have claimed the credit for ensuring Conservative election victories, whether justified or not. It is, however, difficult to see how the electoral system could prevent newspapers participating in election campaigns. Questions of media influence rather raise issues relating to concentration of media ownership.

The final requirement for a satisfactory electoral system is that it should be understood by and acceptable to the electorate. This factor always presents problems for any proposal to change the system. People become used to the traditional voting methods, and a substantial programme of public education would be needed if any change were to be made. The UK electoral system makes it very easy to vote and very easy to count the votes, so that results can be declared very quickly. In the more complex systems, such as the single transferable vote, it can take several days for the final results to be calculated. One factor which makes the UK system particularly understandable and acceptable to the electorate is that, by electing MPs on the basis of single member constituencies, the voter feels a link to a particular individual in Parliament. MPs see it as an essential part of their role to foster that link, and devote much time and effort to helping their constituents to obtain redress for their grievances. In a party list system this link does not exist, which diminishes the role the MP will play in helping individuals.

In conclusion, it can be said that the most striking feature of the UK electoral system is the emphasis it places on achieving a decisive result, manufacturing a clear majority for the most popular party. But it fails in most circumstances to produce a Parliament which is genuinely representative of the spread of opinion in the electorate, and this can lead to disenchantment with the whole political system. It may be that the price of obtaining an artificially decisive result is too high.

QUESTION 2

There is undoubtedly widespread concern about the way the legislative process works and about its final product, statute law. For some time, many of those who have to apply the law, and many of those who have to comply with the law have been unhappy about the way legislation is prepared, drafted, passed through Parliament and published.

Report of the Hansard Society Commission on the Legislative Process.

Explain and discuss. What improvements to the legislative process would you recommend?

Commentary

The essential basis for answering this question is a knowledge of the way the legislative process works, particularly the various stages of a Bill's progress through Parliament. The student who has looked at the Hansard Society Report will be at a great advantage but any student could tackle this question by taking a critical view, working out the defects in the system. Mere description will not be adequate but the student may be able to quote examples of unsatisfactory statutes from other areas of legal study, and this will enhance the answer.

Suggested Answer

The importance of the legislative process can hardly be overstated. It is essential that the law be made in an open, accountable way and that the end result be law which is clear, unambiguous and understandable. But there is now frequent criticism that, irrespective of the substantive merits of legislation, UK statutes are poorly drafted and inadequately scrutinised. Although there is some excuse for this in the pressures on parliamentary time, defects in legislation necessitate further amendment, which simply increases the pressure on time and is an inefficient use of resources.

Government legislation may originate from a variety of sources. There may have been a manifesto commitment to change the law, or a new and unforeseen problem may have arisen. Local authorities, government agencies or pressure groups may have persuaded the government that a change in the law would be desirable. The most carefully elaborated legislative proposals come from the Law Commission, whose reports are, where appropriate, accompanied by a draft bill ready for presentation to Parliament.

It is generally agreed that the quality of legislation is improved if there is consultation with interested parties in advance. It is quite common for the government to precede the final proposals contained in a White Paper with a Green Paper suggesting alternative courses of action and asking those interested to submit comments. There is often direct contact at an early stage between civil servants and interested organisations in the public, private and voluntary sectors. The Law Commission conducts elaborate consultation processes, publishing its preliminary thoughts as a consultation paper and encouraging academic and practising lawyers to respond.

Where legislation is introduced in a hurry, however, such consultation will not take place. Many of the most criticised statutes show defects which interested parties would have been able to identify in advance. There is a particular problem where the government has committed itself politically to the introduction of a controversial law, and dare not accept even reasoned criticism through fear of being seen to weaken.

There is no formal requirement for primary legislation to be preceded by consultation, although such requirements are common in relation to the making of secondary legislation, where parliamentary scrutiny is limited. It could be argued that some such requirement would be desirable, but it is difficult to see how this could be made obligatory, given that circumstances do sometimes require the passage of speedy legislation. It is also debatable whether failure to consult could invalidate legislation, given the doctrine of parliamentary supremacy.

The drafting of legislation is the responsibility of parliamentary draftsmen who operate within the agreed conventions as to how statutes are drafted. Their main problems arise when the government is in a particular hurry, or when revisions have to be made to secure the Bill's passage through Parliament. Sometimes very substantial redrafting has to occur and it is then inevitable that mistakes will be made.

The legislative programme for each session of Parliament is worked out by a Cabinet committee. This usually involves much competition between government departments, most of which will have legislative projects waiting for a chance to be put to Parliament. There have been recurrent complaints from the Law Commission that its proposals are always pushed to the back of the queue for parliamentary time, even where all agree that their enactment would be desirable. But there are items of legislation, like the annual Finance Act, which have to be given priority, and it is inevitable that the government will wish to give prominence to the measures which fulfil its political commitments. Agreement on the programme has to be reached in time for the Queen's Speech at the opening of the new session, though not all government bills are announced then.

Legislation can be introduced into either of the Houses of Parliament, but convention dictates that all measures with constitutional implications and all major financial measures are introduced in the House of Commons. Law reform measures are usually introduced in the House of Lords, where the Lord Chancellor sits. Governments often find it difficult to arrange their legislative programme so that the work is spread evenly between the two Houses over the course of the session. All too often, the House of Lords is underworked during the first half of the session and then has large numbers of Bills sent up to it in the second half. It often has to sit late into the summer and return early in the autumn to complete its consideration of Bills before the session ends, usually in November. Any Bill which does not complete its passage within the session is lost and has to go through all its stages again before it can become law.

This imbalance arises principally from the fact that only the House of Commons is democratically representative, so that it is seen as essential that all important Bills are introduced there first. It is also a waste of time for the Lords to consider a Bill which may be defeated in the Commons, as no Bill can ever become law without the Commons' consent. Were the structure and membership of the House of Lords to be reformed, it would be easier for the legislative programme to be arranged more evenly; until then, this problem cannot be resolved.

To examine the stages of the legislative process, the example taken will be of a Bill introduced in the House of Commons. The introduction and first reading are purely formal; the title is read out and the Bill is ordered to be printed. The second reading is a set piece debate on the principle of the Bill. If defeated, the Bill must be withdrawn but this is unusual unless the government has miscalculated its support. The Bill will then be sent for detailed examination in committee, where it will receive its closest scrutiny. Most Bills are dealt with by a standing committee, consisting of up to 50 MPs, with the parties represented in proportion to their overall strength in the Commons. The committee stage can be dealt with by a committee of the whole House but this time-consuming procedure is used only for non-controversial measures, such as consolidation Bills, where it has been agreed that no amendments are necessary, and, at the other extreme, measures of such importance that all MPs feel entitled to participate in the discussion. The ratification of the Treaty on European Union was dealt with in this way.

Although the committee stage is supposed to be concerned with the detailed scrutiny of the Bill, it is often the case, particularly with controversial measures, that the committee stage is used for a political battle. The Opposition may try to ruin the Bill by wrecking amendments, or delay it by filibustering. To prevent this, the government may get the Commons to pass a guillotine motion, imposing strict time limits for the consideration of amendments. Such a timetable may mean, however, that some parts of the Bill are not actually considered at all at the committee stage if time runs out before they are reached. This is clearly undesirable and contributes to the passage of unsatisfactory legislation. But governments argue that, because the principle of the Bill has been approved at second reading, they are justified in limiting the time available for the Opposition to be obstructive.

There are procedures which could, if more widely used, increase the effectiveness of the committee stage. It is possible for a Bill to be referred to a select committee, or to a special standing committee which can hear witnesses, but these procedures are rarely used because they take more time. It may also be that governments do not wish to have their proposals subjected to such detached scrutiny, especially if they have a large enough majority to force their legislation through.

If the Bill has been amended in committee, the next stage is the report stage at which the whole House can examine the amendments. This stage is often used by the government to reverse amendments which have been made against its wishes. Finally, the Bill will be debated and given its third reading.

The Bill will then be sent to the House of Lords, where a similar pattern of readings is followed, the main difference being that all stages take place on the floor of the House, with very little use being made of standing committees. Because the party struggle is less intense, it is in the Lords that most Bills are given their most detailed scrutiny. Technical and drafting amendments may more easily be accepted by the government, and the range of expertise possessed by members of the House of Lords may enable them to make valuable suggestions for improvements. The quality of legislation would be lower were it not for the work of the House of Lords in this respect.

Provided the legislation has been passed in the same form by both houses, it can proceed to the formality of Royal Assent, but if the Lords have made amendments, the Commons will have to reconsider the Bill. By convention, the Lords will normally defer to the wishes of the Commons as the elected chamber, but if they fail to do so, the government will have to invoke the Parliament Acts 1911 and 1949 to have the legislation passed again by the Commons in the following session, so that it can become law without the Lords' consent.

A final criticism of the legislative process is that, once a Bill has become law, it is published, but on a commercial basis only, which for many statutes means at some considerable cost. Traditionally, ignorance of the law has been no excuse; but could a defendant plead that he could not afford to buy the statute which would have informed him whether his proposed course of conduct would be unlawful?

In conclusion, the main problem with the legislative process is that of inadequate parliamentary scrutiny. Although consultation with interested parties is desirable, the democratic legitimacy of the law is dependent on its having been examined and approved by Parliament, in particular by the elected members of the House of Commons. Although there are genuine problems of pressure of time, it can be argued that changes in procedure and more particularly changes in attitude are needed, so that the scrutiny of legislation is given a higher priority. In the long term, improvements to the quality of legislation would actually save Parliament time, by reducing the need for successive acts on the same topic, each repairing defects in the previous attempt.

QUESTION 3

At a recent general election, ten seats were unexpectedly won by the Green Party. The newly-elected MPs seek your advice as to the means available to them to try to influence government policy, especially on environmental matters.

Advise them.

Commentary

This question touches on a wide range of issues relating to the powers of back-bench MPs; the student should try to be reasonably comprehensive rather than just dealing with legislative processes or select committees. Although environmental issues are used as the example in this problem, no specialised knowledge of that subject is needed. A similar answer would serve if another area was identified. An awareness of political realities will enhance the answer, if it is combined with a good knowledge of the House of Commons' activities.

Suggested Answer

The most important factor in determining how much the new MPs can influence the government will be the size of the government's majority. A government with a substantial majority, as long as its own supporters remain loyal, need not worry about the attitude of opposition parties. At the other extreme, a minority government will be dependent on the votes of other parties, which may be able to exact a high price in policy terms, even to the extent of insisting on places in a coalition government. But even where a government has a comfortable working majority, parliamentary procedures offer opposition and back-bench MPs a variety of opportunities for the exercise of influence, and a skilful use of such procedures will maximise their effect. Although government business generally has priority, the new Green Party MPs will find opportunities to make their presence felt in Parliament.

The largest single item in the House of Commons' timetable is the consideration of government legislation. The Green Party MPs may seek to speak in the second reading debate, but the party's greatest opportunity for influence will be achieved by getting one or two of its MPs onto the standing committees which subject bills to detailed scrutiny. This will provide the opportunity to propose amendments, though these will only succeed if they can attract the support of some government MPs; the government, provided that it has an overall majority in the House of Commons, will have a majority on each standing committee. Any amendments agreed to in committee can be reversed by the House of Commons as a whole at the report stage, but there is always the chance that the government will accept reasoned amendments in order to avoid delay in passing the legislation.

Other forms of legislation may provide opportunities for intervention. Private Bills, especially those promoted by local authorities to facilitate developments, may have major environmental implications, and there are opportunities for back-bench MPs to call for debates on the floor of the House, as well as participating in the quasi-judicial committee stages. There are various methods by which an MP can propose legislation, but most of these provide no real chance of success. To have the best chance of getting a Private Member's Bill debated and even enacted, the MPs should enter the annual ballot for the right to promote a Bill on one of the Fridays reserved for that purpose. Competition is very great; most back-benchers enter the ballot, whether or not they have a Bill ready to propose. If one of the Green Party MPs were to be successful in gaining a high place in the ballot, that would give an excellent opportunity to change the law. However, the government would ensure that any Bill to which it was opposed would be defeated, so the MP needs the benevolent neutrality of the government, if not actual support. A modest environmental measure, perhaps for the better preservation of bats, would stand the best chance of success.

Matters of environmental policy will also be dealt with by secondary legislation, but the opportunities for MPs to scrutinise this are not great. Although the most important statutory instruments may require the approval of the House of Commons, most do not and will become law unless a negative resolution is proposed and passed against them. There is a joint committee of Lords and Commons on statutory instruments which examines all instruments laid before Parliament, and has the power to draw matters of concern to the attention of the House, though not in respect of the substantive content of the instrument.

Many environmental matters are the subject of European Community legislation, in which national Parliaments have no direct involvement. There is, however, a Select Committee on European Legislation, which examines proposed EC legislation in the interval between its proposal by the Commission and its approval by the Council of Ministers. The House of Commons has resolved that no minister should agree to a proposal in the Council of Ministers until the committee has had a chance to examine the proposal and, if the committee sees matters of concern, the House should have a chance to debate the issue before any decision is taken in the Council meeting. Although ministers do endeavour to adhere to this procedure, the extension of qualified majority voting in the Council of Ministers means that the UK minister may be unable to prevent the adoption of EC legislation against Parliament's wishes. The Green Party MPs may find it better to influence EC institutions directly, perhaps through the Green MEPs elected in other countries.

Apart from legislation, much of the House of Commons' time is spent on various forms of debate. Although most debate is at the government's initiative, there are a certain number of opposition days, when the opposition can choose the subject for debate. Most of these are used by the largest opposition party, but, by agreement, the Greens may be allocated a half day to debate a subject of their choice. Further, there is an adjournment debate every sitting day, with MPs' right to choose the topic being allocated by ballot. The relevant minister will be required to reply to the debate. Such debates are unlikely to change the government's policies, but are a useful method of publicising an issue, and identifying the government's views on it.

One of the most obvious ways for the Green Party MPs to make their presence felt is by asking parliamentary questions. To obtain maximum publicity, questions should be set for oral answer, often in an oblique form in the hope of surprising the minister with an embarrassing supplementary question. But MPs are subject to restrictions on the number of questions they can table, because of the likelihood of the system becoming clogged and, question time being strictly limited, only some 10 to 20 questions can be dealt with on any day. Any questions not reached are given a written answer, as are all questions where a written answer is requested. This procedure, while not attracting such immediate publicity as Question Time, is extremely useful as a means of obtaining information about the government's actions and policies.

In recent years, the departmentally related select committees have provided MPs with enhanced opportunities for scrutiny of the executive and the Green Party MPs would certainly hope to obtain a place on the Environment Committee. Competition for places is intense and, while places are formally allocated by the Committee of Selection, in practice the party whips have a considerable influence over the allocation of places between parties. The government will have a majority on each committee, and the major opposition party will take the bulk of the remaining places, but determined lobbying by the Green MPs should secure them a place. Select committees do generally try to operate in a non-partisan way as far as possible, and are more likely to influence the government if they do so operate. The opportunities for questioning witnesses in public, and obtaining information from government and other sources make select committees an excellent forum for MPs to operate in.

The Green Party MPs are likely to find themselves a focus for attempts to lobby the government and other authorities. The new restrictions, imposed as a result of the Nolan Committee report into standards in public life, forbid paid advocacy of any cause. This is unlikely to present any problems for the Green Party MPs, as the financial state of most environmental organisations would preclude the payment of consultancy fees. Any such fees, and any other benefits, such as foreign travel, must be fully declared in the Register of Members' Interests. Unpaid advocacy and the general making and facilitating of contacts — indeed the whole networking process — are going to be one of the most useful ways in which the Green Party MPs can help the green movement. Environmental pressure groups have often been seen as outsiders, not directly involved in the political process and kept at a distance from places of influence. Some groups of course prefer that status, believing that the inevitable compromises needed to 'make friends and influence people' are a betrayal of the cause. But others would argue that a voice closer to the internal workings of government will have more effect in practice than any amount of public protest and direct action.

In conclusion, there is a range of methods available to the new Green Party MPs to try to influence the government. While such a small group will have no substantial power, unless a combination of circumstances were to leave them holding the balance of power in a hung Parliament, they can, with political skill, make good use of the opportunities available to them. They may find the dominance of the major parties frustrating, and they will need to seek allies within those parties to achieve anything. But they will have opportunities, particularly to obtain information, which they would not have had but for their electoral success.

QUESTION 4

Did the reform of select committees in 1979 have any significant impact on the balance of power between Parliament and the executive?

Commentary

To answer this question, the student will need to explain how the reformed system of select committees is structured and then to identify those features of the system which have an impact on how effective they can be. The membership and how it is chosen, the powers of the committees and the inter-relationship between members of different parties are all relevant. The assessment of how significant the impact has been is an arguable matter; some might be more critical, others more complimentary. What is important is that the student should construct a convincing argument, whichever standpoint is chosen.

Suggested Answer

The House of Commons uses select committees to perform tasks, such as investigation and scrutiny, which cannot be adequately performed on the floor of the House. Only in committees can witnesses be questioned and evidence examined. Before 1979, there were select committees to examine some subjects, such as nationalised industries, and science and technology, but there was no organised system. In 1978, the Select Committee on Procedure recommended that a rational structure of committees be created, by relating them to government departments. This recommendation was accepted and put into effect immediately after the 1979 general election, mainly on the initiative of the then Leader of the House, Mr Norman St John Stevas.

In 1979, a select committee was created to examine the work of each of 12 government departments, together with their associated agencies, boards, quangos and nationalised industries. Further committees were added to deal with Scottish and Welsh affairs, and in 1994, a Northern Ireland select committee was created. Changes in the structure of government departments, such as the division of Health from Social Security, or the creation of the Department of National Heritage, have been followed by the appropriate amendments to the structure of the select committees covering those areas. The only areas that were initially deliberately excluded from the select committee system were the Lord Chancellor's and Law Officers' departments, because of concern that investigations might be conducted into inappropriate subjects, such as the appointment of individual judges, or the conduct of particular cases. But in 1991 it was agreed that the remit of the Home Affairs Committee should be extended to cover the general functions of those departments. It is therefore now the case that select committees cover the whole range of governmental activities.

Membership of select committees is confined to back-bench MPs, who are chosen by a Committee of Selection. It was hoped that this method of selection would diminish the influence of the party whips, but it appears that in practice each of the main parties agrees on its nominations, leaving the committee with little to do. There are normally just 11 places on each committee, and places are keenly sought after. For long-serving MPs, who have lost the ambition or expectation of serving on government or opposition front bench, the select committees offer an alternative and enhanced back-bench role. For newer MPs, a place on a select committee offers an opportunity to make a name for oneself, with the hope of ultimate promotion to the front bench.

It is accepted that the government, provided that it has an overall majority in the House of Commons, will be entitled to have a majority of members on each select committee. This caused problems during the 1987–1992 Parliament, when the Scottish Affairs committee could not be formed, because there were not enough Scottish Conservative back-bench MPs to form a majority for the committee. In the following Parliament, English Conservatives were used to make up the numbers. Although it is generally straightforward to allocate seats as between the two main parties, the distribution of seats for the minor parties has sometimes caused problems which had to be resolved by a vote of the whole house. The Opposition is allowed to nominate the chairperson of some committees, though the government will provide most chairpersons. Committee members can hold their places for an entire Parliament, and, though there is inevitably a turnover of membership due to promotions to the front bench, resignations and deaths, members can develop a considerable expertise.

Select committees have the power to send for persons, papers and records. Any individual, other than a member of either House of Parliament, may be formally summoned to appear, though in practice committees need do no more than issue an invitation, which will invariably be accepted. Many witnesses will indeed welcome the opportunity to give evidence before such a highly-regarded body. Others may be less co-operative; the brothers Kevin and Ian Maxwell declined to answer questions from the Social Security Committee about their late father's fraudulent use of pension funds, because they were facing criminal proceedings. The committees themselves have no coercive powers. All they can do is to refer the matter to the House of Commons, which has the power to punish those found to be in contempt, but is unlikely to be willing to do so except in an extreme case. No attempt was made to punish the Maxwells in this way.

Members of either House, including in particular government ministers, can only be invited, not summoned to appear. The government promised in 1979 that ministers would appear when invited, and they have complied with this, though it took four increasingly pressing invitations to persuade Mrs Edwina Currie to appear before the Agriculture Select Committee when it was investigating the incidence of salmonella in egg production. Although the House of Commons does have the power to force one of its members to attend a committee, such a power is never in practice going to be used against a government minister, as long as the government retains its overall majority. It is in any case always possible that the minister who willingly attends the committee meeting may be less than helpful in actually answering the questions.

The most interesting issues arise in relation to the appearance of civil servants before select committees. Traditionally, civil servants were not directly accountable to Parliament. Instead, they were responsible to the minister, who had to account to Parliament for their actions. But select committees can bypass the minister by calling the civil servants themselves to give evidence, creating an awkward, three-sided relationship between minister, official and committee. The government has issued, in successive versions, guidance for officials appearing before committees which, though it exhorts officials to be as helpful as possible, reiterates that they remain subject to the instructions of ministers in giving evidence. The guidance suggests that, where issues of the conduct or misconduct of officials are concerned, the official should suggest to the committee that the minister should give evidence instead. Some serious disputes have arisen where ministers have refused to permit particular officials to attend, instead appearing themselves or sending the permanent head of the department to give evidence. The Defence select committee had difficulty investigating the Westland affair because the relevant officials were not allowed to attend. Although the House of Commons could force officials to attend the committee, the government majority is unlikely to permit this, and the officials would be put in an impossible situation if they were ordered by the minister to remain silent. In such a situation, the committee is in practice helpless.

The guidance to officials also identifies various classes of material on which no information should be given to the committee without the minister's approval; these include advice given to ministers, confidential personal information, sensitive economic information and matters under international negotiation. While it is acceptable to assert that some matters are too sensitive to be discussed openly in committee, this list appears to cover some matters which would be of legitimate concern to an investigating committee.

Even more complex issues arise in relation to executive agencies which, while remaining part of government departments, are supposed to operate with a degree of autonomy. Although the governent stated that the creation of these agencies was not intended to alter the arrangements for accountability, their existence has limited the scope for scrutiny through parliamentary questions, and increased the need for other methods of scrutiny to be developed. The government has accepted that, for matters concerning the day-to-day operation of an agency, the head of the agency is the appropriate witness to be called by a select committee, though reserving the minister's right to control the answers given. The select committee seems to be the best method available for parliamentary scrutiny of these agencies, and it is to be hoped that there will be further development of practice in this area.

The most striking feature of these committees is the ability of MPs from different parties to work together, symbolised by the fact that when hearing witnesses they sit together round a table, unlike the confrontational arrangement of the chamber of the House of Commons. Where possible, a consensus is reached and a unanimous report issued. There are some instances where party divisions have prevented this, but not so many as to diminish the effectiveness of the committees. Each committee can choose what topics to examine within its own remit; it will usually conduct one or two major investigations each session, as well as responding quickly to matters of immediate concern. The government has no direct control over the choice of topics and, while it may try to exert an influence behind the scenes, this has not prevented committees choosing subjects which have gravely embarrassed the government. Investigations like that into the Westland affair have lifted stones which the government would certainly prefer to have left unturned.

Although it is clear that select committees have the potential to enhance the powers of the back-bench MP to scrutinise government actions, it is very difficult to assess just how much impact they have had in practice. Some of their reports, such as the reports of the Home Affairs committee into the 'sus' laws have been followed by statutory reform, but in most cases other pressures have contributed to persuading the government to act. A select committee report may simply be the last straw. The government has undertaken always to make a formal response to select committee reports; this does at least force the government to consider and justify its attitude to the issue. It is very difficult for a government to dismiss a unanimous select committee report out of hand; there is always the risk that the subject will arise again to embarrass the government.

It was never likely that the introduction of the reformed select committees would transform the House of Commons into as powerful a legislative chamber as the US Senate, before whose committees even the most powerful have to tremble. But the committees have succeeded in supplying back-benchers with a source of detailed information and in encouraging the development of expertise within Parliament. Their reports have given the public access to insights into the inner workings of government and the televising of their hearings shows the people that the House of Commons is not just a beargarden but is working on their behalf.

The existence of select committees has now become an established part of the parliamentary system. Their impact can perhaps best be assessed by trying to imagine the furore that would be caused, both inside and outside Parliament, by any attempt to abolish them.

QUESTION 5

'It is vital for the quality of Government, for the effective scrutiny of Government and for the democratic process, that Members of Parliament should maintain the highest standards of propriety.' First Report of the Committee on Standards in Public Life.

Why have MPs been subjected in recent years to criticisms of their standards of propriety? What steps have been taken to meet these criticisms? Do you think these steps will be sufficient to restore the reputation of MPs?

Commentary

This question is concerned with a topic which has come to prominence in recent years, and is therefore likely to be popular with examiners seeking an alternative to the more traditional topics. Because the Nolan Committee is still sitting, further developments may occur at any time, so the student who keeps up to date with the news will be at a considerable advantage. Reading the newspapers is an essential task for students of constitutional law.

Suggested Answer

Recent years have seen the appearance of the term 'sleaze' in the vocabulary of journalists describing the conduct of MPs. There has come to be a perception that the behaviour of MPs does not comply with the highest standards of integrity. This led to the establishment of the Nolan Committee, whose report has been followed by changes to the rules governing the conduct of MPs, which it is hoped will in time improve the reputation of Parliament.

Criticism of the conduct of MPs has developed because of two related issues. First, it has never been the rule that MPs must devote themselves wholly and exclusively to their Parliamentary duties. Indeed, it was only in 1911 that MPs were first paid a salary; before then, MPs had either to have inherited wealth, to work at a profession or to accept the sponsorship of trade unions. The hours of sitting, starting in the late afternoon, were designed for the convenience of those with other occupations. Even today, a considerable number of MPs continue in their previous profession, thereby preserving some security for themselves and their families in case of a change of political fortunes.

Secondly, there were very few specific rules as to what an MP could or could not do. Reliance was placed instead on the general good sense of MPs, a shared but unarticulated understanding of what was or was not the 'done' thing. But changed circumstances meant that this shared understanding broke down, leaving MPs with no way of telling whether their behaviour was acceptable or not. In particular, MPs found increasing opportunities to earn money, not from an occupation separate from their seat in Parliament, but from the very fact of being MPs.

Criticism has been concentrated on two main areas. First, many Labour MPs have traditionally been sponsored by trade unions, with the union contributing usually a modest sum towards the MP's office costs and a more substantial contribution towards election expenses. Such sponsorship has always been open, and is payable only from the union's political fund, to which no union member can be obliged to contribute. But it does have the effect of committing the MP to what may be seen as a sectional interest. It is possible that political change within the Labour Party may diminish the appeal to the unions of this form of sponsorship, and some of the proposals of the Nolan Committee will impinge upon it.

The other area, which has attracted concern on a much wider scale, is the development of parliamentary consultancy. Various organisations pay retainers to MPs, in return for such services as making useful contacts with government departments, arranging meetings with ministers, putting down parliamentary questions, suggesting amendments to legislation and generally keeping an eye on anything which may affect the interests of their client. Concern increased further when MPs, not content with a single consultancy, contracted themselves to firms of consultants or formed such firms themselves, even touting openly for clients. Prime Minister John Major was led to describe this as a 'hiring fair' for MPs. The final straw in the view of many was the revelation that some MPs were apparently willing to accept payment in return for asking parliamentary questions on behalf of commercial interests.

The principal rule governing the conduct of MPs was a resolution made by the House of Commons in 1947 which forbade any MP to 'enter into a contractual agreement with an outside body controlling or limiting the Member's complete independence and freedom of action in Parliament'. But the mischief which this resolution was intended to address was any attempt by outsiders to compel MPs to vote or speak in a particular way. It was not clear how it applied to an MP who chose to accept a consultancy. Most MPs felt themselves to be perfectly entitled to speak on behalf of their client's or sponsor's interests in the House, regarding this as an exercise of their freedom of action, not a restriction on it.

There had always been an obligation on MPs to reveal any pecuniary interest in any matter on which they wished to speak or vote. In 1974 it was decided to formalise this by establishing a register of Members' interests. MPs are required to enter on this register a wide range of external interests, from employment, consultancy and sponsorship to gifts, hospitality and overseas travel. This had the desirable effect of increasing the transparency of MPs' activities though MPs could enter the information in an uninformative way. Some declared their employment by firms of consultants, but did not identify the clients of those consultants. Nor were the fees paid revealed, though most Labour MPs declared the amount of their trade union sponsorship. The existence of the register may even have had an adverse effect by persuading some MPs that, provided they made a full entry, they had complied fully with their obligation of disclosure and could not be in breach of the 1947 resolution, even if they accepted money to ask a question or speak in a debate. The impression left in the minds of the general public was that a company could virtually buy the services of an MP. The government decided to set up a committee under the chairmanship of Lord Nolan to investigate this whole area.

The report of the Nolan Committee, while finding no evidence of unlawful corruption, recommended various steps to be taken to restore confidence in the conduct of MPs. Firstly, it recommended reiteration of the 1947 resolution, banning MPs from entering into contracts which require them to act in Parliament as representatives of outside bodies. It further recommended that MPs should be banned from working for parliamentary consultancy firms with multiple clients. The register of Members' interests should be strengthened and clarified to include details of MPs' remuneration from consultancy contracts.

These recommendations were referred to a select committee of the House of Commons which, in one respect, went even further than the Nolan Committee. It proposed a complete ban on paid advocacy; no MP would be allowed to speak in the Commons on any matter on behalf of the organisation that was paying them. All that consultant MPs would be allowed to do was to act outside Parliament and any such contracts would have to be fully declared and registered. The select committee rejected the proposal that remuneration be revealed, but this was overturned on a free vote of the House of Commons. In addition to the ban on paid advocacy, MPs now have to declare, within certain bands, the amount they are receiving for their consultancy contracts. This requirement took effect from April 1996. To enforce these new rules, an independent Parliamentary Commissioner for Standards has been appointed, who reports to a new Select Committee on Standards and Privileges.

The Nolan Committee rejected the suggestion that MPs should be exclusively committed to their parliamentary activities; they are therefore still permitted to have outside employment, practise a profession or be directors of companies. Some argue that all such outside activities should be banned, but this would deter many able persons from seeking a seat in Parliament. Politics is a peculiarly precarious activity; one's career may be destroyed by a slump in the popularity of one's party or a change in constituency boundaries. To retain contact with one's profession is sensible and may well enhance one's usefulness as an MP.

The ban on paid advocacy is likely to lead to a reduction in the number of organisations willing to pay an MP for consultancy services and, where consultancy continues, a reduction in the amount companies and others are willing to pay. It is likely to be some time before the full implications of the new rules are established, and the new Parliamentary Commissioner for Standards will have to give rulings on disputed matters. A question has already been raised as to whether an MP sponsored by a trade union may speak on general trade union issues. This has been held to be permissible though any specific advocacy would no longer be permitted. Trade unions may well abandon sponsorship if its effect is to preclude sympathetic MPs from speaking on their behalf.

Some MPs suggested that, because opportunities for outside earnings were reduced, there should be a substantial increase in MPs' pay. In 1996, MPs awarded themselves a 25 per cent increase. It is notable, however, that an unusually large number of MPs announced in 1995 and 1996 that they would stand down at the next election, and the new rules may be a factor in this. Research conducted for the Nolan Committee gave striking evidence of the low reputation of politicians; only 14 per cent of the public questioned would trust a politician to tell the truth! The effectiveness of the Nolan recommendations can best be judged when the reputation of politicians is examined in a few years' time.

QUESTION 6

Consider the following situations in the light of the rules on parliamentary privilege.

(a) Giles, a back-bench MP, said during a debate in the House of Commons that the directors of the three largest UK fertiliser companies met together regularly to fix prices, in breach of both UK and EC law. The Minister of Agriculture asked Giles to send him further details of the accusation and also suggested that Giles inform the European Commission. Giles wrote to both the minister and the Commission from his parliamentary office. The managing director of one of the companies is threatening to sue Giles for defamation.

(b) A private member's Bill to outlaw fox-hunting is to be debated next week in the House of Commons. Reynard MP is the parliamentary consultant to the British Horse Society; he is paid £2,000 a year for his services, and has declared this in the register of Members' interests. He has been told by the Society that they will end his consultancy immediately unless he votes against the Bill. Animal rights activists have told Reynard that they will picket his home and his office unless he votes for the Bill.

(c) During a debate in the House of Commons on the decline in moral standards, Pecksniff MP accused Deadlock MP of fathering an illegitimate child. This accusation was false, and Deadlock was so annoyed that he punched Pecksniff in the voting lobby. The following day, the *Daily Broadsheet* published a report of the debate, including a mention of Deadlock's accusation. The *Daily Tabloid* published a front page article under the headline 'Deadlock in Love Child Scandal' not mentioning the rest of the debate.

Commentary

When dealing with questions on parliamentary privilege, it is important for the student to remember that there are two perspectives, that of the courts, and that of Parliament itself. These do not necessarily coincide; it is possible for the courts not to accept that a particular issue is protected by parliamentary privilege, even though that is how Parliament would regard it. The student should therefore take both points of view into account.

Suggested Answer

(a) This problem is concerned with the fundamental privilege of Parliament, freedom of speech. This is protected by Article 9 of the Bill of Rights 1689, which states:

That the freedom of speech and debates in Parliament ought not to be impeached or questioned in any place out of Parliament.

As a consequence, the courts have accepted that words spoken in the course of parliamentary proceedings are absolutely privileged. No action for defamation can be brought in respect of such words, nor can they even be cited in court to support an action for defamation arising from words spoken outside Parliament, as in *Church of Scientology* v *Johnson-Smith* [1972] 1 QB 522. Giles can therefore face no legal action over what he said in the debate.

As for the letter written by Giles to the minister, the position here is less clear. If Giles had given the details orally in the course of the debate, this would be protected as a proceeding in Parliament. Does the writing of a letter count as a proceeding in Parliament? In 1957, the MP G. R. Strauss had written a letter to the minister outlining complaints from a constituent about an electricity board.

The board considered the letter defamatory and threatened legal action, which the MP suggested might be a breach of privilege. The Committee of Privileges felt that the MP's letter was a proceeding in Parliament and should have the protection of absolute privilege, but the House of Commons disagreed and voted to dismiss the complaint of breach of privilege. Although suggestions have been made by various select committees that the position should be clarified by a formal extension of privilege to correspondence between MPs and ministers, no such ruling has been made.

Because correspondence is increasingly used by MPs as the best way of raising issues with a minister, parliamentary questions being reserved as the second line of attack, it can be argued that the absolute privilege should be extended. Indeed, MPs are now encouraged to deal with the new executive agencies directly by letter rather than by asking a question of the minister in the House of Commons. However, an MP's correspondence on official matters will have the protection of qualified privilege, and it can be argued that this is sufficient. Why should an MP be immune if he or she is maliciously passing false information to a government minister or official? But the reason for absolute privilege is that even the unfounded threat of legal action might operate to deter MPs from performing their proper function without fear or favour. Anything which reduces the effectiveness of MPs is undesirable.

As far as the letter to the European Commission is concerned, it would be difficult to argue that this is entitled to absolute privilege as a proceeding in Parliament, as EC institutions are completely separate from UK institutions. Giles would certainly be able to claim qualified privilege, however, so that he will be protected if he has acted without malice.

(b)   Provided that Reynard has made a full declaration of his agreement with the British Horse Society, he will not be in breach of any rules by voting on the fox-hunting Bill, whether for or against. His problem is that two different groups are attempting to force him to vote in particular ways. It is a clear breach of privilege for any outsider to attempt, by bribery or threats, to influence an MP, and any such attempt would be subject to punishment as a contempt of Parliament, as well as possibly amounting to a criminal offence. But it is not clear how this rule relates to the practice of parliamentary consultancy. This issue was raised in 1947. W. J. Brown an MP, was appointed by a trade union to further its interests in Parliament, but when political disagreements arose between them, the union threatened to withdraw from the contract, causing Brown financial loss. The Committee of Privileges was concerned mainly with the propriety of the original contract and, having decided that it was proper, found no breach of privilege in the decision to terminate it. But they confirmed that any agreement which purported to bind an MP to behave, vote or speak in a particular way would be improper. In some later instances, the threat by a trade union to withdraw sponsorship from an MP has been classed as a breach of privilege. On each occasion the union withdrew the threat as soon as the issue of privilege was raised, and no punitive action was taken.

It therefore seems probable that any express threat from the British Horse Society, or any subsequent decision to withdraw sponsorship with immediate effect, would be regarded as a breach of privilege, though there would be nothing wrong with a decision to terminate the contract in due course in accordance with its terms. The Society might be satisfied to reflect that in any case, an MP is likely to feel inclined to support the causes for which he has accepted a consultancy. The new rules introduced as a result of the Nolan Committee report will, however, prevent Reynard from speaking during the debate.

Any physical action taken by the protesters may be a breach of the criminal law; an offence under the Public Order Act 1986, assault or criminal damage. Reynard's best course of action, if subjected to harassment, may well be just to call the police. But it will also be a contempt of Parliament to molest or threaten an MP. In the case of the *Sunday Graphic*, 1956, a newspaper was held to be in contempt when it published an MP's telephone number and incited its readers to ring him up and complain about his actions in Parliament. The House of Commons has the power to order an outsider to appear at the bar of the House to be reprimanded, but this power is rarely used. It is probable that, as happens if persons demonstrate in the public gallery, any protesters will be handed to the police to be dealt with.

(c) Because Pecksniff's statement was made during a debate, he is protected by the absolute privilege conferred by the Bill of Rights. Deadlock cannot bring any legal action against Pecksniff for defamation, even if Pecksniff knew the accusation was false. Only if he repeated the statement outside Parliament could Deadlock sue him. Deadlock could, however, refer the matter to the Speaker as a possible breach of privilege, if Pecksniff is abusing his parliamentary immunity; MPs have been reprimanded in such circumstances.

As far as the assault by Deadlock on Pecksniff is concerned, there are various possible consequences. Deadlock has apparently committed a criminal offence, possibly an arrestable offence as defined by s. 24 of the Police and Criminal

Evidence Act 1984. Although MPs were once entitled to freedom from arrest, this no longer applies to criminal proceedings. Deadlock may therefore be arrested and charged with a criminal offence, and dealt with by the criminal courts in the same way as any other person. It is, however, possible for the House of Commons to exercise its right to regulate its own proceedings. It has from time to time had to deal with disorderly conduct by MPs. It may suspend the MP from the House for a time; the MP is not paid during that time and cannot take part in any of the House's activities. The ultimate sanction available against an MP is expulsion from the House, but this has only been used in extreme circumstances, such as conviction for a grave criminal offence, or gross contempt of the House. It is unlikely that Deadlock's behaviour would be regarded as justifying such an extreme sanction, though he would certainly be expected to apologise as was Ron Brown MP when in 1988 he damaged the mace during an overheated debate.

So far as newspapers are concerned, absolute privilege only extends, under the Parliamentary Papers Act 1840, to material published by or under the authority of either House, such as Hansard. But a newspaper has qualified privilege for any fair and accurate report of parliamentary proceedings made without malice, as in *Wason* v *Walter* (1868) LR 4 QB 73. The report does not have to be verbatim to be protected. In *Cook* v *Alexander* [1974] QB 279, it was held that a parliamentary sketch, provided it was honest and fair comment, was entitled to qualified privilege. It therefore appears that the *Daily Broadsheet* may be able to claim qualified privilege for its report. The *Daily Tabloid*, however, is hardly in a position to assert that it is reporting parliamentary proceedings at all, let alone in a fair and accurate way. It will therefore be susceptible to an action in defamation, and cannot plead any privilege as a defence.

QUESTION 7

What purposes are served in a democratic state by a second legislative chamber? To what extent does the House of Lords fulfil those purposes?

Commentary

Questions on the House of Lords are usually concerned with its composition and functions, and will normally require some evaluation or criticism. This question requires the student to discuss in general terms the purposes of a second chamber, before examining the House of Lords itself. A mere description would not be adequate; evaluation is essential, though a student could be more or less critical of the Lords than the suggested answer is, according to personal opinion. References to legislatures in other states, though not essential, will enhance the quality of the answer.

Suggested Answer

In most liberal democracies, the legislature consists of two chambers. Only in smaller states is a single chamber, or unicameral, legislature found to be satisfactory. The respective powers of the two chambers will vary according to the constitutional structure of the state. In Britain, the House of Lords and House of Commons have developed over the centuries, and, as with much of the British constitution, their relationship is to be found in both statute and unwritten convention.

It is an essential element in any democratic state that the legislature should consist of representatives of the people. In a bicameral legislature, both chambers would usually be representative, but with the people represented in different ways. In a federal state, such as the USA or Germany, the separate constituent parts of the federation will be represented in the second chamber. The US Senate consists of two senators from each state, regardless of size. Even in non-federal states, such as France, the second chamber consists of representatives of geographical areas.

The House of Lords, however, cannot be described as consisting of representatives of the people. The existence of the two separate Houses of Lords and Commons derives from the medieval idea that the different classes of society should be separately represented. Such class representation cannot be reconciled with modern egalitarian ideas, but the continued presence of hereditary peers in the House of Lords shows that the peerage retains its privileged right to a voice in Parliament.

The representation of other groups in the House of Lords is arbitrary and erratic. Bishops of the Church of England have seats, but the clergy of other faiths and denominations do not, unless ennobled as a personal honour. The Lords of Appeal can ensure that the judiciary is represented, but doctors, accountants and industrialists have seats only as individual recipients of honours.

It can be argued that, because the United Kingdom is, at present, a unitary state, there is no need for separate geographical representation, and representation on some other, occupational basis would be desirable. But most members of the House of Lords represent only themselves, a bizarre anomaly in a modern democratic state.

One of the principal roles of a second chamber is to act as a check on the first and a safeguard against the concentration of too much power in any one institution. The powers of a second chamber can vary from a mere power of delay to a complete veto, according to the constitution of the state. In Britain, as the House of Commons became more representative of the people, the convention developed that the House of Lords, as an unrepresentative assembly, should not reject measures, particularly financial measures, which the Commons had approved. When the House of Lords broke this convention in 1909, the Parliament Act 1911 was passed to remove the Lords' general power to reject legislation, replacing it with a power of delay, initially for two years, reduced in 1949 to one year.

It is significant that the House of Lords retains the power to reject any Bill to extend the life of the House of Commons, thus making the House of Lords a safeguard against any attempt to subvert democracy by postponing elections. In other matters, the Lords' power to act as a check on the House of Commons, where the influence of the government is dominant, is reduced but not eliminated. To become law within a single session, it is still necessary for a Bill to be passed in identical form by both Houses. Because of its unrepresentative nature, the House of Lords is hesitant to reject legislation or insist on substantial amendments against the wishes of the House of Commons. But it has exercised that power where it has felt that the proposed legislation would be unfair or undemocratic. For example, in 1984 it rejected a proposal to cancel elections to the Greater London Council before its abolition, and in 1990 and 1991 it rejected the War Crimes Bill, forcing the government to invoke the Parliament Acts to ensure its passage. The House of Lords can therefore act as a check on the Commons.

A third task performed by a second chamber is to share the onerous work of scrutinising legislation. Modern governments require the enactment of large amounts of increasingly complex legislation. In Britain, some 50 to 70 Acts are passed each year. It is an essential element in the democratic process that all legislation should be scrutinised by the legislature, and that governments be required to justify their proposals in both substance and detail. Because legislation can be introduced in either House, it is common practice for some legislation, particularly non-controversial measures, to start their passage in the House of Lords where detailed scrutiny can be given, thus saving time in the over-pressed House of Commons.

The House of Lords is considered to play a particularly useful role in the scrutiny of legislation. Among its members are experts in many fields, legal, medical, scientific, technical and ethical, whose comments may be of particular value. Whereas in the House of Commons the intensity of the party struggle may detract from the technical scrutiny of legislation, members of the House of Lords may be able to take a more detached view, ensuring that the legislation, whatever its substantive merits, is of good quality. Without the House of Lords, the quality of legislation would be impaired.

A fourth purpose which can be served by a second chamber is to assist in the scrutiny of the executive. Whether a government is fully accountable to both chambers will vary from state to state. But it is usual for both chambers to play a part in questioning the government and investigating its activities. In Britain, the government is ultimately accountable to the House of Commons alone, through the convention of ministerial responsiblity. But some government ministers will sit in the House of Lords, all government departments will be represented, and it is therefore possible for members of the House of Lords to question the government, both orally and in writing. The House of Lords has established some specialist select committees which can carry out investigations. An important innovation in recent years concerns the scrutiny of proposed European Community legislation, where the House of Lords plays a particularly useful role. Its reports are highly regarded.

Although members of the House of Lords have no constituents to represent, many of them are committed supporters of particular causes, which they use their status and position to promote. Many pressure groups and voluntary organisations find the House of Lords a more useful focus of their lobbying activities than the House of Commons, where party allegiance is expected to prevail over all other interests.

The House of Lords' greatest inadequacy as a second chamber is its non-representative nature, which precludes it from claiming any democratic legitimacy. But, subject to that major deficiency, it performs many of the functions of a second chamber with reasonable efficiency. Its abolition without replacement would leave the government majority in the House of Commons in a dangerously powerful position, and would lead to a reduction in the quality of legislation.

6 Prime Minister and Cabinet

INTRODUCTION

It is ironic that these topics will be included in any constitutional law course, in spite of the fact that they are matters purely of convention, not law in the strict sense. This chapter includes what must be the classic question on the relationship between Prime Minister and Cabinet. Although questions in this area are often in essay form, problem questions may also be set to give variety. The material for these two types of answers will be similar, but the way they are set down will be different and must be more focused.

For all these questions, it is essential for the student to show familiarity with current political developments. Imagine the different answers to a question on the Prime Minister that needed to be written before and after the fall of Mrs Thatcher.

QUESTION 1

How far is it true to say that Britain has moved from a system of Cabinet government to a system of Prime Ministerial government?

Commentary

This is one of the classic subjects for debate in constitutional law, and there are as many opinions on it as there are commentators. The conclusion reached by the student is of much less importance than the quality of the arguments displayed. Because the question addresses change in the constitution, the student must show an awareness of historical developments. It will also be desirable for the student to make comparisons between different Prime Ministers. Any reference to contemporary developments will impress the examiner, though the core of the answer will consist of the classic examples of Prime Ministers using their powers, or being prevented from doing so by their Cabinet.

Suggested Answer

When Bagehot wrote his classic study of the British constitution in 1867, he identified the Cabinet as the central controlling institution, the principal of the 'efficient' parts of the system. But when in 1963 Richard Crossman provided a new introduction to Bagehot's work, he wrote:

> The post-war epoch has seen the final transformation of Cabinet Government into Prime Ministerial Government.

Many commentators have agreed with him, particularly when describing the prime ministership of Margaret Thatcher. Others have pointed to her downfall as demonstrating that the fundamental nature of British government remains collective not individual. The Cabinet, if it so wishes, can still rule.

In the British constitution, both Cabinet and Prime Minister are creatures of convention. Their functions and powers are not defined by law, but have developed gradually in order to provide a form of government answerable to Parliament rather than to the Monarch. The Cabinet developed from the practice of government ministers meeting in private, in the absence of the Monarch, to agree on policies to be presented to Parliament. No legal rules defined which minister was to be regarded as most important. But the position of First Lord of the Treasury, with responsibility for government finance, inevitably made the holder first, or Prime, Minister.

Initially, the Prime Minister was described as 'primus inter pares' or first among equals. Although by the nineteenth century some Prime Ministers, such as Gladstone, were exercising a dominant influence, others, particularly if they sat in the House of Lords, were little more than chairmen of the Cabinet. In the present century, it has become an established convention that the Prime Minister must sit in the House of Commons and political practice now concentrates intense attention on the position of Prime Minister.

The Prime Minister's powers derive almost exclusively from convention and the Royal Prerogative, not from statute. Whether such powers are exercised by the Prime Minister alone, or by the Cabinet collectively, may be determined by established convention, but will often be a matter of political practice or expediency. Even conventions may change over time. The decision to ask the Monarch to dissolve Parliament and call a general election was at one time taken by the Cabinet, but since 1918 the Prime Minister has made that decision, after such consultation with colleagues as appears desirable at the time.

The initial creation of a new government provides the first illustration of the inter-relationship between the Prime Minister's powers and political practice. By convention, the Monarch calls on the leader of the party with a majority in the House of Commons to form a government. The new Prime Minister then has the power to select all the members of the new administration. The Cabinet is therefore of the Prime Minister's own choosing and could be expected to reflect his or her ideas. But in practice, the Prime Minister's choice will be constrained. Leading members of the party will expect important posts, preferably those which they shadowed while in opposition; former political favours may need to be repaid. The longer a Prime Minister remains in office, however, the more opportunity there is for the Cabinet to be reshaped according to the Prime Minister's real preferences. It is now accepted political practice for there to be frequent reshuffles; ministers whose performance is seen as inadequate, or who are not fully in sympathy with the Prime Minister's policies can be removed. For example, Margaret Thatcher was able to remove the so-called 'wets' from her administration. The dismissal of ministers can, however, weaken a Prime Minister by providing a focus for party discontent, or even by being perceived as an act of desperation.

Once the government is formed, the Prime Minister has a decisive voice in the processes by which it operates. Because of the increasing complexity of modern government, meetings of the full Cabinet can deal with only a fraction of government business. The Prime Minister, who approves the agenda, can decide which matters are discussed there, and can keep controversial items off the agenda, though this will be subject to political constraints. Michael Heseltine resigned from the Cabinet when unable to raise the Westland affair there.

The Prime Minister, as chairperson of the Cabinet, can lead and control the discussion there. Because it is not the practice to take votes, the Prime Minister normally concludes discussion by summing up the sense of the meeting, which will be entered in the minutes. It is a matter of personal style whether the Prime Minister allows a genuine consensus to develop or attempts to dominate the debate. But no Prime Minister can be sure whether a Cabinet discussion will lead to the desired result. In the last resort, the Prime Minister cannot insist on the adoption of a policy against the wishes of the rest of the Cabinet.

The Cabinet forms the apex of a hierarchy of cabinet committees, sub-committees and working groups, and most government business will now be dealt with outside the full Cabinet. The Prime Minister now has considerable freedom in establishing and staffing such committees, and can, by careful selection, ensure that only those likely to favour his or her opinion are involved in the taking of the decision. Decisions made in a Cabinet committee are generally as final as those made in the full Cabinet, and ministers remain bound by collective responsiblity even if they were not party to the making of the decision. The existence of Cabinet committees used not to be publicly admitted, but since 1992 the identity and membership of several have been officially revealed. A Prime Minister may even avoid the use of such formal bodies and use wholly informal working groups to take sensitive decisions. Margaret Thatcher used such a group when deciding to ban trade union membership at GCHQ, with other ministers being kept in ignorance until the decision was publicly announced. This clearly shows how the Prime Minister can exercise a dominating influence over the decision-making process, though the exclusion of ministers who feel they should be more involved may ultimately cause political problems.

The Prime Minister has a general responsibility for government policy and is therefore entitled to intervene in almost any aspect of the work of any department, subject only to the limits imposed by energy and enthusiasm. All Prime Ministers are expected to take a particular interest in economic and foreign affairs. Diplomacy is now conducted to a great extent by summit meetings, and the regular meetings of the European Council are the main focus for developments in the European Union. In other matters, a Prime Minister may allow departmental ministers to develop their own policies within an overall strategy, or may insist on involvement in all developments.

It has been suggested that, because Prime Ministers are now so involved in all developments, a Prime Minister's Department should be created, but no such institution has been formally established. The Prime Minister does have the assistance of a range of support services. The Cabinet Office, headed by the Cabinet Secretary, will work closely with the Prime Minister. The Prime Minister's Private Office is staffed by the most promising young civil servants. A Prime Minister will also engage policy advisers from outside the civil service, though problems have arisen where these advisers are thought to have too much influence. Nigel Lawson resigned as Chancellor of the Exchequer when Margaret Thatcher insisted on retaining an adviser who had publicly criticised his economic strategy.

It could be argued that the present situation falls between two stools, by accepting the dominant position of the Prime Minister without providing enough support. The establishment of a Prime Minister's Department on an official basis would provide the ultimate proof that a system of Prime Ministerial government had been established.

There can be no doubt that recent years have seen an increasing concentration of media attention on the Prime Minister. Surveys suggest that the Prime Minister gets more publicity than all the rest of the Cabinet put together. The broadcasting of Parliament, especially the regular televising of Prime Minister's Question Time, has created a perception that the Prime Minister is the government, whatever may be the reality. Elections are described as if they were a contest between party leaders, and it can be argued that elections give the Prime Minister a personal, not just a party, mandate. This strengthens the hand of a successful Prime Minister, but also increases the likelihood that a party's response to unpopularity will be to replace its leader. Even Margaret Thatcher's dominance after 11 years in office did not save her from that fate.

It is very difficult to envisage a return to the days when the Prime Minister was only first among equals. Even a Prime Minister who does not wish to dominate the government would find it impossible to reverse the popular perception of the dominant leader. There are very considerable powers available to a Prime Minister who wishes to make full use of them, and such a Prime Minister will overshadow the rest of the government as Margaret Thatcher did. But the Cabinet remains as the forum in which fundamental issues have ultimately to be decided, and no Prime Minister can ignore or evade the objections of the majority there to the policies he or she wishes to pursue. There have been times when Britain has approached very close to having a system of Prime Ministerial government. But the Cabinet remains among the efficient rather than the dignified parts of the Constitution. The picture drawn by Bagehot is still recognisable.

QUESTION 2

Last year, Peter became Prime Minister when his party won a general election with a majority of 30 seats. He promised, during the election campaign, to provide a massive expansion of higher education. He has now decided that this can only be achieved if a special tax is imposed on graduates. He has discussed this privately with the Chancellor of the Exchequer, who agrees with the scheme. No other ministers have yet been informed, and several of them are likely to be critical of the plan.

What steps can Peter take to ensure that:

(a)   the scheme is adopted as government policy;

(b)   the necessary legislation is passed through Parliament;

(c)   the public accepts the need for the new tax?

Commentary

This question is principally concerned with the powers of the Prime Minister, but it also includes material from other parts of the syllabus, particularly the legislative process. The extent to which material on pressure group activity and policy formation would need to be included would depend on whether the course takes such a political slant. The student will be expected to demonstrate a clear understanding of the conventions governing the Cabinet and of the legal rules governing the passage of legislation. The answer will be greatly enhanced by an awareness of political realities. Too often students' answers read as if this was an abstract theoretical problem, whereas it could easily happen in practice. Because this question is in the form of a problem, the answer should take the same form: do not answer it as if it were an essay.

Suggested Answer

The British Prime Minister has a considerable range of powers and means of influence available to ensure the adoption of his or her policies. Indeed, it is often argued that the British system of government has become one of Prime Ministerial government. But there are constraints on the Prime Minister's powers, and even determined Prime Ministers may find that they fail to ensure the adoption of their preferred policies.

(a) The most formal means available to have the scheme adopted as government policy is to have it agreed in a meeting of the Cabinet. This will ensure that all ministers are bound, by the convention of collective Cabinet responsibility, to support it in public, whatever their private misgivings. Any minister who feels unable to support the policy must, by convention, resign. It would be most unlikely in practice that any such matter would be raised in Cabinet without extensive prior consultations with the ministers directly affected, such as those at the Department for Education and Employment. To avoid a possibly embarrassing defeat, the Prime Minister is sure to take soundings generally among his colleagues, so that he can take the matter to Cabinet having already satisfied himself of a majority there.

Most issues are not, however, dealt with by the full Cabinet, because of pressure of business, but are instead referred to Cabinet committees. There are both permanent and temporary committees and sub-committees. Peter, as Prime Minister, selects the membership and remit of all these bodies. It would therefore be possible for him to refer this scheme to a committee whose membership was carefully selected to provide a majority in favour of it. The Chancellor of the Exchequer and the Secretary of State for Education and Employment would have to be members, but Peter would have a fairly free hand in selecting the other members. It would be to Peter's advantage to chair the committee himself, giving extra power to guide the discussion.

It is accepted practice that, if matters have been decided by a Cabinet committee, they will not be discussed again by the full Cabinet. Only if there is disagreement within the committee, or the matter proves to be one of extreme sensitivity, will it be referred up to a Cabinet meeting. It is therefore quite likely that this scheme could be adopted as government policy without the involvement of some members of the Cabinet, who will none the less remain bound by collective Cabinet responsibility. This gives rise to the possiblity that a minister who feels he or she is being bypassed may resign, thereby revealing splits in the Government which the Opposition can exploit. The resignation of

Michael Heseltine over the Westland affair is an example of this. But it is only with the greatest reluctance that most ministers would take such a step, as resignation is often a path to political oblivion.

Once adopted as government policy, the scheme must be supported in public by all members of the government, down to the most junior Parliamentary Private Secretary. The civil servants in the Treasury and Department for Education and Employment will be instructed to prepare the necessary legislation and administrative procedures, instructions which they are bound to obey. Normally such a major proposal would be announced in the Queen's Speech at the opening of the next session of Parliament, but the government may propose legislation at any time.

Peter is justified in feeling that gaining the adoption of his scheme as government policy is the most important step in its progress.

(b)   The next hurdle is the passage of the necessary legislation through Parliament. Because this is a measure affecting taxation, it will be introduced in the House of Commons, where the government has a comfortable majority. Peter need not therefore be particularly concerned about the attitude of the opposition parties; indeed, vehement criticism of the Bill by them may well encourage the loyal support of his own back-bench MPs.

The task of getting the legislation through lies with the whips, who must ensure a disciplined turnout of MPs to vote on the measure. After the formal introduction and first reading, the second reading provides the opportunity for the House of Commons to debate and vote on the principle of the Bill. Defeat at second reading will force the withdrawal of the Bill, but this is a rare occurrence. The whips will inform Peter in advance of potential revolts, and any measure likely to be defeated will be withdrawn for amendment before the government suffers the embarrassment of defeat. After second reading, the Bill will be referred to a standing committee for detailed examination. The government will have a majority on this committee proportionate to its overall majority, so it should have no difficulty in getting the Bill safely through this stage, though it may have to accept any amendments on which its own supporters insist. If the Opposition parties attempt to delay the bill by filibustering, the government can ask the House of Commons to pass a guillotine motion restricting the time allowed for discussion. Once the committee stage has been completed, the government will have to decide whether to accept any amendments made in committee, or to get them reversed by a vote of the whole House. Finally the vote on third reading will complete the Bill's passage through the House of Commons.

The whips' careful use of persuasion, cajolery and coercion will normally ensure the passage of all legislation to which the government is committed. But back-bench revolts have become more common in recent years, as it is no longer the convention that any defeat will force the government to resign. Only defeat on a vote of confidence, announced as such, will force a resignation, as in 1979. It is possible for a Prime Minister to make a vote on a particular piece of legislation into a matter of confidence in order to demand his party's support, but this may be regarded as a sign of weakness not strength, forcing back-bench MPs to choose between their beliefs and their political survival.

The Bill will then be sent to the House of Lords, where a similar pattern of readings will be followed. If it is classified as a Money Bill, then, under the Parliament Acts 1911 and 1949, the Lords have the power to delay it for only one month. If it is a general measure, the Lords can delay its passage for one session, but it is unlikely that the House of Lords would push opposition to the Bill that far. It is the accepted convention that the will of the House of Commons, as the democratically elected House should prevail. There has only been one example in the last 40 years of the government needing to invoke the Parliament Acts to get legislation passed without the approval of the House of Lords and that was the War Crimes Act 1991.

Voting in the House of Lords is somewhat unpredictable. Although there is on paper a Conservative majority, there are a large number of cross-bench Lords without a fixed party allegiance. This Bill is likely to arouse the keen interest of those Lords concerned with higher education, and the final result of the votes cannot be predicted. If amendments are passed, the Bill will have to go back to the House of Commons, where the government will have to decide whether to accept them or to persuade the House of Lords to concede. Only when the Bill has been passed by both Houses in identical form can it proceed to Royal Assent and become law.

(c)   In trying to get his scheme accepted by the general public, Peter's greatest asset is the opportunity to influence the media. The Prime Minister has a press office, which meets regularly with the journalists accredited to the Lobby to brief them on government business. All the arguments in favour of the scheme would be advanced and opposing arguments rebutted, and it could be expected that some at least of this material would find its way into the press. It is vital for any Prime Minister to cultivate good relations with the media; one might note the award of honours, on the Prime Minister's recommendation, to various newspaper editors and proprietors.

It is likely that this scheme will provoke many individuals to write to their MPs, especially as its effects will be felt most strongly by the articulate and educated. It will therefore be desirable for all MPs of the government party to be supplied with material suitable for explaining and justifying the scheme to their constituents, thus keeping both the MPs and their constituents happy.

It may be that the scheme will provoke protest and demonstrations from students, but these can probably be ignored and are as likely to turn public opinion in favour of the scheme as against it. This is particularly true where protests turn violent. Even the demonstrations against the community charge or poll tax played a limited role in forcing the government to abolish it. In the last resort, it must be remembered that there are as many as four years to go before the next general election. Even if the tax is unpopular Peter can reasonably hope that it will have ceased to be a matter of major concern by then.

The above discussion demonstrates clearly that, once a measure has been adopted as government policy, its chances of becoming law are very high. Very little government-sponsored legislation is rejected by Parliament, and public opinion can rarely be mobilised so as to prevent the government pursuing its policies. The greatest problems for the Prime Minister lie in getting the initial agreement of his or her colleagues, but even here the influence of a determined Prime Minister can be hard to resist.

QUESTION 3

What is meant by the convention of individual ministerial responsibility? How has it been affected by recent developments in Parliament and government?

Commentary

The first part of this question is deceptively simple. Although it is possible to give a brief restatement of the traditional doctrine, that alone would not be sufficient. A deeper analysis is needed, identifying the difficulty in establishing how ministers are supposed to behave, with examples drawn, if possible, from recent practice. The second part of the question gives the student useful hints as to where to look for changes. In Parliament, the reform of select committees has made an impact. In government, changes to the structure and organisation of departments are making it increasingly difficult to apply the traditional doctrine.

Suggested Answer

Traditional constitutional doctrine states that each minister is responsible to Parliament for the work of his or her department. This is intended to ensure that government departments are ultimately accountable, through Parliament, to the electorate. Such accountability is essential in a democracy, and is an elaboration of the general accountability of the government as a whole to Parliament. It is well established that the ultimate sanction to enforce this is the power of the House of Commons to force a government to resign by passing a vote of no confidence in it. Similarly, a minister who loses the confidence of the House of Commons has to resign, though in practice, a Prime Minister who knew that a minister was facing defeat in such a vote would require an immediate resignation before any vote occurred. But how the doctrine operates in less extreme circumstances is more difficult to ascertain.

The classic instance used to describe the doctrine of ministerial responsibility is the Crichel Down affair. Civil servants in the Ministry of Agriculture refused to honour a promise made to a landowner when his land was compulsorily purchased for military use, that he or his heirs would be given the opportunity to repurchase the land when it was no longer needed. There was no suggestion of corruption or other gross impropriety; rather it was a plain case of maladministration. The minister was not directly involved, but when a critical report was published, he felt obliged to resign, being the person ultimately responsible. This course of action was praised as particularly honourable.

In the 40 years since then, it has become clear that this was not a typical example of the doctrine of ministerial responsibility in operation. Rather, it was the unpopularity of the government's whole agricultural policy which led to the loss of back-bench support for the minister. The only other example since then of a ministerial resignation for departmental, rather than personal fault is the resignation of Lord Carrington and his junior ministers from the Foreign Office when Argentina invaded the Falkland Islands. Here, the apparent misjudgments by the Foreign Office could be said to have cost many lives, making it infinitely more serious than the average case of faulty administration.

What then does the doctrine of ministerial responsibility amount to in normal circumstances? Its starting point is the right of MPs to question each minister about the activities of the department and the corresponding duty of the minister to answer. Ever since all Crown servants other than ministers were excluded from the House of Commons at the beginning of the eighteenth century, the minister has been the only person available for questioning. When government activity was much less, it was reasonable to expect ministers to know what was going on in their departments. But even as government activity increased, it remained the expectation that the minister should be able and willing, given reasonable notice, to answer questions on any aspect of the department's work. This provided one of the principal means by which an individual could seek redress for grievances, as the complainant in the Crichel Down affair eventually did. Many such grievances would be dealt with without publicity, and even those which did reach the floor of the House of Commons would conclude with an explanation, an apology and a promise of redress from the minister, without the issue of resignation even being raised.

From the 1960s onwards, other means of redress were developed, to supplement or even replace the traditional method. In 1967, the Parliamentary Commissioner for Administration, or Ombudsman, was introduced, providing an alternative course of action for an MP whose constituent was aggrieved by an act of maladministration. As the PCA's reports and recommendations are almost always accepted in full by the government, and appropriate redress offered, there is no need to invoke the doctrine of ministerial responsibility, and no question of resignation is ever raised. The other development was the immense growth of judicial review, which provides a means of redress wholly outside the political process. A finding by the High Court that a department had acted ultra vires may provoke the Opposition to derision, but is not taken as a ground for threatening the minister's political survival. It is possible to imagine that in extreme circumstances, a judicial ruling could bring the minister's future into question. In the case of *Re M* [1994] 1 AC 377, it was held that government ministers could be punished for contempt of court; if such a punishment were ever imposed, the minister would surely be forced to resign.

It was stated above that one of the bases for the doctrine of ministerial responsibility was the fact that only the minister was present in Parliament to be questioned, but recent developments have altered this. It was always possible for civil servants to be called to give evidence to select committees, and this became much more important with the establishment of the revised departmental select committees in 1979. The Osmotherly rules, which were issued as guidance for civil servants, confirm that a select committee may demand the attendance of an individual civil servant, though the minister may suggest to the committee that another civil servant, or the minister in person, may appear instead. Such advice would normally be accepted, and in any case the civil servant remains subject to the minister's instructions in answering the committee's questions. But it has become common to see civil servants appearing before select committees, and MPs are finding this form of scrutiny in some ways more satisfactory and effective than questioning the minister in the traditional way. No longer is the minister the only person who can be called to account by Parliament.

The development which is likely to have the greatest impact on the traditional doctrine of ministerial responsibility is the reorganisation of the government under the Next Steps programme. This was intended to improve the management and efficiency of the government, by converting those parts of the civil service which provide services to the public into separate agencies, each under the control of a chief executive. Ministers, assisted by a central core of civil servants, would lay down the general policy for each agency, leaving the agency to put that policy into operation.

Concern was expressed as to how these new arrangements could be reconciled with the traditional understanding of ministerial responsibility, especially as no institutional provision was made for any new form of parliamentary accountability. But some new procedures seem to be developing. As agencies were established, ministers developed the practice of replying to parliamentary questions about the work of agencies by simply informing MPs that they had passed the matter to the chief executive, who would answer the MP by letter. MPs were concerned that this procedure provided inadequate scrutiny, in particular because such replies would be private. After a long campaign by MPs, it has now been agreed that such replies will be published in Hansard, like written answers from ministers, making them matters of formal record. This does, however, carry the implication that the minister is not responsible or accountable for the operations conducted by the agency, as he or she would have been before the reorganisation.

To follow up a complaint relating to an agency, the MP has limited scope for raising the matter on the floor of the House. It is, however, possible for the chief executive of an agency to be called before a select committee, and this is becoming the normal practice where a large number of complaints are giving cause for concern. The Child Support Agency is an example where the relevant select committee conducted a thorough investigation. If there is direct accountability of the agency to Parliament by means of the detailed scrutiny by a select committee, the responsibility of the minister becomes almost irrelevant.

Major difficulties remain, however, in establishing accountability where matters fall between the clearly operational, with which the minister is not concerned, and the matters of high policy for which the minister alone remains accountable. The situation could become as difficult as that which used to exist in the nationalised industries, where ministers were not accountable for the day-to-day running of the industry, but were consistently interfering in what should have been managerial decisions.

In conclusion, it is clear that the shouts of 'Resign!' which greet any minister whose department has been at fault are little more than a traditional ritual. Crichel Down, far from being the typical example, is in fact unique. It is difficult to imagine any circumstances in which a minister would feel an obligation to follow that precedent in the absence of personal fault. It would perhaps be desirable if more attention were paid to improve the means by which Parliament scrutinises the executive directly, rather than trying to revive a doctrine which took shape in a more leisured age, when the minister read and even wrote his own despatches. The arrival of executive agencies may provide the opportunity for the development of new means of scrutiny, if Parliament wishes to perform this function more effectively.

QUESTION 4

Consider the following situations in the light of the convention of ministerial responsibility.

(a) In his Budget speech, the Chancellor of the Exchequer announced his intention to impose VAT on books and newspapers. Twenty government back-bench MPs have told the whips that they will vote against this proposal, and if necessary against the whole Budget. The government's overall majority is 15.

(b) Julia, the Minister of Transport, proposed to the Cabinet that extra safety barriers be erected along all elevated sections of motorways, but her proposal was rejected on grounds of cost. Last week, 40 people died when a coach crashed off a motorway, an accident which the safety barriers would have prevented. Julia told Boot, a journalist, about the rejection of her proposal, and he has published an article blaming the rest of the Cabinet for putting lives at risk.

(c) Lag, a prisoner, brought an action for damages against the Home Office after he was injured by a dangerous psychopath with whom he was forced to share a cell. During the hearing it was revealed that civil servants in the Home Office had destroyed some prisoners' records. The Home Secretary did not know this had happened, but the Opposition are calling for his resignation.

(d) Palliser, a junior minister in the Home Office, was seen by PC Plod, a police constable, in conversation with a man in an area of Hampstead Heath frequented by male prostitutes. PC Plod reported this to his superior officers, but was told that orders 'from above' were to remove all records of the incident.

Commentary

This problem covers various different aspects of ministerial responsibility. The student's first task will be to identify and explain the particular facet of the convention that may apply in each case, being careful to describe and illustrate how the convention actually operates in practice. An awareness of political realities, and even a familiarity with the attitudes of the tabloid press, will be most useful.

Suggested Answer

(a) The convention of ministerial responsibility requires above all that the government must have the confidence of the House of Commons. If it loses that confidence it must resign, either to be replaced by another government in which the House of Commons does have confidence or, more usually, to cause a general election. The issue raised in this problem is to identify the circumstances in which a government defeat in the Commons will be taken as an indication of such a fatal loss of confidence. It was thought at one time that any defeat on a major issue would demonstrate a loss of confidence and force the government's resignation, but over the last 20 years this has changed. It is clear that any defeat on a vote of confidence, moved as such by government or Opposition, will make the government resign. This occurred in 1979, when the Labour government lost a vote of confidence and immediately called a general election. This government could adopt the high risk strategy of making the vote on VAT into a vote of confidence, if it felt sure that this would force the 20 rebel back-benchers to support it. But if the 20 were to persist in their rebellion, the government would, if defeated, have no choice but to resign.

Defeat on one aspect of the Budget would not in itself force the government to resign; it would merely cause political embarrassment. In recent years, the government has been forced to rescind an increase in VAT on fuel, without any threat to its survival in office. Defeat on the entire Budget, however, presents a more complex problem. Traditionally, the votes on the Queen's Speech and the Budget were seen as being inherently votes of confidence, but it is not clear whether this is still the case. However, it can be argued that it is both a political and a legal necessity for the government to get its financial proposals accepted by the House of Commons. A Finance Act must be passed each year. Were the Budget to be rejected, the only way the government could survive would be to propose and have passed a vote of confidence, and then to introduce a new and acceptable Budget. This would be a political humiliation for the Chancellor of the Exchequer which he or she could hardly survive, but it would be possible for the government as a whole to claim that it retained the confidence of the House of Commons just enough to enable it to continue in office.

(b) The doctrines of collective ministerial responsibility and Cabinet secrecy require all ministers to support government policy and to refrain from revealing discussion in Cabinet. If a minister has a fundamental disagreement with the rest of the Cabinet, and is not prepared to accept government policy, that minister must resign. There have only been a few exceptional circumstances when members of the government have been allowed to express open dissent. For example, during the referendum on Britain's membership of the EC, ministers were permitted by the Prime Minister to campaign for a Yes or No vote as they wished.

It is, however, by no means unusual for ministers, by careful leaking to friendly journalists, to let it be known that they disagree with an aspect of government policy. This may be tolerated by the Prime Minister in a way that openly expressed dissent would not. Even in Mrs Thatcher's Cabinet, the few remaining 'wets' were in practice allowed to speak critically, though obliquely, about government policies. Of course, if Boot maintains the confidentiality of his conversation with Julia, and it may well be in his interests to do so in the hope of future revelations, it is unlikely that it could be proved that Julia is the source of the story. She may therefore get away with the breach of Cabinet secrecy.

It can be argued that it is not justifiable to describe collective ministerial responsibility as a convention, given that ministers do not appear to feel an obligation to suppress all feelings of dissent. Rather they will tread carefully and express their views in carefully coded language. But there is a recognition of the political reality that an openly divided Cabinet cannot hope to survive and few ministers will take a disagreement so far as to resign, or to express dissent so openly that the Prime Minister has no option but to dismiss them.

(c) According to the convention of individual ministerial responsibility a minister is accountable to Parliament for the activities of his department. This gives Parliament the right to question him and imposes on him an obligation to answer. The minister is the only person available for Parliament to question, at least on the floor of the House of Commons. If the minister cannot satisfy MPs, particularly those from his own party, he may lose the confidence of the House of Commons. In extreme circumstances, the House of Commons could force the resignation of a minister by passing a vote of censure against him.

However, it has long been accepted that a minister cannot be personally blamed for faults within his department of which he did not know and of which he could not reasonably be expected to have known. In this problem we are told that the Home Secretary did not know of the destruction of the records; could he be expected to know? It can be argued that the Home Office's record-keeping procedures are not the kind of matter with which any Home Secretary would concern himself, other matters having a much higher priority. There is no convention requiring the Home Secretary to take the blame in this case.

It is true that in the Crichel Down case the minister did resign because of maladministration in his department, but that was an isolated example and, in all subsequent instances, ministers have shown no sign of resigning because of operational faults within their departments. Opposition calls for the Home Secretary's resignation are therefore little more than traditional rituals, unlikely to be heeded. If the government's own supporters reinforce the criticism, the Home Secretary's position will be much weaker, but even then the Prime Minister can protect him by making it clear that criticism of the Home Secretary is criticism of the government as a whole.

The Home Secretary will therefore be able to save his political career by explaining to the House of Commons what has gone wrong, what steps have been taken to put it right and to ensure that it does not happen again, and what has been done to punish those civil servants who were at fault. It is possible that the Home Affairs Select Committee may wish to investigate the matter further, but that committee can call the civil servants involved to appear in person, without involving the Home Secretary himself, unless he wishes.

(d) Personal misconduct by government ministers has, particularly in recent years, been one of the most common causes of ministerial resignation. It appears that any form of personal misconduct, even if it is no way connected with the minister's exercise of his or her official duties, will now be regarded as making the minister unfit to hold office. Any form of sexual misconduct in particular has excited the fervent interest of the tabloid press, making it virtually impossible for the minister concerned to remain in office. Even the express support of the Prime Minister does not seem to suffice to save the position of a minister whose conduct has become the stuff of headlines. If Palliser was in fact engaged in any sort of improper conduct, and if this were to become known to the media, the only possible course of action available to him would be immediate resignation.

In this problem, however, there is the further suggestion that someone in authority is attempting to cover up whatever happened. If this is merely a decision taken within the police force in the lawful exercise of their discretion whether or not to pursue enquiries, then nothing objectionable has occurred. But any political interference in the activities of the police, or of the prosecuting authorities would be improper, and indeed might in some circumstances constitute a criminal offence. If Palliser, or any other government minister were to be implicated in such interference, then, irrespective of what Palliser was actually doing on Hampstead Heath, he would have no option but to resign. Such behaviour would attract the censure of the House of Commons, and no minister can survive that.

7 The Police

INTRODUCTION

The police are usually a popular area of a constitutional law course. Many students can identify with the practical issues of the powers of the police and what they can or cannot do to the citizen, more readily than they can with the more theoretical areas of the syllabus. There are also matters of concern to the whole of the public not just law students.

Problem-style questions are common in this area. To do these questions well it is important to know what police powers are with some degree of accuracy. It is not, however, necessary to learn by heart every section and subsection number of the Police and Criminal Evidence Act 1984. The substance of its provisions is what really matters. You can probably get a good idea from your course of which parts of this Act are being covered. It is not enough, however, just to list the powers of the police. You must show that you understand them well enough to apply them to the facts of the question. Be aware that most police powers are not arbitrary, the police cannot just use the powers as they please but must have 'reasonable suspicion' or 'reasonable grounds to believe'.

Essay questions on the same material are also possible. These commonly invite the student to take a view upon whether the police have too much or too little power or whether there are or are not enough protections for the citizen. It is not necessary or sensible to list every existing police power even if it were possible to do so within the limits of time or space. What is needed is a representative selection of powers to support whatever argument you are making. For instance if you wish to argue that effective policing is made difficult by over-elaborate procedural safeguards, s. 54, Police and Criminal Evidence Act (PACE) 1984 on intimate body search is a good example. If, on the contrary, you wish to argue that some elaborate safeguards for the citizens are in fact useless, then the provisions concerning production orders and journalistic material are a good example. See cases like *R* v *Bristol Crown Court ex parte Bristol Press and Picture Agency* [1986] Cr App R 190.

Accountability and control of the police are important constitutional issues. The police have an odd status. A constable is 'a servant of the state, a ministerial officer of the central power' (*Fisher* v *Oldham Corporation* [1930] 2 KB 364) yet he/she has no employer and certainly does not have to take instructions from the 'central power' upon how to maintain law and order. Control of the police is divided between three bodies, the Home Secretary, the Police Authority and the Chief Constable. There are two issues. Which of these three has the greater degree of control? Which of the three should have control?

QUESTION 1

Jennifer has been arrested for allegedly committing an armed robbery. While being taken to the police station, she escapes from police custody and is pursued. She flees into Brian's house where she has a room. Brian refuses to let the police enter his house, but the police overcome his slight resistance and enter anyway. Jennifer is rearrested in Brian's living room. The police officers search the room. Brian does not object to the search saying: 'You are in anyway, do what you want'. The police do not find anything.

The police then commence searching Jennifer's rented room, despite her strong objections. They find documents there that seem to indicate her involvement in a financial fraud. The police ask Jennifer about this matter while she is standing in the room watching their search. She explains that her solicitor, Peter, deals with her business affairs and that they will have to ask him about the documents.

The police then start taking Jennifer to the nearest police station. On the way they stop at her solicitor, Peter's, office. The police ask to look at his files concerning Jennifer's business affairs. Peter refuses, but, despite his protests, the police search for and find the files and remove them.

Advise the police as to the legality of their actions and advise Jennifer, Peter and Brian on any means of redress that they might have.

Commentary

This is a fairly typical problem question on PACE 1984. The first thing to do is identify the main police powers that are likely to be in issue. Here it is fairly obviously entry and search of property. The standard student mistake is the same mistake that the general public makes: to believe that the police must have a search warrant. This is only necessary in a minority of cases. There are four other main means of securing legal entry and all of them arise in this problem. Section 17 allows entry to property, s. 18 allows search of the arrested person's home, s. 32 permits search of the premises where the person is arrested and last, and by no means least, consent can be obtained. Make sure that you know these powers and the difference between them.

Suggested Answer

The first question to ask is whether the arrest of Jennifer is lawful because many of the subsequent police powers are dependent upon this. According to s. 24,

PACE 1984 robbery is an arrestable offence. Under s. 25 a police officer must have reasonable suspicion that Jennifer committed the crime. According to Lord Devlin in *Shaaban Bin Hussien* v *Chong Fook Kam* [1970] AC 492, 'suspicion in its ordinary meaning is a state of conjecture or surmise where proof is lacking'. Jennifer must have been informed that she was under arrest and given a non-technical reason why; s. 28 and *Abbassy* v *Metropolitan Police Commissioner* [1990] 1 All ER 193.

Provided that it was a lawful arrest the police are entitled to pursue her when she escapes. Section 17, PACE 1984 permits the police to enter Brian's premises, irrespective of his wishes, to recapture a person who is unlawfully at large. *D'Souza* v *DPP* [1992] 1 WLR 1073 makes clear that this must be a genuine pursuit. *Chapman* v *DPP* [1988] Crim LR 842 makes a similar point that the police must be genuinely seeking to arrest someone, whom they reasonably believe to be on the premises. There seems to be a real pursuit here. If Brian's premises comprise two or more separate dwellings then the constable may only search the parts where the constable reasonably believes Jennifer to be and the parts of the premises used in common. Jennifer's room and the living room would seem to qualify. Under s. 17, though, the search must only be for Jennifer and for no other purpose.

Under s. 117, PACE all police powers may be exercised using reasonable force so it is lawful to overcome Brian's 'slight resistance'.

It appears that Brian consents to the search of his living room. This is not governed by PACE itself, but by Code of Practice B on Searching Premises which comes with the Act. This strongly advises that written consent should be obtained by signature on an official form, 'Notice of Power and Rights', which police are obliged to serve under the Code. According to the Code, Brian should not normally be able to consent to the search of a tenant's room. The difficulty with the Code is that it is not law. If Brian freely consents, how can a tort be committed?

Anyway, the search of the living room for things other than Jennifer is probably legal under s. 32, PACE. Jennifer has been rearrested and there is no reason to doubt the legality of the arrest. A police constable may search the premises where the person is arrested for evidence relating to the offence for which she was arrested. The constable must have reasonable grounds for believing that such evidence is there. It is conceivable that there would be evidence of an armed robbery at Jennifer's home. *R* v *Beckford, The Independent*, 21 June 1991, insists that the officer's belief must be genuine.

As Jennifer is again under arrest, s. 18 could be used to justify the search of her room. These are premises occupied or controlled by the arrested person and the constable only needs reasonable grounds for suspecting that there is evidence of that offence or a connected or similar offence on the premises. A suspected armed robber might well have evidence of her crimes in her room.

The police search must be confined to trying to find evidence of the offence for which Jennifer was arrested. If, however, during that search the police uncover evidence of other offences they do not have to ignore it, but can seize it under s. 19. This might allow the confiscation of the documents. There could be reasonable grounds to believe that they are evidence of an offence.

What Jennifer says about her solicitor, Peter might arouse suspicion about his role in her business affairs. It would not, however, be enough to justify his arrest as his role is not connected with any particular offence. Without arrest the search powers under ss. 18 and 32 are not usable. Incidentally, under Code of Practice C the police should have cautioned Jennifer before questioning her.

Jennifer should be taken to a designated police station as soon as practicable; s. 30, PACE. Stopping on the way for further inquires is permitted under this section and under common law; *Dallison* v *Caffery* [1965] 1 QB 348. Peter clearly does not consent to the search. Jennifer's file is clearly trade, business or professional records held in confidence. Therefore the police would need to use the special procedure under s. 9 and schedule 1, PACE and apply inter partes to a circuit judge for a production order. Search warrants are only permitted for serious arrestable offences. Under s. 116 and schedule 5 possession of firearms or serious financial gain make this a seriously arrestable offence depending upon which offence, robbery or fraud, is being investigated. These files are not exempt from this procedure as they are unlikely to be legally privileged under s. 10. They were not created for trial purposes and could be furthering a criminal purpose; *R* v *Central Criminal Court ex parte Francis and Francis* [1988] 3 All ER 775. On the facts given no such production order was sought and the police actions are completely illegal.

If we consider Jennifer, on balance the police actions seem legal. Secondly, Brian has little to complain about unless unreasonable force was used against him. Peter could sue in tort for trespass and perhaps gain damages. Alternatively he could make an official complaint under The Police Act 1996. If he was successful he would have the satisfaction that the police officers responsible would be disciplined.

QUESTION 2

Polly is arrested by PC Keen in the act of burgling a private dwelling house. PC Keen tells her why she has been arrested and Polly immediately confesses to the burglary and tries to explain. Polly is taken to the police station where she declines to repeat her confession. She asks to see her solicitor, Devious, but Inspector Lucky, who is in charge of the investigation, refuses to admit a clerk sent by Devious on the grounds that 'we will have no dealings with that firm'. Polly is held for 48 hours. Keen and Lucky are interviewing her and she asks for the tape recording to be stopped. Her request is granted and then she confesses. Polly is, in fact, mentally handicapped, but it would not be obvious to someone who did not know her. Several days later PC Keen and Inspector Lucky meet in the police station canteen to agree upon their notes of both of Polly's confessions.

The judge at her trial admits the evidence of both her confessions. Polly is convicted of burglary.

Advise Polly on her possible remedies.

Commentary

This problem concerns the correct police procedures for interviewing an arrested suspect. Much attention has recently been focused upon this area of the law because of changes to the so-called 'right of silence' in the Criminal Justice and Public Order Act 1994. If there are defects in police procedure, which a question like this is inviting you to spot, then the problem arises of whether the court will accept the alleged confession. There is much conflicting case law on this point. To do well on a question like this you must show that you are familiar with the current procedure and are able to make sense of the conflicting cases in order to apply them to the facts.

Suggested Answer

The first question to be answered is whether the arrest of Polly is lawful. Burglary is an arrestable offence under s. 24(1), PACE 1984. According to s. 24(4) PC Keen may arrest her in the act of committing burglary if he has reasonable grounds for suspicion. 'Reasonable grounds' means that PC Keen must have some kind of factual basis for his suspicion. In *Shaaban Bin Hussien v Chong Fook Kam* [1970] AC 492 it was held that 'suspicion in its ordinary meaning is a state of conjecture or surmise where proof is lacking'. PC Keen seems to have complied with s. 28, PACE 1984 by telling her that she is under arrest. A non-technical explanation of the reason for arrest must be given; *Abbassy* v *Metropolitan Police Commissioner* [1990] 1 All ER 193.

PC Keen then seems to have committed a breach of procedure which could be important. Under PACE Code of Practice C he should have cautioned Polly before questioning her. This might cast doubt upon whether her alleged confession will be admitted in court; *R* v *Bryce* [1992] 4 All ER 567. We will look at this issue in greater detail after we have considered other possible breaches of police procedure.

Polly is then taken to the police station as she should be under s. 30, PACE 1984. On arrival she should have been informed that she has a right to see a solicitor under s. 58, PACE 1984. Delay is permitted for a maximum of 36 hours if the crime is a serious arrestable offence. According to s. 116, PACE burglary is not necessarily such an offence. It will only be so if it involved 'substantial financial gain' for Polly or 'serious financial loss' to the householder. We do not have enough facts to know how much Polly stole, but it is doubtful that this is a serious arrestable offence. Even if it was, a police superintendent may only authorise delay if he has reasonable grounds for believing that seeing a solicitor will lead to interference with evidence, harm to other persons, alerting of other persons or hindering the recovery of property. In effect the superintendent has to believe that the solicitor is in league with criminals and will himself commit a crime. As *R* v *Samuel* [1988] 2 WLR 920 explained, such cases would be rare and there seems no evidence to support Lucky's decision. He has not the rank to make it either.

On the other hand, an inspector does have the power to exclude clerks; *R* v *Chief Constable of Avon and Somerset ex parte Robinson* [1989] 2 All ER 15. Code of Practice C states that this should only be done if the clerk's identity is in doubt or if they are not of suitable character, for example they have criminal convictions. If Inspector Lucky is concerned about Devious's firm he should notify the Law Society. In this case he should allow Polly to contact another solicitor or use the duty solicitor.

Polly refuses to answer questions at the police station. Under s. 34 Criminal Justice and Public Order Act 1994 this failure can be drawn to the attention of a court trying Polly and the court may draw adverse inferences from her failure to answer. A solicitor's advice not to answer was not a sufficient excuse in *R* v *Condron, The Times,* 4 November 1996, but I would suggest that a denial of any legal advice might be.

Holding Polly for 48 hours is illegal. Extensions over the basic 24 hours are possible under s. 42, PACE 1984, but this is not, as we have seen, a serious arrestable offence and Lucky is not a superintendent.

Under PACE Code of Practice E the interview with Polly must be tape recorded. The stopping of the tape, even if it is at Polly's request, would cast serious doubt on the validity of her confession. *R v Bryce* (1992). PC Keen and Inspector Lucky should have made contemporaneous notes of the interview. Agreeing them several days later in the canteen is a serious breach of Code C and could well lead to the confession being inadmissible: *R v Keenan* [1989] 3 All ER 598.

As Polly is mentally handicapped an 'appropriate adult' should have been present at the interviews; Code C. The Code does not explain how the police discover whether a person is handicapped. At any trial the jury should be warned that no adult was present: s. 77, PACE 1984. Cases such as *R v McKenzie* 1992 NLJ 1162 have expressed considerable doubt whether such 'confessions' should be admissible. It is also possible that the lengthy interrogation of a vulnerable person like Polly might be held to be 'oppression' under s. 76, PACE 1984; *R v Miller, The Times*, 24 December 1992. If this is so then the confession should automatically be excluded.

If s. 76 does not apply, the court must use its discretion under s. 78 when they may exclude evidence if it has 'an adverse effect on the fairness of the proceedings'. Court rulings on this have not always been consistent. It does seem, however, that 'significant and substantial' breaches of the Act and its Code will lead to exclusion; *R v Keenan* (1989). *Samuel* and *Bryce* also support this approach. It is not unknown though for the courts to admit evidence if they are convinced of its strength and they consider that the technical breaches of the rules made no difference; *R v Alladice* (1988) 87 Cr App R 380.

On balance, I consider that there are too many illegalities for the court to ignore and the court would refuse to admit Polly's alleged confession.

QUESTION 3

PC Sweet sees Alfred walking down the High Street. He knows that Alfred has several previous criminal convictions. Alfred enters a large department store and PC Sweet follows him. He thinks that Alfred might be carrying a knife. PC Sweet, who is in plain clothes, grabs Alfred from behind and tells him that he is going to be searched for 'unlawful possession'. PC Sweet searches Alfred's pockets. He does not find a knife but does find a dozen credit cards, with different names on them, in Alfred's trouser pocket. PC Sweet tells Alfred that he must now accompany him to the police station. At the police station the custody officer refuses to charge Alfred with any offence and allows him to leave.

Later that day another police officer, PC Sour sees Alfred loitering outside the same department store, now closed. PC Sour asks him what he is doing and for his name and address. Alfred does not reply. PC Sour takes hold of Alfred's arm, informs him that he is under arrest and tries to take him to the police station. Alfred attempts to resist.

At the police station Alfred is searched and the credit cards, which are still in his possession, are confiscated. He is then questioned at length about the credit cards. After four hours he is released without charge.

Advise Alfred.

Commentary

This is another problem involving police powers, but this time dealing with a different area of the Police and Criminal Evidence Act 1984. These are the controversial powers of stop and search, which are thought to be a great intrusion upon civil liberties as they often do not lead to any arrest or further legal proceedings.

As before, to answer a question like this you need to know the police powers accurately, although section numbers are not important. There are also a few useful cases, both from before and after the Act. These are mentioned in the answer.

Suggested Answer

PC Sweet does possess the power to stop and search Alfred, but this power must be exercised in accordance with the law. These requirements are set out in ss.1 to 3, PACE 1984.

First of all he can only exercise this power in a place to which the public has access. A shop would seem to satisfy this test. PC Sweet only has the power to search for certain things, one of which is 'an offensive weapon'. A knife would certainly qualify. It is essential though, under the existing law, that he has reasonable grounds for suspicion that he will find a knife upon Alfred's person. He seems to have no grounds. Code of Practice A warns that previous convictions alone are not enough and Alfred has done nothing else to arouse his suspicions.

Section 2 outlines fairly strict conditions for the search. As Sweet is not in uniform, he must have documentary evidence that he is a police officer. He must also provide his name and police station, the object of the search and his grounds for making it. Presumably a non-technical explanation is sufficient, but PC Sweet does not seem to have complied with the section. 'Unlawful possession' is too vague; *Abbassy* v *Metropolitan Police Commissioner* [1990] 1 All ER 193. Grabbing Alfred is also questionable. 'PACE' power may be exercised using 'reasonable force' under s. 117, but surely Sweet should announce himself and his intentions before touching Alfred. Search of the trouser pockets is permitted as it does not involve removal of any garment.

Discovering the credit cards might well arouse reasonable grounds for suspicion of some kind of theft offence. Such offences usually carry a power of arrest under s. 24, PACE 1984. PC Sweet should question Alfred so that Alfred can dispel or confirm the suspicion; *Ward* v *Chief Constable of Avon, The Times*, 26 June 1986. In any case there is no indication that Sweet actually arrests Alfred. Under s. 28, PACE and *Abbassy* v *MPC* (1990) he should tell Alfred that he is under arrest and explain why. As he has not done this it looks like voluntary attendance at the police station under s. 29, PACE. Alfred is free to leave at any time.

Perhaps the custody officer realises that Alfred is not under arrest and that is why he lets him go. Otherwise, the officer should decide whether there is enough evidence to charge Alfred or whether detention is necessary in order to obtain it; s. 37.

PC Sour is perfectly entitled to ask Alfred questions. This has always been the law and is confirmed by Code of Practice A. Alfred is perfectly entitled not to answer. Several cases have made the point that a police officer is not entitled to restrain or detain a person in order to ask questions. That person is entitled to resist, using reasonable force. It is then the police officer who commits assault; *Kenlin* v *Gardner* [1967] 2 QB 510. The person does not commit the offence of obstructing a police officer in the execution of his duty (now s. 89(2) Police Act 1996) because the police officer is not performing his duty. He has no legal right to detain in these circumstances; *Collins* v *Wilcock* [1984] 1 WLR 1172. On the other hand, a light tap on a person's shoulder in order to gain their attention, is perfectly acceptable; *Donnelly* v *Jackman* [1970] 1 WLR 562.

Therefore it seems unlikely that Alfred has committed any offence. There is a case that states that if a person is 'abusive, uncooperative and positively hostile' to a police officer, they commit the s. 89(2) obstruction offence; *Ricketts* v *Cox* (1981) 74 Cr App Rep 298. This case is doubted and does not seem to apply to the facts here. As the cases above held, refusal to answer police questions is not an offence. Nothing in part 3 of the Criminal Justice and Public Order Act 1994, the so-called abolition of 'the right of silence' changes this. It merely means that, if there is an eventual criminal prosecution, failure to answer questions may be drawn to the attention of the court and inferences drawn from the failure.

It is a common misconception that s. 25, PACE 1984 makes it an offence to refuse to give a name and address. The section is merely designed to give a police officer a power of arrest where he would otherwise lack one. Some offences, such as obstructing a police officer in the execution of his duty (see above), do not carry their own power of arrest. Therefore, in certain circumstances, the police are given a power of arrest for offences that are usually non-arrestable. These circumstances are know as the 'general arrest conditions' in s. 25. One of them is where a police officer cannot discover a person's name and address. It cannot be used against Alfred because, as we have seen, there is no reasonable suspicion that he has committed any offence, such as obstructing a police officer, in the first place. PC Sour's actions are therefore an unlawful arrest. Alfred is quite entitled to resist, using reasonable force and does not commit the offence of assaulting a police officer in the execution of his duty under s. 89(1), Police Act 1996; *Swales* v *Cox* [1981] QB 849.

If Alfred had been under arrest, a routine search to 'ascertain ... everything which a person has with him' would be legal (s. 54, PACE 1984). This reverses the result of the pre-Act case *Brazil* v *Chief Constable of Surrey* [1983] 3 All ER 537. Anything which the custody officer 'has reasonable grounds for believing ... may be evidence relating to an offence' may be seized. The credit cards would come under this. The wording makes clear that it does not matter that he was arrested for another offence entirely. On the other hand, Code of Practice C suggests that Alfred should only be questioned for the offence for which he was arrested, not about the credit cards. If this is so, even the four hours detention is too long. He can only be detained in order to obtain evidence of the offence for which he has been arrested; s. 37.

As the police had no legal power to act, Alfred seems to have suffered several assaults and false imprisonment. Alfred could be well advised to sue in court. A police complaint is also possible, but no compensation is payable.

QUESTION 4

'The present arrangements enshrined in the Police Act 1964 create confusion about the respective roles of the Home Secretary, police authorities and Chief Constables.'

Police Reform Cmnd. 2281.

Consider whether the Police Act 1996 remedies this confusion.

Commentary

The organisation and control of the police is an important constitutional issue. The basis of the current arrangements was made in The Police Act 1964 when control was split between the Home Secretary, police authorities and Chief Constables. Since that date case law has expanded on the responsibilities of this triumvirate. The 1996 Act alters the balance. The object of this essay is to consider how the balance has changed.

To answer the question it is obviously essential to know what the Police Acts 1964 and 1996 say. If you do, it is a fairly easy essay to write! The structure I have adopted is simply to go through the functions of the three institutions involved and comment upon how they have changed.

Suggested Answer

Before the nineteenth century there was no organised statutory police force, although there had always been local constables. When police forces were established they were on a local basis, the Metropolitan Police first in 1829 followed by borough and county forces. There has always been a fear of a centrally controlled national police force.

In 1962 a Royal Commission studied the organisation of the police. There had been some disquiet about corruption and excessive local authority interference in some forces. For example, the Chief Constable of Brighton had been dismissed and this led to the famous case of *Ridge* v *Baldwin* [1964] AC 40. The Royal Commission's recommendations were implemented in the Police Act 1964. Local authority control was decreased in favour of the Home Secretary and the Chief Constable. The Police Act 1996 continues this process and increases the power of the Home Secretary.

Back in 1962 it was thought that there were too many, small, local forces. The 1964 Act encouraged amalgamation. Section 32 of the 1996 Act allows the Home Secretary to compel amalgamation.

Many of the 'reforms' of the police first surfaced in the Police and Magistrates' Courts Act 1994 and were consolidated in the Police Act 1996. One of the most controversial was the change in the membership of the police authority for each force. Police authorities were thought to be too large and therefore unwieldy and unbusinesslike. The number of members is reduced to 17. Nine of them are appointed by local councils. Three are magistrates. The remaining five 'independent members' were originally to be appointed by the Home Secretary. The compromise is that they are appointed by the other members from a short list prepared by the Home Secretary. They are also in the minority, so that the influence of the Home Secretary is diminished.

The function of the police authority is to 'secure the maintenance of an efficient and effective police force for its area' (s. 6, Police Act 1996). This used to mean that the authority had overall control. Under the new Act the Home Secretary sets 'local policing objectives' for each force (s. 37), 'performance targets' (s. 38) and may devise Codes of Practice on how the authority should carry out its functions (s. 39). This gives a Home Secretary power at least to 'influence' what a local police force is required to do.

More important still is control over the budget for each force. This used to be controlled by the police authority. By refusing to pay for certain things the authority could very much influence what the local police could do. For instance, in 1984, at the time of the miners' strike, South Yorkshire refused to pay for the use of police horses. In *R* v *Home Secretary ex parte Northumbria Police Authority* [1987] 2 All ER 282 the local Chief Constable wanted riot equipment and CS gas, but the police authority did not want to provide it. The Home Secretary wanted Chief Constables to have this equipment and the police authority was overruled. It is clear under the 1996 Act that the Home Secretary can decide how much money each police force should have (ss. 41 and 46) and set a 'minimum budget'.

The police authority decides who should be in charge of its force by appointing the Chief Constable and the Assistant Chief Constables (ss. 11 and 12). Under the 1964 Act this was with the 'concurrence' of the Home Secretary. Now his 'approval' is required. This just reflects increased involvement by the Home Secretary in the selection of these senior officers. Similarly, the authority may 'retire' the Chief Constable or Assistant 'in the interests of efficiency or effectiveness'. Again the approval of the Home Secretary is required. Under s. 42 the Home Secretary has his own power to remove Chief Constables.

We have already seen that the Home Secretary has certain controls over each police force. He also has the power to make detailed regulations upon how the police operate (s. 50) and he appoints Her Majesty's Inspectors of Constabulary who report to him on the 'efficiency and effectiveness' of each force (s. 54). Annual reports are required from both the police authority (s. 43) and the Chief Constable (s. 44). Although the Home Secretary possessed these powers under the Police Act 1964 he had one thing lacking: the power to tell the police what to do if he was dissatisfied with what he read in their reports. He now has the power in s. 40 'to give direction to police authorities after adverse reports'. Failing his statutory powers, the Home Secretary may always fall back on his general prerogative power to maintain the peace of the kingdom; *R* v *Home Secretary ex parte Northumbria Police Authority* (1987).

In London the Home Secretary has more direct control over the police. There is no police authority and the Metropolitan Police Commissioner deals with him directly.

The Commissioner is the equivalent of the Chief Constable outside London. What powers does the Chief Constable possess? Section 10 of the Police Act 1996 merely notes that 'a police force ... shall be under the direction and control of the Chief Constable'. A number of court cases have confirmed that although Chief Constables have a legal duty to keep the peace and enforce the law, how they do it is a matter for their discretion; *R* v *Oxford ex parte Levey, The Times*, 1 November 1986; *R* v *Chief Constable of Devon and Cornwall ex parte C.E.G.B* [1982] QB 458. Lord Denning put the Chief Constable's or Metropolitan Police Commissioner's position most clearly in *R* v *Metropolitan Police Commissioner ex parte Blackburn (No. 1)* [1968] 2 QB 118: 'No Minister of the Crown can tell him that he must, or must not, prosecute this man or that one. Nor can any police authority tell him so. The responsibility for law enforcement lies on him. He is answerable to the law and the law alone.' The courts could intervene if the Chief Constable failed to enforce the law, but in fact never have.

The Chief Constables even have their own organisation, the Association of Chief Police Officers, which has its own National Reporting Centre. Through this they can liaise directly with the Home Secretary and Chief Inspector of Constabulary.

There is little accountability to the public in any of these arrangements. Section 20 allows local councillors to question the police authority at council meetings. The Home Secretary has general ministerial responsibility for the police.

Successive Home Secretaries have declined to answer questions about the operational activities of the police stating that these are the responsibility of the Chief Constable. There were many examples of this during the 1980s, such as the policing of the miners' strike. Each police force has to make 'arrangements for obtaining the views of the community on policing' (s. 96) but these liaison committees are consultative only. If a person is individually affected by a police action then they can, of course, make an official complaint under Part IV of the 1996 Act. This could lead to disciplinary action against a constable. If the complaint is a serious one it could, also, be supervised by the Police Complaints Authority.

Analysing the arrangements under the Police Act 1996 it seems that the Home Secretary is the most powerful actor. The Chief Constable may have operational control, but it is pretty clear that if the Home Secretary wants to 'influence' what a police force does he can persuade the Chief Constable. After all the Home Secretary controls his budget, his promotion prospects and can send in HM Inspectors. The police authority is often bypassed as the Home Secretary deals directly with the Chief Constable.

8   Freedom To Protest

INTRODUCTION

This is sometimes known as the law of public order. There are a number of criminal offences involved so, occasionally, it is treated as part of a criminal law syllabus. It, however, concerns a very important civil liberty, that of protest against the government or other powerful bodies, so historically it has been an important constitutional law issue. How far may the citizen lawfully go to indicate their dislike of government? According to the British tradition of civil liberties citizens may protest in any way that they want, as long as they do not break the law.

To study this subject we need to know, fairly accurately, which laws may be broken. Problem questions are common in this area. All that you need to do is to identify which laws may have been broken or offences committed. Many students find essay questions more demanding: you have to have a point of view, argue it and marshal evidence to support it. You may be asked whether you think that there is sufficient liberty to protest or whether you approve of the Criminal Justice and Public Order Act 1994 for example.

There is a lot of duplication in the laws on this area. The old common law such as breach of the peace remains. Added to this was the Public Order Act 1936. Some of that Act still remains although much of it was replaced by the Public Order Act 1986. On top of that the Criminal Justice and Public Order Act 1994 creates additional criminal offences and police powers. It is perfectly possible for the same set of facts to give rise to liability under several different laws. The more one looks at a public order problem the more offences one can see. Under examination conditions this is not a problem, time will limit what you can identify. If it is an essay you have to be sensible about what you are going to cover. Select material to support your argument.

If you are considering a problem question only deal with the legal issues raised by the facts. For instance, if you are given a set of facts indicating fairly minor public disturbances it is unlikely that you would be expected to consider riot. A reasonably high level of violence would indicate riot.

QUESTION 1

A group called the West Country Panthers hire a council owned hall in order to hold a public meeting. The meeting is to protest against proposed increases in the excise duty on cider. Six local police officers insist on being present at the meeting, despite the express wish of the West Country Panthers that they should not be. The leader of the Panthers, Jethro X, speaks from the platform and exhorts the crowd to 'throw out these unwanted police officers'. Some of the crowd forcibly remove the officers.

Led by Jethro X, the Panthers then march a kilometre to the main police station to demonstrate against 'police harassment'. Their procession blocks the traffic, some shop windows are broken and some cars are damaged. Many pedestrians flee in alarm. The police arrest Jethro X and 50 other West Country Panthers.

Advise the police on any public order offences that may have been committed.

Commentary

This is a fairly standard sort of problem. The 'mix' of offences is always different but certain 'clues' should be apparent. Look for key words. This is a 'public meeting', so several control powers exist. Speeches call to mind ss. 4 and 5, Public Order Act 1986. Marches and processions are also governed by the same Act. Look out for interference with traffic on the highway: obstruction of the highway is common in such problems.

Suggested Answer

It seems that the local council has freely allowed the West Country Panthers to use its hall. It is not a public assembly within the meaning of s. 14(1), Public Order Act 1986 because it is in a hall. Section 17 defines a public assembly as 'an assembly of 20 or more persons in a public place which is wholly or partly open to the air'. This does not mean that the police are powerless to act. They have their common law duty to prevent a breach of the peace.

The facts here are quite similar to *Thomas* v *Sawkins* [1935] 2 KB 249. There, a public meeting was held in a public library. Police officers insisted upon being present against the wishes of the organisers. The case arose from the attempted expulsion of one of the police officers. It was held that the police officers had a right to enter and could remain if they had a reasonable apprehension that there would be a breach of the peace. Some commentators have thought that this was only because it was a public meeting but it is nowadays clear that this power of entry also applies to private dwellings: *McLeod* v *Commissioner of Police for the Metropolis* [1994] 2 All ER 553. It is also clear, from the same case, that the officers must genuinely believe that a breach of the peace is imminent. Breach of the peace has defied precise definitions. The preferred explanation today is that it is some kind of violence or threat of violence, actual or anticipated; *R* v *Howell* [1982] QB 416; *Percy* v *DPP* [1995] 3 All ER 124. This supplants Lord Denning's view in *R* v *Chief Constable of Devon and Cornwall ex parte CEGB* [1982] QB 458, which claimed that breach of the peace could merely be interference with the work of others. The violence does not have to be committed by the person dealt with by the police. Provoking it in others is enough; *R* v *Howell* (1982).

On the facts given the police might suppose that violence could occur. Jethro X's speech is even more likely to be a breach of the peace. It is also likely that he commits an offence under s. 4, Public Order Act 1986. His words are threatening and are intended or likely to cause the police officers to fear immediate violence. Inciting an audience has long been an offence under this section; *Jordan* v *Burgoyne* [1963] 2 QB 744. It would justify Jethro's arrest.

When the West Country Panthers start marching, there is even more reason for the police reasonably to fear a breach of the peace. It seems from the case law that the police can take any reasonable measures to prevent a breach of the peace. They can attempt to disperse the crowd; *Duncan* v *Jones* [1963] 1 KB 218. They can try to prevent the procession moving to where a breach of the peace may occur; *Moss* v *McLachlan* [1985] IRLR 77. It is clear from these cases that the police may arrest those breaching the peace. The most likely offence that they would be charged with is obstructing a police officer in the execution of his duty (now s. 89(2), Police Act 1996). The police are doing their duty in preventing a breach of the peace, so refusing to obey their instructions is a commission of the offence.

This is a procession so under s. 11, Public Order Act 1986 Jethro X should give the police at least six days notice that the march is planned. It is an offence not to do so. There is no requirement to give notice if 'it is not reasonably practicable'. This was intended by Parliament to excuse 'spontaneous' protests of this type from the need to give notice. Unfortunately there is no case law to confirm this yet. In any case it may still be a breach of the peace. If the Panthers come to a halt it would be a public assembly, as mentioned previously, as there are over 20 of them and they are now out in the open air. Under s. 14, if a senior police officer reasonably believes that serious public disorder, serious damage to property or serious disruption to the life of the community or intimidation of others will result, then he can impose conditions on the place, duration and number involved in the protest. The police's breach of the peace power mentioned earlier is much more flexible and they would probably prefer to use this.

A number of public order offences are likely. A s. 4, Public Order Act 1986 offence is committed as bystanders are put in fear of violence. As the bystanders are at the very least caused harassment, alarm or distress by this threatening behaviour an offence under s. 5, a less serious public order offence, is committed. The most serious offence, riot, can be committed by those who are 'part of the crowd using unlawful violence'; *R v Jefferson* [1994] 1 All ER 270. There are well over 12 participants, (s. 1) but a 'common purpose' might seem to be lacking. According to *Jefferson* a common purpose can be fairly vague; in that case it was 'football hooliganism, celebrating England's victory in an unlawful manner'. Perhaps protesting against tax on cider, in an unlawful manner, would be enough.

Violent disorder only requires threats or acts of violence by three or more people, which put persons of reasonable firmness in fear (s. 2). As with riot, violence against property is enough (s. 8). Affray has no minimum number of participants and merely requires violence against the person putting persons of reasonable firmness in fear (s. 3). There are people nearby so this requirement is met; *R v Sanchez, The Times*, 6 March 1996.

Last but not least the protestors have blocked the traffic. This is obstruction of the highway under s. 127, Highways Act 1980. It is no defence that no obstruction was intended; *Arrowsmith v Jenkins* [1963] 2 QB 561.

The police have many possible offences at their disposal and ample powers to intervene and stop the protest. Their only problem is the practical difficulty of stopping and arresting 50 angry people.

QUESTION 2

Gotham is a small city in the North of England. As a result of government spending cuts, Gotham District Council's Education Committee became extremely short of funds, and so they decided to sell, for development, one half of the playing fields of the local comprehensive school. This caused tremendous opposition locally, and a 'Parents Action Committee' was formed. However, the sale went ahead, and work began on the site. The Action

Committee at once initiated a plan of 'peaceful disruption' involving all-night vigils at the site and constant demonstrations by day. To keep its spirits up, the Action Committee plays music and sings protest songs, particularly during the night. These demonstrations were, at first, peaceful but then began to turn ugly, with the parents and building workers taunting each other. The demonstrations take place largely on adjoining common land, but tend to overflow into the road and onto the site itself. A group of more militant parents has now 'occupied' the site by lying down on it.

The Chief Constable of Gotham City is being pressed by the Council and the developers to do something about this situation. Advise him.

Commentary

This problem is designed to raise the issue of large public protests and how the law might apply to them. As well as the 'standard' old 'common law' and offences under the Public Order Act 1986 you need to consider the newer Criminal Justice and Public Order Act 1994. Although it seems that the government's intention was not to legislate directly to deal with protests as such, some of the Act's provisions are wide enough to cover such events. These create the offences of 'aggravated trespass' and the concept of a 'trespassory assembly'. Lastly the question asks the classic civil liberties question: even if offences are being committed, does this oblige the police to act?

Suggested Answer

The Chief Constable should be advised that his powers to deal with the parents' occupation are considerably increased by the Criminal Justice and Public Order Act 1994. First, however, it should be pointed out that the police already had both common law and statutory powers to deal with this type of matter before the 1994 Act.

If the police officers present have honestly and reasonably formed the opinion that there is a real risk of an imminent breach of the peace, both in place and time, then they may take reasonable preventative action; *Moss v McLachlan* [1985] IRLR 77. A breach of the peace was defined in *R v Howell (Erroll)* [1982] 2 QB 416 as acts or threats of violence against other people or even acts or threats likely to provoke violence. *Percy v DPP* [1995] 3 All ER 124 confirms this interpretation. It seems clear from the parents and building workers taunting each other that a breach of the peace may occur. This entitles the police officers present to disperse the protestors or indeed, the building workers! It also gives the officers power to enter the land which may be private property; *Thomas* v *Sawkins* [1935] 2 KB 249. If the protestors refuse to leave, this would be obstruction of a police officer in the execution of his duty under s. 89(2), Police Act 1996 (*Duncan* v *Jones* [1936] 1 KB 218).

The 'taunting' could well qualify as an offence under the Public Order Act 1986. Threatening, abusive or insulting words likely to cause harassment, alarm or distress are prohibited by s. 5. If any of the words carry with them threats of violence, then it is possible that the more serious s. 4 offence is committed. This outlaws threatening, abusive or insulting words uttered with the intent to cause another person to believe that immediate unlawful violence will be used against the person threatened. Even provoking that other person to violence is covered, confirming the old case of *Jordan* v *Burgoyne* [1963] 2 QB 744.

Under the same Act, a senior police officer could exercise his power of control under s. 14 over 'an assembly of twenty or more persons in a public place which is wholly or partly open to the air'. He could place conditions on the place, duration and maximum number of the assembly. It would be an offence to disobey.

It should be noted that some of the demonstrations overflow onto the road. According to *Arrowsmith* v *Jenkins* [1963] 2 QB 561 wilful obstruction of the highway under s. 137, Highways Act 1980 can be committed even if there was no intention to obstruct traffic and even if no one was actually obstructed.

The Criminal Justice and Public Order Act 1994 grants some new powers to the police to deal with trespass. The most obvious one here is aggravated trespass under s. 68. The parents are trespassing by being present on the old school playing fields and these fields certainly qualify as 'land in the open air'. The Act is unclear on this point so far as s. 68 is concerned, but it is usually possible to trespass on common land. The building workers are engaged in a 'lawful activity' and the parents are intending to obstruct or disrupt that activity. Actual disruption does not have to be proved; *Winder* v *DPP, The Times,* 14 August 1996. Any police officer in uniform may arrest for this offence. Under s. 69 a senior police officer could also direct them to leave. It would be an offence to fail to leave as soon as practicable.

It is also likely that the protestors are covered by s. 61 of the 1994 Act and that therefore a senior police officer may direct them to leave the land. There must be two or more parents and they are obviously trespassing. They have a common purpose in residing there. Even common land is included under this section. The other elements that need to be proved are that the occupier has taken reasonable steps to ask them to leave and that the parents have either damaged the land or used threatening, abusive or insulting words or behaviour towards the occupier's employees or agents. Alternatively the other element could be that the protestors had six vehicles with them. This seems unlikely on the facts. Damage could be merely trampling the grass down; *Gayford* v *Choulder* [1898] 1 QB 316. As we have seen earlier, the parents have almost certainly used, at the very least, abusive or insulting words to the building workers who could well be employees of the occupier. To fail to leave as soon as reasonably practicable is again an offence.

From the point of view of the Chief Constable both s. 61 and s. 68 give him the ability to 'clear' the site. It is an offence for any person who knows of the directions to return within a three month period.

Although this protest is definitely not a 'rave', it is just about possible that it meets the definition in s. 63. They are on land in the open air. Trespass is not necessary. There might be one hundred or more of them. They are present during the night. It is doubtful though that their music is 'amplified' or of such a 'loudness and duration' as to be 'likely to arouse serious distress to the inhabitants of the locality'. The parents' musical tastes are unimportant. 'Music includes sounds wholly or predominantly characterised by the emission of a succession of repetitive beats' which means that 'ordinary' music is covered by the Act, not just rave music.

The ability to apply for a four day ban in a five mile radius under s. 70 might seem attractive to the Chief Constable. The assembly is a 'trespassory' one and probably involves 20 or more people but it seems unlikely that it is causing significant damage to land of historical, archaeological or scientific importance. 'Serious disruption to the life of the community' is just about possible but the local authority and Home Secretary would have to agree to such a ban. This seems unlikely in these circumstances.

So it is clear that the Chief Constable has a number of 'dispersal' powers at his disposal. He does not, however, have to use any of them if it seems inappropriate to him, despite the wishes of the Council and the developers. Even following the passing of the Criminal Justice and Public Order Act 1994 it would seem that *R* v *Chief Constable of Devon and Cornwall ex parte* CEGB [1982] QB 458 still applies. There, according to the Court of Appeal, clear breaches of the criminal law were being committed by trespassers occupying a site. Despite this the Court was content to rely on the Chief Constable's discretion and would not order or advise him to do anything.

QUESTION 3

... there are many ways in which public meetings or processions may fall foul of the law, both civil and criminal. Just as important is what is likely to happen in practice ... Much depends on 'the policeman on the spot'.

Bailey, Harris and Jones. *Civil Liberties, Cases and Materials.*

Discuss.

Commentary

This is the dreaded discussion essay. It is a bit different from the straightforward question which asks for a view upon whether civil liberties are unduly restricted or not. You are being asked to consider a very specific issue, the amount of discretion built into the law. The question is also confined to meetings and processions. There is therefore no need to list every possible public order offence. You are being asked about police powers of control. If we look at them closely we can see that police officers are often faced with difficult choices. The powers to control meetings and processions under the Public Order Act 1986 should spring to mind but so should the new powers in the Criminal Justice and Public Order Act 1994 and common law concepts like breach of the peace.

Suggested Answer

Even before the enactment of the Criminal Justice and Public Order Act 1994 the police had many powers, both statutory and common law, at their disposal to control public meetings and processions. Although many of these powers are characterised by quite complex requirements before they can be used, those requirements are very much a matter of interpretation. The formula used in the Public Order Acts is 'the senior police officer'. This simply means the most senior officer present, meaning that 'the policeman on the spot' often has much discretion about the decision that he takes. Such decisions are rarely challenged in the courts.

A public meeting or procession may well be held on the public highway. Such events have no special legal protection and would usually be a criminal obstruction of the highway. According to *Arrowsmith* v *Jenkins* [1963] 2 QB 561 no intention to obstruct is necessary and it is irrelevant that the highway is not completely blocked. *Hirst* v *Chief Constable of West Yorkshire* [1987] 85 Cr App R 143 tries to moderate this by insisting upon the right to demonstrate and protest, but it seems from the facts that this defence will only succeed if the obstruction was very minor.

A police constable has a common law duty to prevent a breach of the peace occurring; *Lavin* v *Albert* [1982] AC 546. The exact definition of a breach of the peace is uncertain but it seems to involve an act of violence or a threat of violence, including threats of violence against a person's property in their presence; *R* v *Howell* [1982] QB 416 and *Percy* v *DPP* [1995] 3 All ER 214. Both cases make clear that provoking others to violence is also a breach of the peace. An important point is that the breach of the peace need not actually be occurring, it need merely be 'imminent' in time and space; *Moss* v *McLachlan* [1985] IRLR 77. Therefore the police officer has to anticipate what is about to happen. In *Moss* the police believed that if 'flying pickets' reached a nearby colliery, violence between striking and working miners might erupt. The honest and reasonable belief of the police might be based on past incidents of violence as in *Moss*, or just on what could happen as in *Lavin* where someone was pushing into a bus queue. If a breach of the peace is feared, then the police officer on the spot may take any reasonable action to prevent it. This could involve arrest, stopping a procession as in *Moss* or dispersing a meeting as in *Duncan* v *Jones* [1936] 1 KB 218. It is difficult for someone to challenge successfully the lawfulness of a police action. A rare example is *Percy* v *DPP* (1995). Percy had repeatedly climbed the perimeter fence into RAF Alconbury. She could not be bound over to keep the peace, because she was not threatening any violence, nor was it reasonably likely that she would provoke any.

Turning to statutory powers, s. 11, Public Order Act 1986 requires the organisers of a procession to give six days' notice. This enables the senior police officer to fix conditions such as the route or a requirement not to enter a particular public place. The police officer has very wide powers because the conditions depend upon his reasonable belief that there is likely to be serious public disorder, serious damage to property, serious disruption to the life of the community or the intimidation of others. If the police are concerned about serious public disorder they may go further and seek an order banning all processions in the area for a period of up to three months. The application is made by the chief police officer, not the policeman on the spot, and goes via the local authority to the Home Secretary (s. 13). There is no appeal against the imposition of conditions or a Home Secretary's ban. A judicial review was attempted in *Kent* v *Metropolitan Police Commissioner, The Times*, 15 May 1982, but it failed.

The senior police officer has similar, but more restricted powers to impose conditions upon public assemblies (s. 14). These are defined as gatherings of at least 20 people in the open air. There is no requirement to give advance notification to the police and no ban can be imposed. Conditions may be imposed on the same grounds as for processions, but they may only affect the place, maximum duration and maximum number of people involved. Coupled with the breach of the peace power mentioned earlier, this gives the police considerable discretion as to how to deal with a public assembly.

The Criminal Justice and Public Order Act 1994, ss. 70 and 71, expands the powers in s. 14 of the 1986 Act, by creating a new concept of the 'trespassory assembly'. Now the chief officer of police can apply to the Home Secretary via the local authority, for an order banning such assemblies for a period of up to four days. The chief officer must have a reasonable belief that it is a trespass and that this may result in either serious disruption to the life of the community or significant damage to land, buildings or monuments of architectural, archaeological, historical or scientific importance. This section is obviously designed to give the police the legal power to stop the annual Stonehenge and other 'free', pop music festivals. How they judge whether there will be 'disruption' or 'damage' is problematic.

Under the 1994 Act, ss. 63 to 67, the police are given extensive powers to control a particular type of public assembly, 'the rave'. Raves can be forbidden, people can be arrested and vehicles and sound equipment can be seized. A police superintendent decides whether it is a rave, but ordinary police officers implement his decisions. Maybe one knows a rave when one sees one, but the statutory definition could prove very difficult to apply. There is no need for it to be a trespass, at least 100 people must be present, amplified music must be played, at night and the loudness and duration must cause serious distress to the inhabitants of the locality. Finally, music can include 'a succession of repetitive beats'. There can even be doubts about what is music!

A component of both these new powers is the ability to stop people from proceeding to the assembly or rave at a distance of up to five miles from the event. For an assembly it is a radius of five miles. For a rave, it is five miles from the boundary of the site. A police officer could be involved in difficult questions of how far away from the event a person is.

Processions and meetings have no special protection from the civil law. Trespass is a distinct possibility. Nuisance, both public and private is also easily committed; *R* v *Clark (No. 2)* [1964] 2 QB 315. Lord Denning argued in *Hubbard* v *Pitt* [1976] 1 QB 142 that a small picket of an estate agents was not nuisance, because the minor interference with business was outweighed by the pickets' freedom to protest. Unfortunately, the other two judges did not agree with him. Motorway protesters at Twyford Down committed the tort of wrongful interference with business; *Department of Transport* v *Williams, The Times,* 7 December 1993.

In a sense though, none of these civil matters directly involves the police. *R* v *Chief Constable of Devon and Cornwall ex parte CEGB* [1982] QB 458 made clear that the police only had a duty to become involved if a crime or breach of the peace had been committed or was about to be committed. The case also made clear that the decision to become involved was not that of the Chief Constable. The individual policeman on the spot should weigh up the situation and decide for himself what needs to be done.

9 Freedom of Speech

INTRODUCTION

Freedom of speech is one of the most important civil liberties in a democratic society. It enables citizens to say or write what they like. This could include criticism of the government or other powerful institutions and discussion of alternative policies. Without free and open debate it is difficult to see how a democratic system could work.

As it is a civil liberty and not a right, we need to study the various laws that restrict free speech. One can say or write whatever one likes unless there is a law against it. Unfortunately there are a lot of laws that may need to be considered. The main areas would be obscenity, official secrets, breach of confidence and contempt of court. Other relevant laws might be blasphemy, sedition, incitement to disaffection, incitement to racial hatred and civil and criminal defamation. Different constitutional law courses will have different emphases and may concentrate on only some areas. Read the syllabus and listen to what your lecturers and tutors are telling you! If this does not work, a study of past examination papers should usually give you a clear idea of the areas that are required study.

Different lecturers will often have very different ideas of what should be studied. A traditional concern was the freedom of expression of writers and artists. This is reflected in the 'reform' of the law in the Obscene Publications Act 1959. Other laws would probably be considered such as the common law conspiracy to corrupt public morals, and the statutes regulating cinemas, theatre and videos. A more modern way of looking at this area might be to assume that the battle for artistic freedom was won back in the 1960s and 1970s and that the worry now might be whether there is sufficient control over pornographic material. A topical concern here might be paedophilia and as well as the above laws there might be a consideration of the Protection of Children Act 1978.

Other courses might be interested in the freedom of the press. The Broadcasting Acts, the non-statutory procedures for press complaints, contempt of court and defamation might well be the main focus of study.

Yet again there has been recent concern over the government's control over official information. Here one would look at not just the Official Secrets Acts but also the Public Record Acts, breach of confidence and the Spycatcher trials. The *Scott Report of the Inquiry into the Export of Defence Equipment and Dual-use Goods to Iraq and Related Prosecutions* dealt with government accountability to Parliament and public interest immunity. When John Major became Prime Minister he announced that he was in favour of open government and a White Paper of this name was issued in 1993 (Cm 2290). So here we see a number of areas of constitutional law study combining: freedom of speech, Parliament, ministerial responsibility, the control of the Civil Service and even Crown Proceedings. The debate often centres around whether we can rely on the government of the day to make more information available, as John Major suggests, or whether we need something more formal and legally enforceable like a Freedom of Information Act.

It is unlikely, nowadays, that any constitutional and administrative law course would attempt to cover all of the possible aspects of freedom of expression. So our suggested answers only try to cover the main and, we hope, most likely areas.

QUESTION 1

Humbert, who lives in Alphaville, is interested in computing and child pornography. He obtains from his computer images of young children engaged in sexual activity. These he prints out and exchanges with his friends. He also exchanges video recordings dealing with similar subject matter. He is arrested by the police and prosecuted.

In his defence, he wishes to argue that his sexual desires are incurable and that looking at such pictures is beneficial in that it satisfies those desires. He also wishes to argue that some of the computer images are of artistic merit. Eminent psychiatrists and art experts are willing to give evidence on his behalf.

Two days before his trial, the local newspaper, *The Alphaville Record* publishes an article under the headline, 'Hanging is Too Good for Humbert' and reveals that he has previously been convicted for sexual offences. The editor defends publication as in the public interest.

Advise Humbert and the editor of *The Alphaville Record*.

Commentary

This is a fairly typical problem designed to raise most of the main issues on obscenity law. The cases are interesting in themselves and fairly easy to remember. All that is needed is to apply them to the facts. In common with many questions on obscenity the student would also be expected to know about other laws which cover roughly the same area. There are quite a number of them and it is hard to predict which ones would come up in a particular question. So it is best to have a general idea of most of these laws. The examples here are the Protection of Children Act 1978, the Video Recordings Act 1984 and perhaps conspiracy to corrupt public morals.

Another common tactic is to expect students to be aware of quite recent changes in the law, here those made in the Criminal Justice and Public Order Act 1994 will need to be mentioned.

It is hard to make a problem question about obscenity long enough, so it is not unusual to include another area of law in the question. Here it is contempt of court. Again it would be hard to devise a full problem question on contempt. There are only so many points that could be raised.

Suggested Answer

The first offence that springs to mind is that Humbert might have contravened the Obscene Publications Act 1959. Section 1 makes it an offence to publish an obscene article.

Publishing includes any form of distribution. It is not necessary to show that Humbert did this for gain, for distributing or circulating is enough according to the Act. Even if this was not the case, an 'exchange' might well be held to be for gain. 'Article' includes video cassettes according to *A-G's Reference (No. 5 of 1980)* [1980] 3 All ER 816. Whether obscene material stored on a computer was an 'article' was open to doubt until the Criminal Justice and Public Order Act 1994 (schedule 9, para 3) made it clear that the transmission of electronically stored data was covered by the 1959 Act.

The test for obscenity is also set out in s. 1, Obscene Publications Act 1959. It is that the article is obscene 'if its effect ... is, if taken as a whole, such as to tend to deprave and corrupt persons who are likely, having regard to all relevant circumstances, to read, hear or see' it. This test has eluded precise definition. *R v Secker and Warburg* [1954] 2 All ER 683 stated that the material being merely shocking and disgusting was not enough. The famous, though unreported, case concerning the book, *Lady Chatterley's Lover* in 1960 suggested that it meant 'to make morally bad, to pervert, debase or corrupt morally'. The old case, *R v Hicklin* (1868) LR 3 QB 360 mentioned 'exciting impure or libidinous thoughts'. It is not necessary to show that anyone was actually depraved or corrupted, merely that the material has that tendency.

The statutory definition above also demands that the likely audience is taken into account. If it is children, obscenity is more likely to be proved; *DPP v A & BC Chewing Gum* [1968] 1 QB 519 and *R v Anderson* [1972] 1 QB 304. Here though, although the material concerned children, they are most unlikely to be the 'target' audience. This is likely to be adults. Humbert cannot argue that they are likely already to be paedophiles and so incapable of further corruption. The argument that the 'audience' for pornography is already corrupt has not succeeded; *R v Anderson* [1972] 1 QB 304; *DPP v Whyte* [1972] AC 849.

The vague definition of obscenity may not be a problem. The jury will decide. Expert evidence is not permitted to help them on this issue unless the type of obscene material is outside the normal experience of adults. Expert evidence was allowed upon the effects of cocaine in *R v Skirving* [1985] QB 819 and the effects of horrific pictures upon children in *DPP* v *A & BC Chewing Gum* (1968). There seems no justification for this type of expert evidence in this case.

Section 4 of the 1959 Act does, however, permit expert evidence upon 'artistic merit' (*R* v *Anderson; Lady Chatterley*). If the material can be shown to be for the 'public good' it is not obscene. The jury decide first whether material is obscene and then, if it is, whether considerations of public good outweigh this and if publication is desirable. More general arguments and evidence that pornographic material has therapeutic effects has never been permitted; *DPP* v *Jordan* [1977] AC 699 and *A-G's Reference (No. 3 of 1977)* [1978] 3 All ER 1166.

On balance I consider that Humbert's computer images and videos will be judged to be obscene. If this is not so, there are other offences that could be considered. Mere possession of an 'indecent' photograph is an offence under the Protection of Children Act 1978. Section 84, Criminal Justice and Public Order Act 1994 makes very clear that 'photographs' include both the electronic data and the print-out. There is no defence of public good. Similarly there is no such defence to the common law offence of 'conspiracy to corrupt public morals'; *Shaw* v *DPP* [1962] AC 220. Paedophile 'rings' have been dealt with under this offence. Lastly it is highly unlikely that Humbert's videos have been given a classification under the Video Recordings Act 1984 by the British Board of Film Classification. This is particularly so, since the Board was urged to have 'special regard' to videos dealing with 'human sexual activity' in s. 90, Criminal Justice and Public Order Act 1994. It is a criminal offence merely to supply such a video, punishable by imprisonment.

The Alphaville Record is almost certainly guilty of contempt of court. Under s. 2(2), Contempt of Court Act 1981 there needs to be a 'substantial risk that the course of justice will be seriously impeded or prejudiced'. The publication of previous convictions has long been held to be contempt; *R* v *Odhams Press* [1957] 1 QB 73. The proceedings are clearly 'active' because Humbert has been arrested (s. 2(3)).

There is a defence under s. 5 that the risk of prejudice is purely incidental to a 'discussion in good faith of public affairs'. A passing mention in a newspaper article about a forthcoming trial might benefit from this section; *A-G* v *English* [1983] 1 AC 116. Here, though, the main purpose of the article seems to be to discuss Humbert, his trial and his previous convictions. It is a clear contempt.

Indeed, it could be argued that the editor obviously knows about the trial and is deliberately trying to interfere with the administration of justice. This intentional contempt is not covered by the Act (s. 6), but remains as a common law offence; *A-G* v *Hislop* [1991] 2 WLR 219. It would be treated most seriously by the courts if, as would be likely here, the Attorney-General brought a prosecution against the editor.

In conclusion both Humbert and the editor face conviction. In a strange way the contempt might help Humbert. If convicted, he might be able to appeal successfully on the grounds that he did not receive a fair trial; *R* v *Taylor* [1993] 98 Cr App R 361.

QUESTION 2

Jane is a civil servant working for the Ministry of Defence. Because of the nature of her work she had signed the Official Secrets Act on commencing her employment. During the course of her work Jane comes across a document indicating that a British company is selling artillery shells to the government of Fantasia. She knows that this is contrary to British law and contrary to the stated policy of Her Majesty's government. Jane asks a more senior civil servant what she should so. He tells her that the Secretary of State for Defence knows all about it but the matter is to be kept secret.

Jane is still concerned that the law is being broken so she hands over a copy of the document to a journalist who works for the *Sentinel* newspaper. That journalist discovers that there is a D-notice relating to arms sales to Fantasia. He and his editor decide to publish the document anyway.

The government learns about the proposed publication and wants to stop it. It also wishes to punish the parties responsible.

Advise the government.

Commentary

The problem with this sort of question is that at first glance it might seem unclear which area of constitutional law is relevant. The inspiration for the question is fairly obviously the 'Arms to Iraq' scandal, but it is not about the main concerns there of ministerial accountability and public interest immunity. Reading the rubric carefully, what you are actually asked to do with the facts given, is often helpful. Here it tells you that we are looking at the laws protecting government information.

The Official Secrets Act should immediately spring to mind, but so should breach of confidence, even though it is now several years since the Spycatcher trials. As will be seen from the suggested answer there are a few other bits and pieces of law that come in handy for questions like this.

Although this is a problem question, this sort of area is more often examined by means of an essay. The same material could be 'recycled' to answer an essay. With an essay, though, you would be expected to be critical rather than analytical as with a problem.

Suggested Answer

The most obvious avenues for the government to explore are the Official Secrets Acts 1911 and 1989, but there are other possibilities. A civil action, perhaps for breach of confidence, might be possible and as Jane remains a civil servant, she is subject to Civil Service discipline.

Jane has signed the Official Secrets Act. This is a common procedure, but has no legal effect. All it does is warn her that she is in the sort of job that may be subject to the Act. Despite the reforms of 1989, s. 1, Official Secrets Act 1911 remains in force. Breach of this is a serious offence and can be committed by communicating to an enemy information which may be 'prejudicial to the safety and interests of the state'. Jane might well argue that she has not communicated to an enemy and that her actions are not 'prejudicial to the safety and interests of the state'. *Chandler* v *DPP* [1964] AC 763 indicates that only the government can decide what is in the interests of the state. In *R* v *Ponting* [1985] Crim LR 318 Clive Ponting, another civil servant, tried to argue that he was helping the state by revealing to an MP information that ministers were hiding from Parliament. This is the 'whistle blower' argument: he has a duty to expose wrongdoing. In *Ponting* the court ruled that this argument was unacceptable, as in *Chandler*, only the government of the day could rule on what was 'in the interests of the state'. Despite the ruling the jury acquitted Ponting. For this reason, it is unlikely that the government would use s. 1 against Jane or the journalist, who would also be liable.

The old s. 2 of the 1911 Act was replaced by the Official Secrets Act 1989. Geoffrey Robertson QC described it in *Freedom, the Individual and the Law* (p. 168) as replacing 'a blunderbuss with an armalite rifle'. The Act is meant to focus only on those areas where the Crown is genuinely concerned with the revelation of official information. As a Crown servant Jane is definitely affected by the Act. At first it seems that she has committed an offence under s. 2 because she has disclosed 'defence' information. 'Defence', as defined in s. 2(4)(b), includes 'weapons' but only those used by the armed forces of the Crown. Foreign armed forces are not included. Maybe it is possible that foreign weapon sales come under subsection (d), the more general 'defence policy'. Not only this but the prosecution must prove that disclosure of information is 'damaging' to British defence. It is difficult to see how this could be so. Damage to British interests abroad is also mentioned in s. 2 and might be easier to prove on our facts. There is also a 'did not know' defence in the Act. Jane, would perhaps claim that she did not know that this was defence information, as defined by the Act. It would be hard for her to claim that she did not know that it was 'damaging'.

Another government possibility is s. 3 of the Act which protects information relating to 'international relations' in a similar way. Conceivably arms sales to a foreign country might well be connected to foreign policy matters. Again damage to British interests would need to be shown.

It is by no means clear that Jane has committed either offence. *Chandler* v *DPP* (1964) suggests that the courts would accept the government's view upon what was 'defence', 'international relations', or 'the interests of the United Kingdom abroad'. It will be interesting to see if nowadays the courts will be prepared to allow Jane to put forward her own evidence on these issues. We await cases!

The journalist commits an offence if he knowingly receives the information and knowingly passes it on (s. 5). This the *Sentinel* newspaper seems determined to do. It is necessary, however, for the information to contravene the foregoing provisions of the Act for this to be an offence. As we have seen, it is by no means clear that it is 'defence' or 'international relations' information. The journalist also has a 'not damaging' defence.

Under s. 8 it is a specific offence for a Crown servant like Jane to retain the actual document 'contrary to her official duty'. Again, though, for the offence to be committed it has to relate to 'defence' or 'international relations'. This is not certain.

Because of the difficulties of a successful prosecution the government might resort to other measures. The 'D-notice' is just a non-statutory warning issued by a committee of members of the media, civil servants and the military. It is not an offence to ignore the notice. Civil injunctions can be sought to prevent breach of the Official Secrets Act, as occurred in the Zircon Affair of 1986–7. As such an injunction would probably be issued ex parte, the government might be successful in obtaining it. The court would await the full trial before looking into the finer legal points.

There is possibly a very simple way to recover the document. The document and copies of it are personal property that belong to the government. It could simply sue in tort for its return. This occurred in a rather similar case to our facts, *Secretary of State for Defence* v *Guardian Newspapers* [1984] Ch 156. Sarah Tisdall, a civil servant, had handed a document about cruise missiles to *The Guardian* newspaper. Section 10 of the Contempt of Court Act 1981 allows a journalist to protect his sources, but not if it is an issue of national security. This might well be such an issue and the document's return would be ordered.

Jane, as a civil servant, would be subject to dismissal for breach of contract. It was suggested in *R* v *Ponting* (1985) and *A-G* v *The Observer, The Times* [1990] AC 109 that a civil servant concerned about government wrongdoing should report their worries to their superiors, not the press.

The most flexible remedy that the government has, is to seek an injunction for breach of confidence. It is clear that Jane has an obligation of confidence as a civil servant. The government would need to show that it was in the public interest to prevent disclosure: *A-G* v *The Observer, The Times (Spycatcher)* [1990] AC 109. Damage to the security services was the reason for non-disclosure in that case. Here, though, Jane, wishes to reveal breaches of the law. This might be allowed; *Cork* v *McVicar, The Times*, 31 October 1984. It is difficult to know how the courts would balance the need for confidentiality in the civil service against the need to expose wrongdoing. If an injunction was issued, it would not just affect Jane and the *Sentinel*, but other newspapers who could be reasonably expected to know about the injunctions; *A-G* v *Newspaper Publishing* [1991] 2 WLR 994.

Despite the powers available to the government it is uncertain whether the courts would help it prevent disclosure. It is not clear that there are breaches of the Official Secrets Acts. Nor is it clear what the 'public interest' requires under breach of confidence. Following the scandal about Arms to Iraq and the *Scott Report of the Inquiry into the Export of Defence Equipment and Dual-use Goods to Iraq and Related Prosecutions* (15 February 1996) it is to be hoped that the courts would think it desirable for information about illegal arms deals to be revealed in the newspapers.

QUESTION 3

'British law regards free speech as a very good thing so long as it does not cause trouble, at which point it can become expensive speech, visited with costly court actions, fines and damages, and occasionally imprisonment.'
G. Robertson, *Freedom, The Individual and The Law*, 7th edn.

Discuss.

Commentary

This is a very opinionated statement. You can either agree with it, disagree with it or examine both sides of the argument and 'sit on the fence'. Whatever you do, you must show that you have a good knowledge of this area of the law. Also, you must show that you understand the law to a reasonable level. You can do this by making clear that you understood what G. Robertson means in his statement, even if you do not necessarily agree with what he says. Knowledge can also be shown by choosing examples which well illustrate the point that you are making. In this sort of question there is no need to describe the law in minute detail. Pick your examples to suit your argument.

Lastly a good essay needs a good argument. Structure is very important. Think about how you can build an argument to a conclusion. Always work out a plan before starting and, particularly in examination conditions, stick to it!

Suggested Answer

The British are very proud of their 'right' of free speech. In fact, though there is no 'right' of free speech, it is merely a civil liberty. We may write or say anything that we want, as long as we do not break the law. Unfortunately, there are rather a lot of laws that can be broken. As will be demonstrated, speech that is innocuous will be tolerated. If powerful interests are threatened the full weight of the law will be used against the offender.

The Obscene Publications Act 1959 is often cited as a progressive, liberal measure which ushered in the permissive, so-called 'swinging sixties'. It is true that its preamble states that it is 'to provide for the protection of literature', but it is also 'to strengthen the law concerning pornography'. An 'article' is deemed to be obscene 'if its effect ... is, if taken as a whole such as to tend to deprave and corrupt persons ... likely ... to read, see or hear the matter contained ... in it'. (s. 1(1)). This would seem wide enough, but the Act has proved ineffective. Pornography is widely available and there is increasing concern about material involving children. Yet many of the famous obscenity prosecutions have been of books that did not just contain sexual material, but a controversial issue or political message. The trial of the book, *Lady Chatterley's Lover* in 1960 was a famous case, but D. H. Lawrence had long been a controversial author. *Cain's Book* by Alexander Trocchi contained very little sexual material but approved of injecting heroin; *Calder* v *Powell* [1965] 1 QB 509. *R* v *Skirving* [1985] QB 819 involved the promotion of the use of cocaine. *R* v *Calder & Boyars* [1969] 1 QB 151 concerned *Last Exit to Brooklyn* by Hubert Selby Jr. It merely described the seamier side of New York life. *R* v *Anderson* [1972] 1 QB 304 involved the prosecution of the hippie magazine, *OZ*, as much for its political stance as for its sexual content. It is true that in all but *R* v *Skirving* (1985) an acquittal was eventually obtained, but the defendants were put to the trouble and expense of defending themselves. Anderson and his co-defendants were even jailed for a short period.

It may be that the 'public good' defence under s. 4 enabled the defendants to escape conviction by showing, with the help perhaps of expert witnesses, that their work had literary or artistic merit, despite being obscene. We shall never know because juries do not give reasons.

The authorities found a way around this defence in their battle to suppress controversial publications. *IT* was another hippie magazine which, as part of its contents, published contact advertisements for homosexuals. In *Knuller* v *DPP* [1973] AC 435 the proprietor was convicted of two common law offences, conspiracy to corrupt public morals and conspiracy to outrage public decency. Whether these offences even existed was a debatable point, but it did mean that a public good defence could not be used.

Similarly, the homosexual newspaper, *Gay News* was convicted of blasphemy in *R* v *Lemon* [1979] AC 617. This is an extremely rare offence and the House of Lords helpfully redefined it by saying that all that needed to be proved was that the material shocked and outraged Christians. No public good defence could be used, which was a great disadvantage to the defendant. The offending poem was written by a professor of English literature and might have had literary merit.

A remarkable feature of the case law on the Official Secrets Acts is that many of the cases do not involve spies, but simply people protesting about government policies or publishing matters that the government would rather keep secret. *Chandler* v *DPP* [1964] AC 763 involved anti-nuclear protesters wishing to occupy an airfield in protest against nuclear weapons. They were convicted of a conspiracy to enter a prohibited place for a purpose prejudicial to the safety and interests of the state. They were not allowed to put forward evidence that a nuclear free Britain would be in the interest of the state and were convicted, despite the head note of s. 1, Official Secrets Act 1911 saying 'penalties for spying'.

It is no defence to claim that the defendant is revealing issues that the public ought to know as was tried in *R* v *Ponting* [1985] Crim LR 318. If the government says that it is not in the interests of the state the courts must accept it, even though the jury may not. Surprisingly, it is also no defence to show that the information is not, in fact, secret. Aubrey, Berry and Campbell published information about government communications and listening posts. Most of the material was obtained from government publications. It was still an offence under the old s. 2, Official Secrets Act 1911 (*R* v *Aubrey, Berry and Campbell* [1979] Crim LR 284). This Act was 'reformed' in the Official Secrets Act 1989, but the government made sure that areas like security, intelligence, defence, international relations and criminal investigations were still well protected from the prying eyes of journalists.

If the criminal law is inappropriate, the civil law can always be used. In the late eighties and early nineties a large number of cases were commenced in courts all over the world to prevent the publication of Peter Wright's book, *Spycatcher* and its serialisation in newspapers. It was argued that it was breach of confidence and a former intelligence agent like Wright owed a lifelong obligation of confidence to the government. The justification advanced was that this would deter other intelligence agents from following his example. Perhaps it was just that Wright's revelations were a little too uncomfortable. The courts tended to support the government view and issue injunctions against newspapers serialising the book; *A-G* v *Observer* [1987] 1 WLR 1248 and even public libraries stocking the book; *Re Application by Derbyshire County Council* [1987] 1 All ER 385. The injunctions were only lifted when everyone knew of Wright's allegations and there was no point in continuing with the injunctions; *A-G* v *Observer, The Times* [1990] AC 109.

An important point about breach of confidence is that its use is not restricted to the government. Much information is confidential. For instance an employee can often obtain such information. Employers can prevent them telling anyone else by using breach of confidence. Employers need only show some possible detriment or harm to their business.

Contempt of court is also a useful tool with which to silence journalists. Merely to repeat the *Spycatcher* allegations, if the newspaper knew of the injunctions in force, was contempt; *A-G* v *Newspaper Publishing* [1991] 2 WLR 994. Journalists can be forced to reveal their sources if national security requires it; see s. 10, Contempt of Court Act 1981 as explained in *Secretary of State for Defence* v *Guardian* [1984] Ch 156. This is also the case, even if the source's name is only required so that a party may pursue a civil action against them; *X Ltd* v *Morgan-Grampian* [1990] 1 All ER 616.

The most expensive hazard of free speech is, however, being sued for defamation. The defendant has the burden of proving the truth of what he said. There is no defence that what was written was in the general public interest. Huge damages were possible until very recently when the Court of Appeal stated that it could, and would, reduce excessive awards; *John* v *MGN Ltd* [1996] 2 All ER 35. If it is a serious libel of a public figure then a particularly vindictive litigant can always try criminal libel; *Goldsmith* v *Pressdram* [1976] 3 WLR 191.

In conclusion, it may be said that the courts cannot prevent prosecutors and plaintiffs using all the laws at their disposal. It may be that the defendant will be acquitted, as we saw in some of the obscenity cases. In other areas, though, like official secrets, breach of confidence and contempt, the courts have shown themselves only too willing to advance other interests, like national security or the convenience of litigants, over that of freedom of speech.

10 Administrative Law: Extra-judicial Redress

INTRODUCTION

This chapter covers a variety of topics which could be included in constitutional and/or administrative law courses, though not all courses will include all of them, particularly since the growth of judicial review has rendered other methods of redress of less interest to lawyers. But, where they are included, they provide students with relatively straightforward subjects for examination answers. What will in each case make an adequate answer into a good one is the quality of the arguments advanced and the drawing from those arguments of a soundly based and well reasoned conclusion.

QUESTION 1

The processes for the making of delegated legislation are not satisfactory. Parliament grants excessively wide powers to the administration, and then fails to scrutinise adequately the way those powers are used.

Explain and discuss. What reforms would you suggest to improve the scrutiny of delegated legislation?

Commentary

This question addresses two areas, the way Parliament delegates powers to the administration and the way Parliament watches over the making of the subsequent orders, regulations and statutory instruments. The answer will need to be based on an explanation of the place of delegated legislation within the administrative system, though there is no need for a lengthy discussion of the merits and defects of it in principle. The student needs to identify reforms which will address the defects identified in the earlier part of the answer, and justify them by argument.

Suggested Answer

The delegation of legislative powers by Parliament to the administration has long been a feature of the British administrative system. Although such delegation has been criticised as inherently improper, and contrary to the doctrine of separation of powers, it is now accepted as essential. Parliament could not possibly enact all the laws necessary in the complex, modern welfare state; it has difficulty coping with the current amount of primary legislation. A proper distinction has to be drawn between matters of policy and principle, requiring Parliament's full attention, and matters of technical detail, which can safely be left in the hands of the administration. Delegated legislation may be accepted as conceptually satisfactory, but still subjected to criticism on grounds of inappropriate use or inadequate supervision.

There are no constitutional limits on the power of Parliament to delegate legislative powers to the administration, because of the doctrine of parliamentary supremacy, except that Parliament may always revoke any delegation it has made. Parliament has granted the administration extremely wide powers; the Emergency Powers (Defence) Act 1939 permitted the government to make regulations for 'public safety, the defence of the realm, the maintenance of public order and the efficient prosecution of the war'. It is difficult to imagine any subject not covered by such a provision.

Control over the extent of delegation is in the hands of Parliament when it passes the enabling Act, but a government with a secure majority in the House of Commons can be sure in most circumstances of obtaining whatever delegated powers it wants. Indeed, Parliament may easily fail to realise the implications of an enabling Act. There is general agreement that parliamentary scrutiny of legislation is unsatisfactory, especially where pressures of time lead to the imposition of guillotine motions, leaving some provisions of a Bill unexamined by committee. Whether regulations are subject to affirmative or negative resolution may appear to be a mere technical detail, but, as will be seen, is in fact of major importance.

The only specific machinery for the scrutiny of enabling legislation is the House of Lords select committee on the scrutiny of delegated powers, which was set up in 1992. This committee examines enabling legislation when it is introduced into the House of Lords, considers the justifications offered by the government for seeking such powers, and then reports to the Lords in time, normally, for the committee stage of the Bill. It performs the very useful function of drawing to the Lords' attention any delegation it considers excessive or undesirable. This forces the government to offer a public justification of its proposals, and has on occasion helped to force the government to accept amendments to the legislation. It is significant that this valuable addition to parliamentary scrutiny of legislation is in the House of Lords, where the government cannot rely on the passive obedience of its back-bench MPs. It would clearly be desirable for the House of Commons to establish some such committee, or for a joint Lords and Commons committee to be set up, but the potential for government embarrassment is likely to prevent the acceptance of any such proposal. Reliance will have to continue to be placed on the vigilance of individual MPs in standing committees instead.

The most controversial form of enabling provision is the so-called Henry VIII clause, which permits the government to make delegated legislation which amends other primary legislation. This is regarded by many as constitutionally improper, on the grounds that the amendment of parliamentary legislation should only be conducted by Parliament itself. It can, however, be justified where the draftsmen have been unable to assure themselves that all possible clashing legislation has been suitably amended. It is also possible to justify the provision in the European Communities Act 1972 which authorises the government to use delegated legislation to implement European Community laws as they are made, including amendments and repeals of earlier UK statutes. Schedule 2 of the 1972 Act imposes restrictions on the use of this power, and in any case the EC law will have passed through, and been scrutinised during, the EC's own legislative processes. Very serious concern was expressed in Parliament during the passage of the Deregulation and Contracting-Out Act 1994, which gives ministers unprecedented powers to make orders which amend or repeal previous legislation, if the minister considers this would relieve business of an unnecessary burden. But the government was able to ensure the passage of the Act with only minor amendments to the procedural safeguards on the making of such orders, demonstrating the limited control that Parliament can actually exercise at this stage over a government with a working majority.

Turning to examine the scrutiny of the delegated legislation itself, it is normally the practice that delegated legislation has to be laid before Parliament, though there is no obligation to include such a requirement in any enabling Act. There are various procedures which may be selected; the instrument may simply have to be laid, or laid in draft, and Parliament may or may not have an opportunity to vote on it. Parliament's greatest opportunity for control arises where the instrument is subject to affirmative procedure, that is, it has to be approved by a vote of each House, in draft or in its final form, before it can come into effect. This means that the government has to find time for debates in both Houses, though in the Commons less controversial measures can be debated in a standing committee rather than on the floor of the House. The provisions of the Parliament Acts 1911 and 1949 do not apply, so the House of Lords retains its veto, though it has only ever used it once in modern times. It is possible for the enabling Act to demand the approval of the Commons only, and this is normal for taxation matters, over which the Lords have almost no control. Affirmative resolution procedure is generally regarded as satisfactory and many commentators would like to see it more widely used.

It is far more common, however, for enabling Acts to impose the negative resolution procedure, which is governed by the Statutory Instruments Act 1946, s. 5. The instrument is laid before Parliament, either in draft, or after the department has made it. During the next 40 days, either House may pass a 'prayer' that it be annulled, forcing the government to withdraw it. The main defect of this procedure is that a prayer will only be debated if time is made available by the government, which it will be reluctant to do. It may decline completely, or move that the instrument be referred to a standing committee, which may debate it, but cannot pass the prayer necessary to annul it. Of course, if an instrument has proved politically controversial, it will be difficult for the government not to concede time for a debate; the whips are likely to be able to ensure that the prayer is defeated, however.

Under both the affirmative and negative procedures, Parliament has no power to amend delegated legislation, unless such a power is granted by the enabling Act. This is an unfortunate rule, as it means the House has to vote against an entire instrument if it is unhappy with just one aspect of it. The instrument will then have to be withdrawn and a new instrument laid, with the whole procedure repeated. As both Houses of Parliament are permitted to amend primary legislation, it is difficult to justify a different rule for secondary legislation. A change to the rule would make parliamentary scrutiny more effective and would ultimately save parliamentary time.

The negative resolution procedure would be even less effective if it depended solely on the vigilance of individual MPs, as the sheer volume of delegated legislation makes it impossible for them to check on all proposals. Since 1973, a joint committee on statutory instruments, drawn from both Lords and Commons, has assisted MPs and Lords in this task. It examines all statutory instruments laid before Parliament and all other general statutory instruments. It can draw the attention of Parliament to the instrument on various grounds concerned with the procedure and legality of the instrument, though not its substantive merits. These grounds include: that it imposes a charge, is retrospective, attempts to exclude review, may not be intra vires, makes an unusual or unexpected use of powers or that there has been delay in its laying or publication. The committee will be given an explanation by the department of its proposals; it can call witnesses from the department if it thinks it necessary.

The committee, a hard-working body, issues reports after each of its weekly meetings, but all too often it is impossible for it to report in time for Parliament to make use of its reports. The 40 day period for prayers against instruments is not extended to allow for scrutiny by the joint committee, though such a provision would clearly be desirable. However, the committee still performs a useful task, ensuring that departments have to justify their proposals; where obvious defects are identified, it is always open to the department to withdraw the instrument itself for amendment and improvement, rather than risk disapproval by Parliament or later legal action on grounds of ultra vires.

As stated above, the joint committee cannot comment on the merits of delegated legislation. Instead, any instrument may be referred to a standing committee, known as a merits committee, where the substance of the instrument may be debated. But the committee's views on the instrument have no legal effect, with any vote to approve or annul having to take place on the floor of the House. The most the merits committee can hope is that the government will take its views into account, and this is entirely in the government's hands. It would be desirable if a merits committee could at least force the holding of a debate on the floor of the House. Until such a reform occurs, debates in merits committees will be of little use.

An interesting development has occurred in relation to the Deregulation and Contracting-Out Act 1994, which, as stated above, gives ministers very wide powers to make statutory instruments modifying previous legislation. Such instruments have to be laid in draft and approved by both Houses, with the period for parliamentary scrutiny extended to 60 days. In the House of Commons, a special committee, the Deregulation Orders Committee has been established, which will consider each draft proposal and hear comments from those affected. It will have the power to approve, amend or reject the proposal. The House of Lords will use its delegated powers scrutiny committee to perform the same function. This new procedure should ensure that these extensive powers are subjected to greater scrutiny than is usually the case with delegated legislation and go some way towards reducing the criticisms of the grant of such wide powers to government ministers.

Although traditionally primary legislation has received much more attention from Parliament, scrutiny of delegated legislation is just as important, as it too creates the law of the land, conferring rights and obligations on citizens. Parliament cannot be said to perform this function satisfactorily, though the blame for this lies primarily in the level of executive dominance, particularly over the House of Commons. But the more extensive the powers delegated to ministers, the more essential it is that Parliament should not neglect scrutiny of its use. The price of freedom is indeed eternal vigilance.

QUESTION 2

'In Britain, Parliament is the place for ventilating the grievances of the citizen ... It is one of the functions of the elected Member of Parliament to try to secure that his constituents do not suffer at the hand of the Government.'

White Paper on the Parliamentary Commissioner for Administration, 1967.

How important is Parliament as a means of redressing citizens' grievances? How effective are MPs in performing this task?

Commentary

This question requires the student to explain why MPs have this role, how it fits into the constitution and what MPs can actually do in practice. It is hardly possible to attempt any quantitative assessment, but any relevant statistics will be useful. The student can usefully make some comparisons with other methods of redress and explain how they interrelate.

Suggested Answer

One of the stock remarks of that traditionally irascible British citizen, Disgusted of Tunbridge Wells, has always been, 'I shall write to my MP about this!'. Every day, MPs receive numerous letters from their constituents, and almost every week they have to set aside times for surgeries in their constituencies where voters can meet them in person. This demonstrates clearly how much this function of MPs is a deep-seated part of the British constitution.

The role of the MP, from as far back as the Middle Ages, has always included bringing the concerns of the constituent to the attention of the authorities, though the unreformed electoral system often meant that the MP had only a patron to please, rather than a wide electorate. But as the system was reformed in the nineteenth century, with extensions to the franchise and redistribution of seats, more MPs had to take account of their constituents' concerns. By the beginning of this century, it was common practice for MPs to take up individual grievances, though there were still MPs in safe seats whose contact with their constituencies was minimal.

Over the last 50 years, however, there appears to have been a considerable increase in the involvement of MPs in the redress of individual grievances. Various factors have contributed to this. The growth of the welfare state and the intervention of the government in new areas have increased the occasions for grievances to arise. All citizens have dealings with public bodies which may give rise to problems; taxation, social security and health are obvious examples. The electorate is increasingly articulate, educated and willing to express dissatisfaction, rather than suffering injustice passively. There has been a growth in campaigning groups, in areas such as the environment, who are likely to try to gain the ear of the local MP. It also appears that MPs have changed their attitudes towards their constituency duties. It has been suggested that, feeling that their influence at Westminster has been reduced by the rigidity of the party system, MPs seek the satisfaction of assisting individual constituents as a replacement for the loss of opportunity to influence government policy. In

selecting candidates, local parties take account of the level of local commitment shown by those seeking nomination. This is particularly important in the
Labour Party, where even sitting MPs have to seek reselection, though similar
issues are considered in all parties where boundary changes lead to a
redistribution of seats. A good constituency MP is far more likely to find a new
seat than one with a reputation for indifference and neglect.

A further relevant factor is that many more MPs can now be described as career
politicians, hoping to remain in Parliament long enough to gain a front bench
position. Such MPs are likely to take much more trouble to cultivate their
constituency reputation, in the hope of securing a personal vote as a cushion
against party unpopularity. It is important to note that the present electoral
system, with its single member constituencies, provides a strong incentive for
MPs to take up individual cases, unlike some other systems. Although assisting
constituents does not guarantee that they will vote for that MP, no MP dare risk
offending a constituent by refusing to help. Many MPs are at pains to ensure
that the local media are informed of their successes on their constituents'
behalf.

The description of Parliament as the place for ventilating grievances is
constitutionally justified as an aspect of the doctrine of ministerial responsibility. The MP is entitled to demand information from ministers and to call
ministers to account. The strength of the party system now means that
Parliament can rarely overthrow the government, but ministers are still under
an obligation to satisfy MPs as to their conduct and that of their departments.
Of course, MPs deal, on their constituents' behalf, with other organisations as
well, but underlying even these is the possibility that, if such organisations are
misbehaving, the minister could be expected to intervene with improved
regulation. Although ministerial resignation has become a rarity, ministerial
accountability on a daily basis remains an active element in the constitution.

There is some evidence of the increasing scale on which people contact their
MPs, for assistance and information, as well as to let off steam. In the 1960s,
MPs each received between 25 and 75 letters a week; by the 1980s this had
risen to 20 to 50 letters every day. These were followed up by MPs writing over
15,000 letters a month to ministers; one minister claimed to send 300 replies to
such letters every week. These figures demonstrate how extensive the use of
MPs is, and contrasts markedly with the 2,000 or so applications for judicial
review made each year. The issues raised by constituents will vary according
to the social make-up of the constituency. In poorer areas, council housing and
welfare benefit problems will predominate; in wealthier areas, health, transport

and education issues will be more common. Most initial contact from constituents is by correspondence, though significant numbers attend an MP's surgery in person.

It appears that MPs will very rarely decline to take up a matter on behalf of a constituent, though most adhere strictly to the convention not to take up a matter raised by any other MP's constituent. Only if a complaint appears totally ill-founded, or if some other means of redress is clearly more appropriate will the MP refuse to become involved. The most usual course of action for an MP who takes up a complaint is to write to the appropriate ministry, agency or other organisation. Civil Service practice ensures that MPs' letters are given priority over other business, and are dealt with at a higher level in the official hierarchy. Where an individual citizen may be fobbed off with a standard letter from a junior official, the MP's intervention will at least provoke a prompt response from someone more senior, even the minister in person. In many cases this may achieve the desired result without further action. If the constituent's complaint was of delay in the administration, the MP will normally be able to speed up the process; if the constituent wanted a decision reviewed, the MP's involvement will ensure a second look is taken.

Most MPs will leave it up to the constituent to decide whether the initial response is satisfactory, but will be willing to take further steps if the constituent is still aggrieved. This may take the form of further correspondence, or more informally, speaking to the minister perhaps in the corridor or voting lobby in Parliament. Failing this, the MP may arrange a formal meeting with the minister to press the case. If all these methods fail, the MP may invoke the formal procedures of the House of Commons. Foremost among these is the parliamentary question, put down for oral or written answer. This will elicit a public response from the minister which will be on the record. It is likely to be most effective where the matter is of a kind to attract attention. Parliamentary questions can be used to embarrass the government by asking a question in abstract terms and then raising the constituent's grievance as a supplementary question. If this still achieves no result, the MP may seek to raise the issue as an adjournment debate; there is a ballot among MPs for the opportunity to choose the topic. By this stage the MP's chances of forcing the government to act will be dependent on the subject having attracted some media attention, or being taken up by one of the political parties.

If the grievance needs thorough investigation, the MP may refer it to the Parliamentary Commissioner for Administration, or another appropriate Ombudsman, though MPs seem reluctant to do this unless the constituent suggests it. Once such a reference is made, the matter is out of the MP's hands, though the MP will probably claim some of the credit if there is ultimately a successful result.

It is very difficult to assess the effectiveness of the MP in obtaining redress, but it appears that they are most effective in dealing with relatively minor and uncontroversial matters which can be disposed of by correspondence. Most government departments and other public bodies will feel able to make a concession or admit a mistake in the relative privacy of a letter. But once the matter has come out into the open, and entrenched positions have been adopted, it becomes very difficult for the MP to force a change of mind on a reluctant government. Only if there is a substantial media campaign, or an investigation by an Ombudsman, can a determined authority be forced to concede defeat.

MPs, however, have some great advantages as redressers of grievances. Their services are free and easily accessible; many MPs take great pains to advertise their surgery times and other means of contact in the local media. Most are assiduous in taking up grievances, and often the mere fact of receiving a letter from an MP, rather than from an ordinary citizen, will induce the authority to give a favourable response. Further, the MP's services are equally useful whether the constituent is asking for the correction of an error or the more favourable exercise of a discretion, where no legal redress would be available. Legal action for judicial review has the advantage of being able to produce a decisive and binding result, but it is limited in scope, and carries financial penalties if unsuccessful.

Although some traditionalists resisted innovations like the introduction of Ombudsmen on the grounds that they would diminish the role of the MP in the redress of grievances, it would seem that neither Ombudsmen, nor the growth of judicial review, have prevented the role of the individual MP from developing and expanding. MPs are clearly continuing to provide a useful and popular means of redress for the aggrieved citizen.

QUESTION 3

How effective has the Parliamentary Commissioner for Administration been in providing redress for citizens aggrieved by acts of maladministration?

Commentary

This is a fairly straightforward question. The answer requires as a basis a description of the jurisdiction, powers and practices of the PCA. To produce a good answer, the student needs to cite some examples of the PCA's work, and to make explicit the criteria against which effectiveness is being judged. Any comparisons with Ombudsmen from other states will enhance the answer.

Suggested Answer

The office of Parliamentary Commissioner for Administration (PCA) or Ombudsman was introduced into the UK in 1967, because of concern that existing methods of redress were inadequate. Following the example of Scandinavian states, it was hoped that an Ombudsman would provide a simple and understandable means by which citizens' complaints could be dealt with. Since 1967, the idea of redress through Ombudsmen has spread widely through both the public and private sectors in the UK, but some disappointment has been expressed that the PCA, the most senior Ombudsman with the most important area of jurisdiction, has not been more effective.

The PCA's powers of investigation cover over 100 government departments and non-departmental government bodies. It appears to be accepted practice that as such bodies are created they are brought within the PCA's jurisdiction, though there may inevitably be some time lag. There are, however, various matters specifically excluded from the PCA's remit by Sch. 3, Parliamentary Commissioner Act 1967. Some of the exclusions can be justified on the grounds that alternative methods of redress are available. The National Health Service has its own Commissioner, though the post has always been held concurrently with that of the PCA. Other exclusions are open to criticism, particularly the exclusion of contractual and other commercial transactions entered into by the government. Governments use contracts as an instrument of policy and their maladministration could easily cause injustice. In recent years there has been an increase in the contracting out to the private and voluntary sectors of services traditionally performed by the government itself, and it is clearly undesirable if this process is excluded from investigation. Personnel matters in both the military and civil services are also excluded from the PCA's jurisdiction, in spite of the fact that sensitive issues may arise. The introduction of a formal appeal machinery for the dismissal of civil servants has alleviated this problem, but in many other countries, complaints from civil servants form an important part of the Ombudsman's work.

A further limitation on the PCA's powers is found in s. 5(2) of the Act, which forbids him to investigate matters which the aggrieved person could have taken to a tribunal, or brought before the ordinary courts, unless he considers that it was not reasonable for the person to have used that remedy. It seems acceptable that, where a specific statutory remedy has been provided, such as the tribunals dealing with taxation or social security, the individual should be expected to use it. There is more difficulty where the remedy is not specific, and those who drafted the 1967 Act cannot have anticipated the huge growth of judicial review. The PCA seems to take the view that it is generally reasonable for a person to use his services rather than seek judicial review, given the cost and uncertainty of that method of redress. There is inevitably some overlap, and there have been cases, such as *Congreve* v *Home Office* [1976] 1 QB 629, where both the courts and the PCA have dealt with the same matter. Given the diminishing availability of legal aid, it is essential that the PCA continue to exercise his discretion under s. 5(2) generously. It is important to note that the PCA's services are free to the complainant, whether the complaint is upheld or not.

The aspect of the PCA's powers that has always caused most controversy is the fact that, unlike virtually every other Ombudsman in the world, he cannot accept complaints directly from the public. Instead, they must be referred to him by an MP. This system was imposed partly because of fears that the PCA would be overwhelmed by the number of complaints, and partly to help preserve the traditional method of redress through Parliament. But it has acted as a severe limitation on the availability of the PCA as a method of redress. The number of complaints referred by MPs has rarely exceeded 1,000 in any year, and more than two-thirds of these are rejected as outside the PCA's jurisdiction. The PCA does try to ensure that all MPs are aware of his services and understand his powers, but this does not seem to be effective. In any case, MPs prefer to deal with constituents' complaints themselves, as they will then get credit and, they hope, votes at the next election.

The lack of direct access creates a circular problem. There is little point in the PCA embarking on any large-scale publicity campaign, when any matters referred directly to him would have to be sent back, and complainants advised to contact their MP. Few people have heard of the PCA and fewer still would suggest to their MP that the PCA might be used. Research indicates that the MP will rarely make the suggestion of reference to the PCA if the constituent does not raise it. The PCA therefore remains underused. Many critics have argued for the abolition of the MP filter, but this is unlikely to occur. Back-bench MPs are happy with the present system, and governments would hardly wish to see the PCA better known and more active. There is the further issue that, if the number of complaints increased substantially, the PCA's staff would have to be expanded, with a consequent increase in public expenditure, always unpopular with governments. When direct access to the Commission for Local

Administration was introduced, the number of complaints shot up from 3,000 to 12,000 a year, and the same would certainly happen with the PCA.

The PCA's function is defined in s. 5(1) of the Act as being to investigate complaints of 'injustice in consequence of maladministration'. The term 'maladministration' was deliberately not defined in the Act, though Richard Crossman gave some examples during the passage of the Bill: 'bias, neglect, inattention, delay, incompetence, ineptitude, perversity, turpitude, arbitrariness and so on'. The Act did, however, make it clear that the PCA was not to reconsider the merits of discretionary decisions taken without maladministration (s. 12(3)); he was not providing a means of appeal against decisions which people did not like.

There were initial concerns that the PCA was taking too narrow a view of maladministration. He was encouraged by the Select Committee to extend his definition to include both bad decisions, that is, decisions appearing at first glance to be unreasonably perverse, and bad rules, that is, rules which produced excessively harsh results in practice. Most cases concern defects in the way decisions are made and unfair treatment of individuals. Common examples are delay, giving incorrect or misleading advice, failing to inform people of their rights and unfairness as between individuals.

The process of investigation is generally seen as painstaking and thorough. The PCA has power to demand all government papers, with the exception of Cabinet papers, which may be withheld by the Cabinet Secretary with the Prime Minister's approval. The PCA has all the powers of a court to summon witnesses and take their evidence on oath if necessary, and can order the production of documents. He is not bound by the Official Secrets Act, Crown privilege or public interest immunity. It is therefore possible for the PCA to go deeply into the decision-making processes of the government and uncover what lies behind the public façade. It would be quite impossible for an individual MP to do this. A striking example is the PCA's investigation into the Barlow Clowes affair, where the Department of Trade and Industry had failed to exercise its regulatory powers properly. This complex investigation resulted in the production of a 120,000 word report detailing a history of maladministration lasting 13 years.

The only problem with the thoroughness of the PCA's investigations is that it makes them slow, averaging over one year, though this is partly explained by the fact that only complex cases get through the MP filter; MPs manage the straightforward cases themselves. As the PCA himself has pointed out, the mere fact that a reference to the PCA has been made may induce a government department which knows that it has not behaved properly to offer immediate redress, thereby avoiding an adverse finding. Only the debatable cases will need full investigation.

The PCA has the power to make recommendations, but has no power to force the government to follow them. However, as a general rule, the government will comply with the recommendations even if reluctant. In the Barlow Clowes case, the government disputed the PCA's finding of maladministration but none the less accepted the obligation to compensate the investors, at a cost of £150 million, by far the largest sum ever paid out on the PCA's recommendation. The PCA has not succeeded, however, in obtaining compensation for those whose properties have been blighted by delays in choosing and building the Channel Tunnel rail link. In general, it is politically very difficult for a government to reject what is seen, by Parliament and the country, as an independent, impartial and thorough assessment of the complaint.

If difficulties do arise in persuading the government to accept the PCA's recommendations, the matter may be taken up by the Select Committee on the PCA which monitors the PCA's activities and the government's response to them. The existence of this committee increases the effectiveness of the PCA by ensuring that any failure to follow his recommendations is followed up. The relevant minister or the permanent head of the department is likely to be asked to appear before the committee to explain and justify the failure and the committee will not hesitate to issue an adverse report. In some countries, Ombudsmen do have the power to enforce their decisions, but such a power is rarely used.

In evaluating the overall effectiveness of the PCA, the first point to make is that he has succeeded, over the last 30 years, in obtaining redress for many hundreds of people who would probably have had no chance of redress in any other way. Those matters which are investigated are dealt with thoroughly and impartially and it is never suggested that the PCA has failed to get to the bottom of the problem and find out the truth. Dissatisfaction is concentrated on the issue of access; the limits on the PCA's jurisdiction and the MP filter have been the subject of sustained and cogent criticism, though reform seems as unlikely as ever. It is perhaps hardly fair to criticise the PCA, not for the cases he deals with, but for those which never reach him because of the obstructions placed in their way.

The hopes of those who initially advocated the introduction of a British Ombudsman may not have been entirely fulfilled, but the PCA has become one essential part of the machinery for redressing the grievances of individual citizens. Even the growth of judicial review during the last 30 years has not removed the need, in Britain as in many other countries, for a citizen's defender in this form.

QUESTION 4

A recent accident at a government research establishment led to the discharge of dangerous chemicals into the environment. The government has decided to set up a scheme to pay compensation to anyone who has suffered ill health as a result. It seeks your advice as to whether it would be preferable to establish a tribunal to deal with disputed claims, rather than referring them to the ordinary courts. It also seeks advice on how any such tribunal should be operated. Advise the government.

Commentary

The underlying material for answering this question is the standard material on the advantges and disadvantages of tribunals. But it gives students a good opportunity to display and apply that material. For a good answer, a critical assessment of tribunals will be needed.

Suggested Answer

There are three reasons why the government would find it wise to set up some machinery for dealing with this matter. First, there are bound to be disputes about eligibility and allegations that mistakes have been made in the initial administrative assessment of such claims. Any attempt to have such disputes dealt with by a purely administrative machinery is likely to be unpopular as it will not be seen to be sufficiently impartial. Secondly, at a more theoretical level, the scheme gives people an entitlement to compensation if they fulfil the relevant criteria. This makes disputes about entitlement judicial rather than administrative in nature. The doctrine of separation of powers, which though not rigidly adhered to in the UK is still influential, requires such disputes to be dealt with by a judicial body, whether court or tribunal. Thirdly, any failure by the government to set up some specific machinery for these disputes will not keep the matter out of the hands of the courts. Dissatisfied applicants may seek judicial review, which is available in respect of any decisions made by public bodies under public law, unless specifically excluded by Parliament. The government should note the case of *Anisminic* v *Foreign Compensation Commission* [1969] 2 AC 147, which demonstrates how difficult it is to draft an exclusion clause which will be effective where the courts are determined that it shall not be. Because the process of judicial review is slow, inconvenient for the applicant and uncertain in its application, the government would be wise to reduce, though not eliminate, its incidence by providing a specialised means of dealing with these disputes.

It is therefore necessary to decide whether disputes should be dealt with by a tribunal or by the ordinary courts. A tribunal, like a court, can be defined as an independent, impartial body with power to make decisions binding on the parties by the application of legal rules to facts established by evidence. The distinction between courts and tribunals lies in terminology rather than substance. The term 'court' is generally used where the body has a general jurisdiction over a wide range of cases, whereas 'tribunal' refers to a body with a limited, often very specific jurisdiction. Both courts and tribunals are, as the Franks Committee asserted in 1957, part of the judicial system; the term 'administrative tribunals' is misleading and should not be used.

If these disputes were to be referred to an ordinary court, they would have to be dealt with by the ordinary judges, whereas a tribunal could be staffed by persons with particular expertise. Tribunals often consist of three people, a legally qualified chairman and two lay members with appropriate qualifications and experience. If this format were adopted, it would be particularly useful to have one member of the tribunal with medical qualifications, as issues about the cause of ill health are likely to be one of the main causes of disputed claims. It would also be helpful to have a person with appropriate scientific knowledge. A further advantage would be that the members of the tribunal, by specialising in dealing with this particular group of claims, would develop a particular expertise and experience, which should enable them to deal with cases more quickly and efficiently.

The scale of this incident is likely to be such that only one tribunal will be needed, sitting near the location of the accident. But if the number of claims is substantial, a group of tribunals may be needed. According to the Council on Tribunals, the best system of organisation is the presidential system, where the tribunals are under the supervision of a president or chairman, who is responsible for organising, co-ordinating and monitoring the work of the tribunals. The appointment of members of the tribunals is generally in the hands of the relevant government department, which has raised concerns as to the impartiality and independence of tribunals. But, under the Tribunals and Inquiries Act 1992, s. 5, the Council on Tribunals may make general recommendations about membership. Further, the Lord Chancellor is responsible, under s. 6 of the Act, for the appointment of the legally qualified chairmen of many tribunals, and, by s. 7, his consent is necessary for the dismissal of tribunal members. This in many ways assimilates the position of tribunal members to that of magistrates, so that concerns about independence and impartiality are no greater than those which can be expressed in relation to the courts. It is generally considered that tribunals' independence should be symbolised, wherever this is practicable, by their sitting in premises separate from the relevant government department.

The government's main concern in practice is likely to be the relative cost of using a tribunal or a court. If there are only a few cases, the expense of establishing a tribunal will hardly be justified, but if there are many, it will certainly be cheaper to refer them to a tribunal. The tribunal members may be part-time or occasional appointees, so cheaper than the full-time High Court or Circuit judge, and there is no need for the elaborate trappings traditionally associated with the higher courts.

The procedures of tribunals are designed to be as simple, straightforward and informal as possible. The Council on Tribunals, which is consulted over the making of tribunals' procedural rules, endeavours to reconcile the desire for simplicity with the need for a procedure to be fair to all parties. But it has proved very difficult in practice to develop a procedure simple enough to enable the average lay person to appear unrepresented. This leads to consideration of a major issue. The government's choice may well be powerfully influenced by the realisation that legal aid is not available for representation before the majority of tribunals. The only exceptions are the Lands Tribunal and Employment Appeal Tribunal, which are virtually equivalent to the High Court, and the Mental Health Review Tribunals, where by definition the applicant's ability to represent him or herself may be impaired. The government can therefore feel quite justified in establishing this new tribunal and refusing to extend legal aid to it. This is likely to leave most applicants with no choice but to attempt to represent themselves, whereas, if these cases were dealt with by a court, applicants would have the chance of seeking legal aid, albeit subject to a stringent means test.

Because they are used to hearing unrepresented applicants, tribunals take a more active part in the proceedings than the traditionally passive judge, and will do what they can to help. For example, they may suggest issues the applicant and the witnesses might like to talk about. The formal legal rules of evidence will not be applied, and witnesses will be encouraged to tell their story in their own words, rather than being tripped up by awkward questioning. But problems will inevitably arise where the inexperienced and inarticulate are trying to represent themselves. It is particularly difficult to avoid the appearance of unfairness where one side is represented, either by a lawyer or an experienced official, and the other is not. Many people, including the Council on Tribunals, have argued that legal aid should be extended to all or most tribunals, but this is most unlikely in the current climate of financial stringency.

If the disputes are referred to the ordinary courts, there is a risk that, because they will have to take their turn with other litigation, cases may suffer considerable delays, which is in itself a cause of injustice. One of the main reasons for establishing tribunals has been to ensure that cases are dealt with more promptly. There have, however, been problems of delay even within tribunal systems, where the number of cases has increased beyond the capacity of the tribunals to cope. An adequately funded tribunal system should still be able to deal with cases more quickly than the courts could, particularly if the procedures adopted are straightforward.

If the disputes are referred to the ordinary courts, then it will be natural to apply the normal procedure for appeals to the Court of Appeal and, with leave, to the House of Lords. If a tribunal is established, it will be necessary to decide what form any appeal should take. The government might take the view that no appeal should be provided, relying instead on the inherent jurisdiction of the High Court to hear cases by way of judicial review. It could be argued that, as the most likely grounds of complaint would be error of law and breach of the rules of natural justice, both of which are well-established grounds of review, that will provide adequate redress. But given the complex procedures involved in judicial review, it might be quicker and cheaper, for both applicant and government, to provide an appeal to the High Court on point of law. A strict time limit could be imposed to make sure appeals are made promptly. It is unlikely to be necessary to set up an appellate tribunal to hear appeals on both fact and law; this is only essential where there are a large number of tribunals whose decisions could diverge without an overall tribunal to give definitive rulings.

In conclusion, it appears that the establishment of a tribunal may be the most satisfactory way of dealing with these cases. The Franks Committee report in 1957, and its rapid implementation enhanced the reputation of tribunals and the quiet but effective work of the Council on Tribunals has ensured that a good standard is maintained. There is now little feeling that tribunals provide only second class justice. Indeed, the victims of this accident are likely to greet the news that a tribunal is to be set up to deal with their claims as a resounding success.

11 Administrative Law: Judicial Review

INTRODUCTION

This chapter covers one of the most important growth areas of the law. Some courses have found it impossible to include it within the general constitutional law course and have hived it off into a separate administrative law or public law course. These questions are designed to cover all the aspects likely to be included in a general, rather than a specialised course.

This subject lends itself particularly well to problem questions, and is for that reason popular with examiners seeking to give a more legal slant to what might otherwise be an excessively political subject. Students will need to demonstrate their legal skills in identifying and applying the appropriate case law.

QUESTION 1

The twentieth century has seen both the decline of administrative law to virtual extinction, and its revival and development to unprecedented heights.

Discuss.

Why has the development of administrative law been so erratic?

Commentary

The basis of the answer to this question will be a description of the way administrative law, particularly judicial review, has developed over this century, illustrated with the appropriate cases. What will make the answer a good one will be the discussion of the reasons for its erratic progress. There are no cut and dried answers on this; the student's answer will be judged on the way the arguments are presented and the evidence marshalled in support.

Suggested Answer

The history of English administrative law can be traced back through many centuries. The prerogative writs of certiorari, prohibition and mandamus were originally developed in the Middle Ages, but first came to prominence with the growth of a more effective administrative system under the Tudors. The seventeenth century sees the first precedents concerning the rules of natural justice (*Baggs Case* (1615) 11 Co Rep 93b) and the doctrine of ultra vires (*Hetley* v *Boyer* (1614) Cro Jac 336).

It was during the nineteenth century that something approaching a system of administrative law was established, in the wake of the Victorian reforms of central and local government, and official intervention in such areas as health, factory conditions and sanitation. The courts were able to use the old prerogative remedies against the new administrative authorities, and to develop and refine the concepts of natural justice and ultra vires, in cases like *Cooper* v *Wandsworth Board of Works* (1863) 14 CB (NS) 180. Maitland pointed out in 1888 that half the reported cases in the Queen's Bench Division dealt with aspects of administrative law. New remedies also became available; in *Dyson* v *Attorney-General* [1911] 1 KB 410, the Court of Appeal confirmed that a declaration could be granted to a person who wished to establish the unlawfulness of administrative action. By the beginning of the twentieth century, it seemed that English law was well on the way to developing a comprehensive and effective system of administrative law.

But during the next 50 years, this promising development was halted; in some respects the law went into reverse. One of the main factors was a conceptual problem about judicial and administrative decisions. Until the nineteenth century reforms, much local administration was conducted through the justices of the peace, and it was natural to describe their power as jurisdiction and their decisions as judicial, whether they were convicting a thief or allocating poor relief. The availability of the prerogative remedies of certiorari and prohibition was also described as being dependent on the decision challenged being judicial. This presented no problems as long as the courts were willing to define decisions as judicial whenever they affected individual rights. But, during the 1920s and 1930s, the courts started to distinguish between judicial and administrative decisions more strictly, confining the definition of judicial decisions to those where Parliament had imposed some kind of judicialised procedure. As a consequence, the rules of natural justice were no longer applied to decisions affecting individual rights where these were classified as administrative; see *R* v *Metropolitan Police Commissioner ex parte Parker* [1953] 1 WLR 1150.

Over the same period, the courts showed some antipathy to the very idea of administrative law, perhaps under the influence of Dicey, who was critical of the French idea of a special body of rules governing the conduct of the administration, assuming that it would give them too much protection. The term '*droit administratif*' was used almost as a term of abuse! Perhaps, as a further effect of this, academic lawyers paid little heed to the subject, and it was not taught except as a minor part of constitutional law.

What was perhaps most unfortunate in these developments was that the courts abdicated their responsibility for protecting the rights of the individual at the very time when the government's activities put those rights most at risk. A notorious example is the case of *Liversidge* v *Anderson* [1942] AC 206, where the Secretary of State had the power to detain persons without trial if he had reasonable cause to believe them to be of hostile origin or associations, a power justifiable enough in wartime. But the House of Lords, with the honourable exception of Lord Atkin, held that the reasonableness of the Secretary of State's belief was not reviewable, turning an objective power into a wholly subjective one. A similarly unfortunate ruling was made in *Duncan* v *Cammel Laird* [1942] AC 624, when the House of Lords held that the Crown had an absolute and unreviewable privilege to withhold documents in litigation, if ministers felt it was in the public interest to do so.

The courts' attitude was not surprising in wartime, but even after the war, the courts remained very reluctant to interfere in the work of the administration in any way. In *Franklin v Minister of Town and Country Planning* [1948] AC 87, the House of Lords refused to apply the rule against bias to an administrative decision taken by a minister, even where Parliament had imposed a quasi-judicial process. In *Smith v East Elloe RDC* [1956] AC 736, the House of Lords accepted as effective a clause excluding judicial review, even where bad faith was alleged. Perhaps the most likely explanation for this lies in the effect of the doctrine of precedent. It will always be difficult to convince a court that the recent precedents should be disregarded and an ancient ruling preferred. A rare example of such a decision was *R v Northumberland Compensation Appeal Tribunal ex parte Shaw* [1952] 1 KB 338, where the Court of Appeal revived the doctrine of error of law on the face of the record after a century of disuse, as a means of controlling the increasing numbers of statutory tribunals.

Overall, anyone surveying the condition of administrative law in the early 1960s would have found a depressing sight. Natural justice was restricted, discretionary power not subject to judicial control, and remedies constrained by ancient rules and obscurities. As a consequence, few applicants considered the risks of litigation to be worthwhile, causing the law to fall yet further into decline. It was generally assumed that the law could not offer a means of controlling the administration, and attention turned to other methods, such as the reform of tribunals and inquiries after the Franks Committee report in 1957, and the introduction of an Ombudsman. Some even advocated the importation of the French system of *droit administratif*, and the establishment of an English *Conseil d'Etat*.

But, to the surprise of many, the English courts showed themselves to be capable of reviving this moribund area of law. In *Ridge v Baldwin* [1964] AC 40, the House of Lords attacked the dichotomy of judicial and administrative decisions, restoring the rule that decisions affecting the rights of subjects were subject to natural justice, even if Parliament was silent on the need for a hearing. This was followed by a stream of cases, extending the right to a fair hearing even into areas which had always been characterised as administrative. Other precedents were reversed. In *Conway v Rimmer* [1968] AC 910, the House of Lords removed the Crown's power to withhold documents in litigation, replacing it with the power of the court to grant public interest immunity. In *Anisminic v Foreign Compensation Commission* [1969] 2 AC 147, the House of Lords found a way of defeating the express exclusion clause which had been held effective in *Smith v East Elloe RDC* (1956), and in so doing extended the courts' powers to review errors of law. In *Padfield v*

Minister of Agriculture [1968] AC 997, the House of Lords rejected the idea of the unfettered and unreviewable administrative discretion.

Why did the courts change the law so radically and so unexpectedly?

One important factor was certainly a change in judicial personnel, with judges used to Diceyan orthodoxy being replaced by others with a less restricted outlook. One of the most influential was Lord Reid, who came to the House of Lords from Scotland, where administrative law had never fallen to such a low ebb. Lord Denning also played a significant part, as he did in so many branches of the law. Some credit is also due to academic lawyers, such as S. A. de Smith and Sir William Wade, whose publications and research into administrative law established it as an important academic subject. It is possible that the courts may have felt that, if the law was not reformed, they would lose out to other methods of redress, such as the Parliamentary Commissioner of Administration, who was introduced in 1967. Such statutory reforms also demonstrated that governments were willing to contemplate improved methods of redress, and the courts would not be risking political controversy if they joined in.

Once the process of revival began, there was no shortage of litigants seeking redress for what would once have been inescapable injustices. Within a few years, a new body of precedents had been built up, and cases decided between 1910 and 1960 are almost always viewed with suspicion. To consolidate this new law, procedural reforms were introduced on the advice of the Law Commission; see the Supreme Court Act 1981, s. 31.

The overall effect has been a huge expansion in the role of judicial review, which now shares with criminal justice the highest profile and the most media attention. Few other branches of the law can show such dramatic changes. It is to be hoped that the courts will maintain their role of protecting individual rights against abuse at the hands of the administration, as they have during the last 30 years.

QUESTION 2

Under the (imaginary) Radiation Protection Act 1993, any person wishing to use radioactive materials must obtain a licence from the Radiation Protection Agency (RPA). On receipt of an application, the RPA must consult any organisation which it considers to be representative of those affected, and must publish notice of the application in the national and local press, and in any other way it considers desirable. The RPA must allow three months for the submission of comments and objections, which should include the name and address of the sender. After considering all representations submitted to it, and giving the applicant a hearing, the RPA may grant or refuse a licence.

The Sulphurous Chemical plc applied for a licence to use radioactive materials in its factory in Coketown. The RPA published notice of the application in three national and two local newspapers, and put up a small notice in the Coketown public library. The RPA wrote to the Coketown Borough Council and the Cokeshire County Council asking for comments. It received a reply only from the Coketown Borough Council. The RPA made no attempt to consult the National Union of Chemical Workers, which represented the majority of Sulphurous Chemical's employees.

The RPA received many objections, including several from an unknown and unidentified group calling itself the Green Anti-Nuclear Faction; the RPA threw these away. A petition signed by 25,000 inhabitants of Coketown was presented the day after the three month submission period had expired, but the RPA refused to accept it.

After completing its consideration and giving Sulphurous Chemical a hearing, the RPA granted the licence.

Consider the validity of the licence.

Commentary

This question is concerned with judicial review, primarily though not exclusively with procedural ultra vires. The student will need to identify and explain the general principle involved, the distinction between mandatory and directory procedural requirements. It is then simplest for the student to work through the problem point by point. Although some issues raised in this type of question may bear a sufficient resemblance to decided cases to be straightforward, others will require the student to argue by analogy. Where issues are debatable, the student will be assessed on the quality of the argument, whichever conclusion is reached.

Suggested Answer

The validity of this licence can be challenged by judicial review, because, as laid down in *O'Reilly* v *Mackman* [1983] 2 AC 237, it concerns the activities of a public body in matters relating to public law. The grounds of challenge mostly concern procedural defects in the way the RPA dealt with the application.

In dealing with procedural defects, the courts have to balance the need to ensure that statutory procedural safeguards are carefully observed against the risk that trivial procedural defects are used as a pretext by objectors seeking to halt or delay an unpopular scheme. To do this the courts have generally drawn a distinction between mandatory and directory procedural requirements. A mandatory requirement is one which is regarded as so essential that failure to observe it justifies treating the decision reached as invalid. A directory requirement is one whose non-observance will not invalidate the decision. In *London & Clydeside Estates v Aberdeen District Council* [1980] 1 WLR 182, Lord Hailsham LC suggested that these two categories should not be regarded as the only two alternatives, but as the extremes of a range of possibilities. An example of a more subtle approach can be found in *Coney v Choyce* [1975] 1 WLR 422, where various detailed publication requirements were only partially complied with. The court held that it was mandatory that there be substantial compliance with the requirement of publication, but that the exact details were merely directory.

It is possible for statute to specify the precise consequences of failure to comply with procedural requirements, but in practice this rarely occurs. It is therefore left to the courts to decide retrospectively whether the failure has invalidated the decision. This area of the law is criticised as uncertain, but some guidance may be obtained from decided cases.

The RPA is required by the Act to publish notice of the application 'in the national and local press'. They published it in three national and two local newspapers. In *Bradbury v Enfield London Borough Council* [1967] 1 WLR 1311, the court held that giving notice was to be construed as a mandatory requirement as it was essential for the protection of the rights of the individual citizen. But in that case there was a complete failure to give notice. In *Coney v Choyce* (1975) substantial compliance was held to be sufficient. It could be argued here that there has been substantial compliance. The size of the petition is evidence that there was widespread awareness of the application. In *Coney v Choyce* it was considered material that all those affected had become aware of the proposal in spite of the defects in the publication. The RPA is given a discretion to publicise the application 'in any other way it considers desirable'. It could be argued that one small notice in the library is hardly sufficient. But any challenge would have to be on the ground of 'Wednesbury' unreasonableness; see *Associated Provincial Picture Houses v Wednesbury Corporation*

[1948] 1 KB 223. It is unlikely that the courts would consider this to be beyond the limits of a reasonable exercise of discretion.

The RPA is required to consult 'organisations which it considers to be representative of those affected'. Consultation is generally held to be a mandatory requirement, as it is a means of protecting the interests of those affected; see *R* v *Secretary of State for the Environment ex parte Association of Metropolitan Authorities* [1986] 1 WLR 1. The consultation of the Coketown Borough Council seems to have been satisfactory. But in *Agricultural Training Board* v *Aylesbury Mushrooms Ltd* [1972] 1 WLR 190, sending a letter which went astray, and failing to make further inquiries was held not to amount to adequate consultation. If the RPA has made no attempt to follow up its letter to the Cokeshire County Council and check that it indeed has no comment to make, it will be considered to have broken a mandatory requirement.

The RPA's failure to consult the National Union of Chemical Workers could be challenged as an unreasonable use of discretion, as in *Secretary of State for Education* v *Metropolitan Borough of Tameside* [1977] AC 1014; no reasonable authority could have failed to consider the Union representative of those affected.

The RPA is required to consider 'all representations submitted to it', but it throws away the objections from the Green Anti-Nuclear Faction. The only possible justification for this is the provision in the Act that objections should include the name and address of the sender. This requirement could be classed as mandatory if it is essential for the conduct of the administration. In *Chapman* v *Earl* [1968] 1 WLR 1315, the failure of a tenant to indicate the proposed rent in an application to a rent tribunal was held to be a breach of a mandatory requirement. However, requirements imposed merely for the convenience of the administration are likely to be classified as directory only. In *Jackson Developments* v *Hall* [1951] 2 KB 488, the requirement that the tenant supply the landlord's name to a rent tribunal was held to be directory. In this problem, the objectors' failure to identify themselves hardly seems of sufficient importance to be treated as breach of a mandatory requirement. Their objections should therefore have been considered.

The petition is rejected because it is submitted one day late. Time limits will be held to be mandatory where they are essential in establishing legal rights and obligations. In *Howard* v *Secretary of State for the Environment* [1975] QB 235, the statutory time limit of 42 days for appealing against an enforcement notice was held to be mandatory, because it determined the legal powers of the local authority. But if no such compelling reasons exist, time limits will be treated as directory. In *James v Minister of Housing and Local Government* [1966] 1 WLR 135, a local authority was held to be entitled to make a planning decision after three months, though regulations imposed a limit of two months. In this problem, as the RPA will be spending some time considering the application, there seems no reason to treat the time limit for receipt of representations as mandatory.

An application for judicial review to challenge the validity of the licence under the Supreme Court Act 1981, s. 31 and Order 53 of the Rules of the Supreme Court could be made by any person with locus standi, that is, with a sufficient interest in the matter. Cokeshire County Council and the National Union of Chemical Workers would clearly have a sufficient interest, as would members of the Green Anti-Nuclear Faction, if willing to identify themselves. In *R v Secretary of State for the Environment ex parte Greenpeace* [1994] 4 All ER 352, Greenpeace was held to have locus standi, as a pressure group with local members, to challenge the licensing of the THORP nuclear plant. It could further be argued that any of the inhabitants of Coketown who had signed the petition would have locus standi. In *R v Inland Revenue Commissioners ex parte National Federation of Self-Employed & Small Businesses* [1982] AC 617, Lord Diplock referred to the desirability of 'a single public-minded taxpayer' being able to challenge the validity of unlawful administrative action.

The most appropriate remedies in this case would be certiorari to quash the licence, or a declaration that it was invalid. It would, however, be open to Sulphurous Chemical plc to make a further application for a licence.

QUESTION 3

The (imaginary) Young Persons' Safety Act 1995 requires any person wishing to run an outdoor pursuits centre to obtain a licence from the county council, which may refuse a licence if it considers the staff or facilities to be unsatisfactory. There is a right of appeal to an Appeal Tribunal against the refusal of a licence.

Crampon applied to the Rockshire County Council (RCC) for a licence to run the Crampon Centre for Outdoor Activities. He completed and submitted the detailed application form. The RCC then asked Abseil, an official, to make inquiries. Abseil visited the Centre, posing as a potential customer, and made other inquiries, after which he prepared a report. This stated that the instructors in horse-riding and canoeing did not have adequate qualifications, and that two years ago, a child had been seriously injured while rock-climbing under Crampon's supervision.

The RCC wrote to Crampon, asking him to give further details of the qualifications of his staff. Crampon replied, giving the details and asking for an opportunity to appear in person before the Council. The RCC refused this request and, after considering Abseil's report and the material supplied by Crampon, refused him a licence, giving no reason.

Crampon then appealed to the Appeal Tribunal, which gave him a personal hearing, but refused to allow him to be accompanied by his solicitor, or to bring his staff to give evidence. At the hearing he was shown Abseil's report and asked to comment on it. The Tribunal rejected Crampon's appeal. Crampon has now discovered that the daughter of one member of the Tribunal died in a canoeing accident 10 years ago.

Advise Crampon.

Commentary

This problem raises a number of issues relating to the rules of natural justice, and is best tackled by working one's way systematically through the problem, picking up each issue as it appears, explaining the law on the point, citing the relevant authority and then applying the law to the problem. The student may quite properly introduce the answer by some general remarks on the topic, but should not attempt to answer this, or any other problem, by writing an essay. It is the ability of the student to select from the material they have learnt what is relevant to the question that marks out the competent student.

Suggested Answer

This problem concerns various apparent breaches of the rules of natural justice. These are rules which the courts have developed to ensure that decisions are taken by a fair procedure and with those affected having a full opportunity to state their case. The courts have adopted the presumption that, where Parliament has been silent about the procedure by which a decision is to be made, it must have intended a fair hearing to be given. The rules of natural justice can be excluded by Parliament, but will otherwise be presumed to be applicable. Failure to observe these rules will be a form of procedural impropriety, according to the classification of the grounds of review by Lord Diplock in *Council of Civil Service Unions* v *Minister for Civil Service* [1985] AC 374.

It is first necessary to establish on what basis Crampon can assert the right to a fair hearing. In *Ridge* v *Baldwin* [1964] AC 40, it was held that natural justice applied whenever a decision affected the rights of the individual, and it was made clear in *Re HK* [1967] 2 QB 617 that this applied even if the decision was of an administrative nature. By imposing a requirement that a licence must be obtained for an activity which could previously have been carried on without restriction, the law is affecting the rights of the individual, and so a fair hearing must be given. This was applied, in *R* v *Gaming Board ex parte Benaim* [1970] 2 QB 417, to the grant of gaming licences, and is clearly applicable in Crampon's case.

At what stage in the procedure is Crampon entitled to a fair hearing? There is no general right to be heard during preliminary investigative or preparatory processes. In *Pearlberg* v *Varty* [1972] 1 WLR 534, the House of Lords held that a taxpayer had no right to be heard by the Inland Revenue as they prepared his tax assessment; he would be heard at the proper time before the relevant tribunal. So it is clearly proper for RCC to use Abseil to carry out investigations in a covert manner. But, before the actual decision on the licence is taken, Crampon must be given an opportunity to state his case. Here, it appears that Crampon was not informed of the contents of Abseil's report, or even of its existence, and was merely sent a general request for further details about his staff. Fairness requires that a person be given full details of the charges against him, or the matters being taken into account. In *Fairmount Investments* v *Secretary of State for the Environment* [1976] 1 WLR 1255, a decision was held to be invalid where a planning inspector had based his decision on defects in the building which he had noticed but failed to mention to the parties. Here Crampon is left unaware of the serious charges in Abseil's report and has had no chance to rebut them.

Crampon's request to appear in person before the Council was rejected. As a general rule, fairness is satisfied by the opportunity to make representations in writing, rather than orally. In *Lloyd* v *McMahon* [1987] 1 AC 625, the House of Lords held that a district auditor had acted fairly in offering councillors an opportunity to make written rather than oral representations to him. Had RCC given Crampon a proper chance to make written representations, that would have been adequate, but it has already been shown that it failed to do so.

The RCC gave no reason when it refused Crampon a licence. There is no absolute rule that reasons must be given, in the absence of a statutory requirement to that effect. But there can be circumstances where fairness does require the giving of reasons, either because of the serious nature of the decision, or because the decision itself was so strange as to require an explanation. In *Doody* v *Home Secretary* [1994] 1 AC 531, it was held that the Home Secretary must give reasons to a life prisoner if he decides the prisoner should serve longer than the term recommended by the judges; questions of individual liberty require the highest standards of fairness. By contrast, in *R* v *Higher Education Funding Council ex parte Institute of Dental Surgery* [1994] 1 All ER 651, the defendants were not required to give reasons for their assessment of the applicants' research record, as there was no general duty to give reasons, and the decision was not in itself aberrant. In Crampon's case, the decision cannot be described as aberrant; if the allegations in Abseil's report are true, they would provide excellent reasons for refusing him a licence. But he could argue that, as the decision will so seriously affect his livelihood, there should be a duty to give reasons in this case. He could also argue that he cannot decide whether to appeal if he is not informed of the reasons for the original decision. Many writers consider that there should be a general duty to give reasons and the courts are showing more sympathy to such claims, so Crampon may be able to establish that the failure to give reasons was another breach of the rules of natural justice.

The breaches of natural justice committed by RCC will render its decision invalid. It can logically be argued that no subsequent procedures can affect that initial invalidity. But the courts have been prepared to hold that, where an appeal takes the form of a full rehearing, it can cure any defects in the initial process. This was held by the Privy Council in *Calvin* v *Carr* [1980] AC 574 and confirmed by the House of Lords in *Lloyd* v *McMahon* (1987). But this is dependent on the appeal itself being conducted fairly, which is open to question in Crampon's case.

Crampon asks for and is refused permission to be accompanied by his solicitor. There seems to be no absolute right to legal, or other, representation. In *R* v *Maze Prison Visitors ex parte Hone* [1988] AC 379, it was held that disciplinary proceedings against a prisoner could be fairly conducted without legal representation. But in *R* v *Home Secretary ex parte Tarrant* [1985] QB 251, the court held that an adjudicating body must consider in each case whether to permit legal representation, and that an unreasonable refusal could invalidate the proceedings. That case concerned prisoners who were facing serious charges and whose detention would make it very difficult to prepare their own defence. It is difficult for Crampon to demonstrate that it is unreasonable to make him present his own case, given that he can make full use of legal assistance in the preparation for the hearing.

Crampon is not allowed to bring his staff to give evidence. In *R* v *Hull Prison Visitors ex parte St Germain (No. 2)* [1979] 1 WLR 1401, it was held to be a breach of the rules of natural justice to refuse to allow prisoners to call relevant witnesses. In this case, Crampon's staff, whose qualifications and experience are clearly important in deciding his suitability to hold a licence, must be relevant witnesses, and the Tribunal is in breach of the rules of natural justice in refusing to admit their evidence.

At the hearing, Crampon is shown Abseil's report, a very belated compliance with the rule that a person must be told the charges against him. But this fails to give Crampon an adequate time to prepare any defence to the accusations in the report. In *R* v *Thames Magistrates' Court ex parte Polemis* [1974] 1 WLR 1371, it was held to be a breach of the rules of natural justice to allow a defendant only a few hours to prepare a defence. Crampon is in effect given no time at all.

The final substantive issue is the allegation that one member of the Tribunal may be biased. The presence of one biased person in an adjudicating body will be enough to invalidate its decision. The extent of bias necessary to invalidate a decision has been formulated by the courts in various ways, including a 'real likelihood' of bias and a 'reasonable suspicion'. The House of Lords, in *R* v *Gough* [1993] AC 646, has attempted to lay down a general test, applicable to all adjudicators including members of tribunals; was there a 'real danger' of bias? The court itself will decide whether the facts of this case can create such a real danger; any involvement of Crampon or his staff in the child's death would clearly give rise to such a real danger, but it could be argued that, in the absence of such a factor, the connection is too remote.

How should Crampon challenge the decisions of RCC and the Tribunal? In the absence of any further appeal, he will be able to seek judicial review, by making an ex parte application for leave within three months of the Tribunal's decision, under Order 53, RSC. The case will then be heard in the Divisional Court of the Queen's Bench Division. The most appropriate remedy for Crampon to seek would be certiorari to quash both decisions. He could ask for mandamus in addition, to force them to reconsider his case. Although the award of these remedies is at the discretion of the court, there seems no reason why he should not be successful in his legal action. But whether he will eventually obtain the licence he needs will depend, rightly, on his suitability.

QUESTION 4

As a result of last month's election, the Radical Party took control of Yarford Borough Council. Since then, the Council has taken the following decisions. Consider whether there could be any legal objection to them, and who would be able to make any such objection.

(a)   The Council has a statutory power to license sex shops. The previous Council had validly granted Dolores such a licence, but the new Council, which had promised in its manifesto to get rid of sex shops, has written to her informing her that her licence has been revoked with immediate effect.

(b)   The Council announced that it would never grant planning permission for the demolition of any listed building, although it has the statutory power to do so.

(c)   At a Radical Party meeting, Yarford councillors agreed that they would license the showing of films strictly in accordance with Radical Party policy, which would be agreed in countrywide party meetings.

(d)   The Council ordered the closure of a registered caravan site, ostensibly on grounds of defective drainage. During the election campaign, several Radical Party candidates had made racist remarks about the gypsies who live on the site.

(e)   The Council has ordered a new Daimler limousine for the mayor's use, although the existing mayoral car was only two years old and in perfect condition.

Commentary

This question raises a variety of issues about the control of discretionary powers. The student will have to identify the particular grounds of challenge most appropriate to each case, though it should be noted that no two academics agree exactly on the categorisation of the grounds of challenge. The same cases can easily appear as authority under a variety of headings. It can safely be assumed that judicial review will be the method of challenge, but the question specifically raises the issue of locus standi.

Suggested Answer

(a) The effect of the original grant of the licence to Dolores is to confer on her legal rights. Whether these rights may be revoked will depend on the terms of the relevant statute. It may be that there is no power at all to revoke a licence granted for a particular term, in which case the purported revocation is ultra vires and void, and can be challenged by Dolores in an action for judicial review. On the other hand, if there is a power to revoke the licence, that power must be exercised in accordance with the rules of natural justice, because it is a decision affecting individual rights. In *R v Barnsley MBC ex parte Hook* [1976] 1 WLR 1052 and *R v Wear Valley DC ex parte Binks* [1985] 2 All ER 699, the revocation of licences by a local authority without a fair hearing was held to be invalid. Dolores could challenge the decision by judicial review, seeking an order of certiorari to quash the Council's decision.

The fact that the Party had promised in its manifesto to get rid of sex shops cannot affect the invalidity of its actions. In *Bromley LBC v Greater London Council* [1982] 1 AC 768, the party's commitment to reducing London Transport fares did not justify a subsidy which was found to be unlawful. It will of course be lawful for the Council to exercise its statutory powers in the light of those policy commitments which can lawfully be taken into account, but it will still have to adopt the proper procedure.

(b) The Council has a discretion over the granting of permission for the demolition of listed buildings. It is entitled to adopt a general policy for the exercise of that discretion, but that does not permit it to adopt a rule and to refuse to depart from it. In *R v London County Council ex parte Corrie* [1918] 1 KB 68, the Council was held to have acted ultra vires in adopting a rule against the sale of pamphlets in parks and refusing even to consider making an exception to it. In *Attorney-General ex rel Tilley v Wandsworth LBC* [1981] 1 WLR 854, the court declared invalid a council's decision never to use a statutory power to rehouse homeless families with children. It would therefore appear that the Council's announcement is invalid, and could be challenged by any person with a sufficient interest, under the Supreme Court Act 1981, s. 31(3). The most likely applicant for judicial review is a person whose application for planning permission has been rejected.

There is, however, nothing unlawful in the adoption of a policy, provided that consideration is given to each individual case. In *British Oxygen v Board of Trade* [1971] AC 610, a decision to refuse the plaintiff an investment grant, in accordance with a stated policy, was held to be valid, because consideration had been given to the individual application. The easiest way to prove that such consideration has been given is to offer the applicants an opportunity to state their case, orally or in writing. In *R* v *Secretary of State for the Environment ex parte Brent LBC* [1982] QB 593, the Secretary of State's refusal to hold a meeting with the council or hear representations from it was held to have demonstrated that he would not even consider departing from his predetermined policy, and so led to the quashing of his decision.

The Council would therefore be well advised to adopt a procedure which shows its willingness to consider individual applications; it can then lawfully reject any applications which it does not feel justify a departure from its policy.

(c) Discretionary powers must be exercised by the persons to whom Parliament has entrusted them, not by anyone else, unless Parliament has authorised the transfer or delegation of the powers. The licensing of films is a power entrusted to local authorities and cannot be exercised by anyone else. In *Ellis* v *Dubowski* [1921] 3 KB 621, the council decided to permit the showing of films only if they had been approved by the British Board of Film Censors, the film industry's self-regulatory body. This was held to amount to a surrender of the council's discretion to the Board, and was therefore invalid.

It is, however, lawful for an authority to use the guidance of some other body, provided that it retains the ultimate exercise of the discretion in its own hands. In *Mills* v *London County Council* [1925] 1 KB 213, the Council's policy was to show only those films approved by the Board, but, unlike in *Ellis* v *Dubowski* (1921), it reserved its right to make its own, different decisions when it thought fit. This was held to be valid.

This principle has been applied in cases concerning the relationship between local authorities and political parties. In *R* v *Waltham Forest LBC ex parte Baxter* [1988] QB 419, a meeting of Labour Party councillors agreed a party line to which all the councillors adhered when the matter came to the vote in the council meeting, even though some had previously disagreed. This was challenged as a surrender of discretion by the individual councillors, but this challenge was rejected by the court. Each councillor retained the right to vote as he or she thought fit, so the ultimate decision remained in their hands. There could be no objection to the adoption of a party line; indeed the court recognised it as an essential part of the political system.

If the ruling Radical Party were to get the Council to adopt a resolution that decisions on licensing were to be transferred to the party meeting, that would clearly be unlawful, and could be challenged by way of judicial review by any cinema owner, or actual or potential cinemagoer. But if it remains merely as party policy, with the actual decision being made in each case by the Yarford Council, it would be difficult for any legal challenge to succeed.

(**d**)   It has to be assumed that the Council does have the power to order the closure of the site. But that power, like all discretionary powers must be exercised for proper purposes only, and the decisions based on relevant considerations. As Lord Greene MR said in *Associated Provincial Picture Houses* v *Wednesbury Corporation* [1948] 1 KB 223:

> The exercise of such a discretion must be a real exercise of discretion. If, in the statute conferring the discretion, there is to be found expressly or by implication matters to which the authority exercising the discretion ought to have regard, then in exercising the discretion it must have regard to those matters. Conversely, if the nature of the subject-matter and the general interpretation of the Act make it clear that certain matters would not be germane to the matter in question, the authority must disregard those irrelevant collateral matters.

As the quotation makes clear, if the statute expressly states which factors are relevant to the exercise of the discretion, it will be unlawful to use the power to achieve other purposes. In *Sydney Council* v *Campbell* [1925] AC 338, the power of compulsory purchase of land was stated in the statute to be available for improvements to the city. It was held to be unlawful to use the power to purchase land with a view only to profiting from its increase in value. Where the statute does not expressly identify the relevant factors, it will be up to the court to identify them by implication. In *Congreve* v *Home Office* [1976] 1 QB 629, the power to revoke a television licence, though not limited by the words of the statute, was held to be improperly used to punish those who had lawfully avoided a price increase by renewing their licences early.

In this problem, it is not clear whether or not the relevant statute prescribes the considerations which could validly be taken into account in deciding whether to close the site. In either case, it is likely that defective drainage would be a proper factor to be considered, and if the decision to close the site has been taken for that reason alone, there would be no ground of legal challenge. However, the question implies that the decision may have been taken for the wholly improper reason of racism. The Race Relations Act 1976 requires local authorities to exercise their functions without racial discrimination, so a decision to close the site made for racist reasons would be unlawful and could be challenged by an action for judicial review, brought by an occupier of the site, or any other person with a sufficient interest. This might well include the Commission for Racial Equality. In *R v Secretary of State for Employment ex parte Equal Opportunities Commission* [1995] 1 AC 1, the House of Lords held that the Commission was entitled to seek judicial review as a means of exercising its statutory function of promoting the equality of the sexes.

Difficulties may, however, arise in establishing the actual motive behind the Council's decision. If it cannot be proved that the Council had a racist motive, the existence of a proper motive, public health, will make it impossible to challenge the decision. What if it can be proved that both factors were taken into account? In *R v Inner London Education Authority ex parte Westminster City Council* [1986] 1 WLR 28, the courts invalidated a publicity campaign organised by ILEA because it combined the lawful purpose of informing the public with the unlawful purpose of persuading the public to protest against government policy. It would therefore appear that any evidence that racist motives played a part in the making of this decision would render it invalid and subject to challenge by way of judicial review.

(e)   The courts have established a general principle that local authorities owe a fiduciary duty to their ratepayers and now council taxpayers. As Lord Diplock said in *Bromley LBC v Greater London Council* [1982] 1 AC 768:

This includes a duty not to expend those moneys thriftlessly, but to deploy the full financial resources available to it to the best advantage.

This principle has been used to challenge various forms of extravagant expenditure by local authorities, including over-generous wages, as in *Roberts v Hopwood* [1925] AC 578, and transport subsidies, as in the *Bromley* case itself. It is possible that the decision to buy a new mayoral car could be challenged as a breach of the Council's fiduciary duty, though the impact on each individual council tax payer would be far less than in those cases.

The other possible ground of challenge would be unreasonableness or irrationality, described by Lord Greene in the *Wednesbury* case as 'something so absurd that no sensible person could ever dream that it lay within the powers of the authority.' This ground of challenge is very difficult to establish, requiring as it does an extreme degree of unreasonableness. It could be argued that this extravagant purchase of an unnecessary car could be so regarded, though the Council might be able to offer a plausible explanation.

This decision could be challenged by means of judicial review. The courts generally accept that any council taxpayer has locus standi to bring such a case, on the basis that there is a direct link between the tax paid to the council and the council's expenditure; see *Barrs* v *Bethell* [1982] Ch 294 and *Arsenal FC* v *Ende* [1979] AC 1. The expenditure of local authorities is also subject to audit, where its validity and propriety may be examined; see *Lloyd* v *McMahon* [1987] 1 AC 625.

QUESTION 5

The divorce between public and private law, proclaimed by Lord Diplock in *O'Reilly* v *Mackman* [1983] 2 AC 237, has not been a happy addition to English administrative law. It has caused problems for litigants, without aiding the development of a coherent system of judicial review.

Discuss.

Commentary

This question deals with the complex issue of the division between public law and private law procedures. The student will need to explain the background to this development, and then examine *O'Reilly* v *Mackman* itself in some detail. The ensuing problems and how the courts have dealt with them should then be discussed. A good answer might make some reference to other legal traditions and should certainly offer suggestions as to whether the law should be reformed and, if so, how.

Suggested Answer

In the civil law tradition, the distinction between public and private law is the primary and fundamental classification of law. It is traceable back to the jurist Ulpian, writing in 200 AD, and is among the first rules mentioned in Justinian's *Institutes*; to this day it forms one of the first lessons for the student of civil law. But in English law, which developed incrementally and without a theoretical framework, the distinction between public and private law was almost unknown. Principles such as ultra vires and natural justice were applied indifferently to public and private bodies and, with the exception of the rules limiting the liability of the Crown, the same laws of tort, contract and property applied to public and private bodies. Indeed, Dicey's analysis of the rule of law depended heavily on the absence of any division. He praised the English use of private law as a means of controlling the activities of the government, and compared it favourably with the strictly separated French system of *droit administratif.*

The only area where the distinction between public and private law was important was in relation to remedies. The prerogative remedies of certiorari, prohibition and mandamus were available only against public bodies, defined by Atkin LJ in *R* v *Electricity Commissioners* [1924] 1 KB 171 at 205 as 'any body of persons having legal authority to determine questions affecting the rights of subjects'. But the private law remedies of injunction, declaration and damages were equally available against public and private bodies, with the exception of the immunity of the Crown from injunctions, preserved by the Crown Proceedings Act 1947, s. 21(1)(a). Litigants against public bodies therefore had a choice of remedies, but unfortunately could not combine remedies from the two groups in the same proceedings, until the introduction of the application for judicial review in 1978.

This new procedure adopted many features from the prerogative remedies, such as the need to obtain leave to make an application, and the short time limit, now set at three months. All applications for certiorari, mandamus and prohibition had to use this new procedure. Applications for injunction, declaration and damages could also use it where the case concerned matters for which the prerogative remedies were available and appropriate. In effect, if an injunction or declaration was sought against a public body, on grounds arising from public law, the new judicial review procedure was available. But the new rules did not use any conceptual terms such as 'public law'. If there was any legal principle underlying the changes, it was not openly expressed.

What was left uncertain was the boundary between those claims for injunction and declaration where judicial review procedure should be used and those where the normal High Court procedure was still applicable. Did it matter which procedure was used? The Law Commission had specifically addressed this issue and had recommended that the new procedure should not be exclusive. But when the issue came before the House of Lords, a stricter rule was adopted.

O'Reilly v *Mackman* [1983] 2 AC 237 concerned various prisoners who wished to challenge decisions taken by prison Boards of Visitors on grounds of breach of the rules of natural justice. Judicial review would clearly have been the appropriate procedure to have used, but instead they started actions by writ in the High Court for declarations, the time limit for judicial review having long since expired. The defendants successfully claimed that the actions should be struck out as an abuse of process. Lord Diplock's justification for this decision was as follows. In the days before the reform of remedies, it was justifiable for applicants to use ordinary High Court procedure rather than the prerogative orders, because of such procedural defects as the absence of discovery and the virtual impossibility of cross-examination of witnesses. But these procedures were now available under the reformed application for judicial review. On the other side, judicial review contained safeguards against the 'groundless, unmeritorious or tardy harassment' of public authorities and applicants should not be allowed to evade these. It was therefore generally contrary to public policy and an abuse of process, for an applicant to begin an action by writ which should have been brought by judicial review. If the case concerned a public body and an infringement of public law rights, judicial review must normally be used, though Lord Diplock conceded that there might be exceptions.

It therefore became essential for the first time for an applicant to identify whether the case was suitable for judicial review or action by writ. This presented two difficulties. First, judicial review is only available against public bodies, not private bodies; they do not have 'legal authority' merely rights and duties under contract. Trade unions, private employers and sporting bodies have all been held not to be subject to judicial review, though it has taken substantial litigation to establish this in some cases; see *R* v *Chief Rabbi ex parte Wachman* [1992] 1 WLR 1036 and *R* v *Jockey Club ex parte Massingberd-Mundy* [1993] 2 All ER 207. But problems arise because of the lack of any conceptual distinction between public and private bodies embodied in English law. The issue was most fully addressed in *R* v *Panel on Takeovers and Mergers ex parte Datafin* [1987] QB 815, and the result was pragmatic rather than theoretically based. The Panel, one of the self-regulatory bodies of the City of London's financial markets, was held to be subject to judicial review, in spite of having no legal authority or even existence! The court pointed out that it was performing a function which, if it did not perform, would have had to be performed by a public body set up for the purpose. If the Panel were held not to be subject to judicial review, its decisions could be arbitrary or unfair and no redress would be available. Subsequent decisions on bodies such as the Advertising Standards Authority, LAUTRO, and university visitors have confirmed the impression that the courts define a body as public in order to subject it to judicial review, rather than subjecting it to judicial review because it is public. In the absence of a specific precedent, it is difficult to tell whether a body without a clearly defined status will be treated as public or private.

The second problem is identifying which issues are regarded as public rather than private law, again in the absence of a theoretical framework. In *O'Reilly* v *Mackman* itself the case was clear; the prisoners' complaint was of breach of the rules of natural justice by a statutory tribunal to which they were subjected by statute, public law in all respects. On the other hand, the rights of public employees in their work derive ultimately from the private law of contract, so judicial review is not appropriate; see *R* v *East Berkshire Health Authority ex parte Walsh* [1985] QB 152. But many cases can be characterised as either public or private depending on the perspective the parties choose to adopt. The GCHQ case, *Council of Civil Service Unions* v *Minister for the Civil Service* [1985] AC 374, was brought as a public law case, by judicial review; in this perspective it concerned a breach of the rules of natural justice by the government in the exercise of a discretionary power. But it could have been treated as a private law matter relating to the contractual right of government employees to belong to a trade union. Conversely, in *Gillick* v *West Norfolk Area Health Authority* [1986] AC 112, the plaintiff brought a private law action complaining that the advice given to doctors infringed her rights as a mother, but the case could have been defined more easily as a public law challenge to the legal validity of the advice.

Particular problems arise where liability in tort or contract is alleged to arise as a consequence of the validity or invalidity on public law grounds of some administrative decision. In *Cocks* v *Thanet DC* [1983] 2 AC 286, a case decided at the same time as *O'Reilly* v *Mackman*, the House of Lords attempted to split up a claim for damages for failure to rehouse a homeless family. If the claim was that the decision that they were not eligible for rehousing was invalid, that was a matter of public law; if it was a claim that the council, having decided they were eligible, had failed to rehouse them, that was a matter of private law. This makes choosing the right procedure very difficult.

The difficulties of attempting to draw the distinctions which the decision in *O'Reilly* v *Mackman* rendered necessary have led the courts to develop the possibility of exceptions to the rule. In *Davy* v *Spelthorne Borough Council* [1984] AC 262, the plaintiff was allowed to proceed with a private law action for damages, even though it depended on establishing the invalidity of a council decision. In *Wandsworth LBC* v *Winder* [1985] AC 461, the defendant was allowed to resist an eviction order by arguing that a rent demand was ultra vires and void. It now seems that, provided the ultimate form of the action is suitable for an action begun by writ, the involvement of public law issues does not matter. In *Roy* v *Kensington Family Practitioner Committee* [1992] 1 AC 624, the plaintiff was allowed to bring a private law action based on the claim that the decision to deprive him of certain payments was invalid.

In the most recent cases, it appears that the courts are unwilling to reject any claim on the basis that the plaintiff has chosen the wrong procedure, unless the procedure chosen is clearly inappropriate. In *Mercury Communications* v *Director-General of Telecommunications* [1996] 1 All ER 575, the House of Lords rejected the assertion that a challenge to the validity of the defendant's ruling in a dispute between Mercury and British Telecom could only be sought by judicial review. The court stated that, as the limits of public and private law were not worked out, the procedural rules should be applied flexibly. This was similar to the opinion expressed by the Law Commission in their 1994 report on judicial review, that continuing flexibility was desirable, to be combined with procedures enabling a case to be transferred to the more appropriate court if the wrong procedure had been initiated. There would seem to be no reason why the concept of abuse of process should not be confined to those cases where a plaintiff is trying to evade a restriction which should be applied to the case, such as a time limit. A litigant who, on legal advice, opts for one of two possible procedures should not be penalised.

The problems thrown up by the decision in *O'Reilly* v *Mackman* can all be traced back to the absence of any conceptual distinction between public and private law in the English legal tradition. It has proved almost as difficult to incorporate the distinction into English law as it would be to incorporate the distinction between common law and equity into a civil law system. Although there are valid arguments for having a special procedure for judicial review cases, these should not lead to the erection of procedural barriers against litigants. It is notable how many of the cases cited have been fought to the House of Lords merely in order to discover by which procedure the substantive issue should be resolved, a great waste of resources. English law should perhaps stick to its traditional concern with practical remedies, rather than trying to adopt concepts which sit uneasily alongside the pragmatic historical development of judicial review.

QUESTION 6

It would, in my view, be a grave lacuna in our system of public law if a pressure group, like the federation, or even a single public-spirited taxpayer, were prevented by outdated technical rules of locus standi from bringing the matter to the attention of the court to vindicate the rule of law and get the unlawful conduct stopped. Lord Diplock, *R* v *Inland Revenue Commissioners ex parte National Federation of Self-Employed and Small Businesses* [1982] AC 617.

To what extent do the rules of locus standi limit the availability of judicial review? Do you consider that the rules should be more or less restrictive?

Commentary

The student needs to start this question by describing and explaining the function of rules of locus standi and then the way they have developed in English law. The central element in describing the current law will be the case itself which, because of its exceptionally unwieldy title, will be referred to as the Fleet Street Casuals case; most examiners will be happy to accept such informal references in an examination. The case contains the most detailed discussion of how locus standi rules are to operate after the reforms in the procedure for judicial review. There are interesting subsequent developments and divergent decisions which need to be explained. Finally the student can express a view for or against Lord Diplock's opinion on locus standi. Either point of view can be justified by argument and the student should not think that the views expressed in this answer are necessarily conclusive.

Suggested Answer

In most areas of law, particularly private law, there has been no need to articulate rules of locus standi, because they are inherent in the substantive rules of law. A tort case can only be brought by the victim, a property claim only by the would-be claimant. In some areas of public law the same is true; a complaint of breach of the rules of natural justice can only be brought by the person who was deprived of a fair hearing.

But in other areas of public law, it has been necessary to develop specific rules to govern the standing of those who bring legal action. The reason is that administrative decisions may affect a range of persons in differing degrees and may cause concern to those who are not materially affected. The decision of a local authority to grant planning permission has its most immediate effect on the landowner, greatly affects the immediate neighbourhood, may have implications for the surrounding areas, and may, if a particularly sensitive area is affected, be of concern to the wider public, expressed through environmental pressure groups. The decision is like a stone dropped in a pond; ripples spread wider and wider across the whole surface.

Who should be allowed to challenge the validity of that decision? Only those directly affected, or those who chose to make it their concern? What if all those affected are happy with the decision? Can outsiders appoint themselves as guardians of the greater public good? It is these issues which rules of locus standi have to address.

Before the 1978 reforms, there were different rules of locus standi for each remedy. For the prerogative remedies, the rules were fairly generous because of their public law nature. The courts expressed their willingness to grant the remedy even to a stranger. In *R* v *Metropolitan Police Commissioner ex parte Blackburn* [1968] 2 QB 118, the applicant was a citizen concerned about the police's apparent failure to enforce laws against pornography and gambling. Although his claim failed on the merits, the court said no objection could be made to his standing. Remedies were granted to those with only a tenuous connection; in *R* v *Cotham* [1898] 1 QB 802, mandamus was granted to a clergyman purely on the basis of his moral concern about liquor licensing.

For the private law remedies of injunction and declaration, however, the courts took the view that in general only those who were particularly affected, over and above the general public, could sue. In *Gregory* v *Camden LBC* [1966] 1 WLR 899, the court even refused to grant a declaration to a neighbour in respect of an invalid planning decision, on the grounds that his legal rights were not infringed; the effect on his amenity was not sufficient. The only way in which a person without locus standi could obtain an injunction or declaration was to seek the assistance of the Attorney-General who, as representative of the public interest, could lend his name for a relator action. But the Attorney-General has a complete discretion as to whether to permit such an action, and has never been willing to authorise actions against central government bodies; ministerial solidarity inevitably takes precedence.

When the application for judicial review was introduced, a conscious attempt was made to find a new formula of words to define locus standi, so as to avoid importing old legal concepts into the new rules. The Supreme Court Act 1981, s. 31(3) states: 'The court shall not grant leave ... unless it considers that the applicant has a sufficient interest in the matter to which the application relates'. The effect of this provision was examined by the House of Lords in the Fleet Street Casuals case. The case arose out of an amnesty offered by the Inland Revenue to Fleet Street casual workers; past arrears of tax would be forgiven in return for future compliance. The applicants sought judicial review of this decision, not because they were in any way affected by it, but because they felt it unfair that some tax evaders should get an amnesty while their members were expected to pay all tax legally due. The Inland Revenue challenged the locus standi of the applicants as a preliminary issue, a procedure which appeared to conform with s. 31(3).

But the House of Lords held that standing should not be dealt with at the stage of asking for leave, except where, as Lord Scarman said, this was necessary to avoid 'abuse by busybodies, cranks and other mischief makers'. Once past that hurdle, the main test is of the merits of the case and, as the Inland Revenue's amnesty was held to be a lawful use of their discretion, the standing of the applicants became of theoretical significance only. The issue was, however, discussed by all members of the House of Lords, their judgments being complicated by the fact that the tax paid by any individual is a private matter, dealt with by the Inland Revenue in confidence. But all agreed that, if the Inland Revenue were committing a serious impropriety, another taxpayer would have locus standi to challenge it. As virtually the entire adult population are taxpayers in one way or another, this can be taken as the abolition of locus standi as a separate requirement. There also appears to be a majority for the view that, in judicial review proceedings, the exact remedy being sought does not matter; the distinction between prerogative and other remedies ceases to matter.

The effect of this decision appeared to be a general liberalisation of the rules on standing. The 'single, public-spirited taxpayer' has been allowed to bring an action for judicial review, in spite of the lack of any particular interest. In *R v HM Treasury ex parte Smedley* [1985] 1 QB 657, a taxpayer challenged, albeit unsuccessfully, the UK's payment of certain sums to the European Community. In *R v Independent Broadcasting Authority ex parte Whitehouse, The Times,* 14 April 1984, the applicant's challenge to the showing of a film on television was based merely on her being a television licence holder, like most other people.

Some of the most interesting issues in relation to locus standi arise from the activities of pressure groups, who are more likely to have the will and the resources to take legal action than private individuals do. As Lord Diplock suggested, the courts have been willing to allow established pressure groups to bring legal actions. In *R v Secretary of State for Social Services ex parte Child Poverty Action Group, The Times,* 16 August 1984 and 8 August 1985, the applicants, a well-known campaigning and advocacy organisation, were held to have locus standi to challenge the defendant's failure to reopen cases where welfare benefits had apparently been miscalculated.

Concern was expressed, however, when a more restrictive attitude was taken in *R v Secretary of State for the Environment ex parte Rose Theatre Trust* [1990] 1 QB 504. The applicant group had been created when the remains of Shakespeare's Rose Theatre were discovered; the members hoped to arrange for the preservation and display of the site. When the Secretary of State refused to schedule the remains as an ancient monument, the group sought judicial review of his decision. The court held that his decision was in any case lawful, but went on to state that the group did not have locus standi. They were mere members of the public, whose standing was not increased by their forming themselves into an action group. This carries the worrying implication that, even if the decision had been invalid, the applicants' challenge would have failed. Furthermore, it is difficult to identify any potential challenger who would have locus standi. The landowners, developers and local authority were all in favour of the development of the site, not its preservation; Shakespeare was unfortunately no longer available.

In three cases decided in 1994, however, the courts seemed willing to return to Lord Diplock's criteria and allow pressure groups to bring actions for judicial review. In *R* v *Secretary of State for Employment ex parte Equal Opportunities Commission* [1995] 1 AC 1, the House of Lords held that the EOC, in its statutory capacity of promoter of equality between the sexes, had locus standi to seek a declaration that employment law, by discriminating against part-time workers, was discriminating against women, contrary to European Community law. The EOC is of course more than a pressure group, having an official status, but this was a promising development. It was followed by *R* v *Pollution Inspectorate ex parte Greenpeace (2)* [1994] 4 All ER 329, in which the well-known environmental pressure group was held to have locus standi to challenge the decision to license the Thorp nuclear reprocessing plant, though its case was strengthened by the fact that it had members in the surrounding area who had fears of being affected by discharges of radiation. But no such considerations arose in the most far-reaching case, *R* v *Foreign Secretary ex parte World Development Movement* [1995] 1 All ER 611. The applicants, whose challenge to the legality of the funding of the Pergau Dam project in Malaysia was successful, were held to have locus standi simply on the basis of being a respected charity known for its lobbying on behalf of the developing world. As the court pointed out, if WDM did not have locus standi, who did, apart from the inhabitants of a remote part of Malaysia whose opportunities to take legal action in the English High Court are limited? This case seems to indicate that issues of locus standi will not be allowed to stand in the way of challenges to unlawful government action.

This indeed is the main argument in favour of generous rules of locus standi; that unlawful administrative action should not be allowed to proceed, irrespective of who is bringing the legal challenge against it. From this point of view, the only restrictions needed are those which ensure that private matters, and those which only affect one person, are not brought to court by busybodies when the immediate victim does not wish it. A person who has been deprived of a fair hearing, but who knows that the result would have been the same anyway, may choose to acquiesce, and should not have the matter raised by a third party.

It can be argued that some further restriction needs to be imposed, to prevent the courts being flooded by cases brought by self-appointed guardians of the public interest, causing delay to the hearing of cases involving genuine personal injustice. But issues of very great general concern may be ventilated by actions brought by individuals. The case of *R* v *Foreign Secretary ex parte Rees-Mogg* [1994] QB 522 raised various important constitutional issues about the Treaty on European Union and its ratification by the UK; the applicant, whose locus standi was not challenged, had no interest other than his concern for constitutional issues.

There are in any case other restraints on ill-founded legal action. Every action for judicial review needs the leave of the court and the risk of having to pay the costs of the action make the vexatious litigant a rarity. To impose restrictions on locus standi would benefit only those public authorities who would prefer it if their unlawful actions went unchallenged.

12 Public Authority Proceedings

INTRODUCTION

The topics dealt with in this chapter are more likely to be included in an administrative law course than in a general constitutional law course, with the exception of public interest immunity, which is of such topical interest that it may be included where the other aspects are not. Students will need to be guided by their own examiners and syllabus.

Examples of both essay and problem questions are included. Good answers will require the student to show skills of legal analysis and application. A student who has studied or is studying tort or contract need not be afraid to bring that extra knowledge into the answer. The law may be divided into discrete subjects for the purpose of teaching and examining, but in reality it is an undivided whole.

QUESTION 1

In 1995, the Home Office decided, as part of its policy of reducing the prison population, to establish hostels where long-term prisoners could spend the last year of their sentences, being gradually rehabilitated into the outside world. One of these hostels was established in Coketown. It was a converted house in a residential area, occupied by eight prisoners, who went out to work during the day, but were otherwise supervised by a warden and his staff.

Consider the liability of the Home Office in the following situations.

(a) White, Black and Gray, who live in the same street as the hostel, consider that it has reduced the amenity and value of their homes. They consider that the hostel should have been established somewhere else.

(b) Brown, who lives next door to the hostel, thinks that the choice of site for the hostel was made because he is a prominent campaigner against Home Office policies; he suspects that there is evidence of this hidden in Home Office files.

(c) The Home Office decided that prisoners convicted of violent crimes could if considered suitable, be sent to the hostel. Reg had been sentenced to 15 years for attempted murder and, because he had behaved impeccably throughout his time in prison, was due for release next year. He was sent to the hostel, obtained a job, and apparently settled in well. But last week, on the way home from work, he went to the pub, got drunk, and punched Green, the landlord.

Commentary

This question raises various issues relating to the liability of public authorities. It is important for students to deal both with the general rules applicable to all public authorities and with the special rules governing the liability of the Crown. The student will not be expected to examine issues of tortious liability in as great depth as would be appropriate in a tort examination, but should concentrate on those aspects peculiar to public authorities. The question also touches on public interest immunity.

Suggested Answer

(a) White, Black and Gray will have to prove that the hostel constitutes an actionable nuisance if they wish to obtain redress. Under the Crown

Proceedings Act 1947, s. 2, the Crown is subject to the same liabilities as any other person in respect of torts committed by its servants or agents, and torts arising from its ownership, occupation or control of property. But there are circumstances in which a body may be able to plead that it has statutory authority. If a statute specifically authorises some activity which will inevitably result in the commission of a nuisance, no action will lie. In *Allen v Gulf Oil Refinery Ltd* [1981] AC 1001, the defendants obtained a private Act of Parliament authorising them to construct a refinery on a particular site, from which some nuisance would inevitably result. They were held to be immune from action, unless they negligently operated the refinery in such a way as to increase the nuisance beyond what was inevitable.

But this defence does not operate where the authorisation is general and the nuisance not inevitable. In *Metropolitan Asylum District v Hill* (1881) 6 App Cas 193, the plaintiff had statutory authority to build hospitals, and chose to build one in a place where it would cause a nuisance. As it would have been possible to exercise the statutory power without causing a nuisance, no defence of statutory authority existed.

In this problem, it appears that the choice of site was in the hands of the Home Office. It can be argued that the hostel could have been established anywhere, including places where it would not have constituted a nuisance.

If therefore the interference which the hostel causes to surrounding property is sufficient to amount to nuisance, White, Black and Gray will be able to sue for damages. They will not, however, be able to obtain an injunction against the Crown to order the closure of the hostel. By the Crown Proceedings Act 1947, s. 21, no injunction may be awarded against the Crown, though a declaration may be awarded instead.

(b) Brown is alleging that the choice of site for the hostel was made maliciously. This would constitute grounds for judicial review, the decision being made for an improper purpose or even in bad faith. Such proceedings would be an appropriate way of getting the decision quashed but would not lead to the award of any compensation to Brown unless he can demonstrate the existence of some established form of liability.

The most likely basis on which he could claim damages would be in terms of misfeasance in a public office. This is committed when a public official knowingly and maliciously makes an unlawful decision which injures an individual. In *Roncarelli v Duplessis* (1959) 16 DLR (2d) 689, the defendant ordered the revocation of the plaintiff's liquor licence because he had annoyed the authorities by his lawful activities in support of an unpopular religious sect. The defendant knew the revocation was unlawful, but chose it as a good way to punish the plaintiff.

It is necessary to prove that the public official knew the decision was unlawful but went ahead with it anyway. To make a decision which subsequently proves to be unlawful does not give rise to any liability. In *Dunlop* v *Woollahra Municipal Council* [1982] AC 158, the Privy Council refused to impose liability on a local authority whose decision, taken in good faith, was later held to be ultra vires.

It is therefore going to be essential for Brown to prove that the decision was taken with the deliberate intention of infringing his rights. The mere invalidity of the decision will not in itself confer any right to damages.

Any attempt by Brown to obtain the documents which he thinks will reveal misfeasance may be met by a claim for public interest immunity from the Home Office. Such a claim may be based on the contents of the particular document, or on the assertion that that class of document needs, in the public interest, to be kept secret. As was made clear in *R* v *Chief Constable of the West Midlands Police ex parte Wiley* [1994] 3 All ER 420, if the Home Office does not think that the public interest would be harmed by revealing these documents, there is no obligation on it to claim public interest immunity.

The case of *Conway* v *Rimmer* [1968] AC 910 established that the decision on disclosure or otherwise rests with the court, not the government. The court has to balance two aspects of the public interest; on the one hand, the public interest in secrecy and confidentiality, and, on the other hand, the public interest in the fair administration of justice. Where necessary, the court may inspect the documents to help it decide whether disclosure should be ordered.

The Home Office may have two possible grounds for arguing that these documents should be kept secret. One is that the security of the hostel, its inmates and neighbours might be compromised if the documents were revealed. This does not appear to be very plausible, though security would generally be taken as a reasonable ground to use as a basis for secrecy. The other ground might be the confidentiality of civil service advice to ministers. It has been asserted in various cases that the candour of public officials, and hence their usefulness to ministers might be impaired if they knew their words might be revealed in later litigation. But the courts have shown themselves very unsympathetic to such claims, refusing to believe that officials, whose advice will in any case be preserved on file, will be frightened by the remote possibility of later litigation into failing to do their job properly. In *Williams* v *Home Office* [1981] 1 All ER 1151, this argument concerning candour was rejected and documents relating to penal policy revealed. In that case, inspection of the documents revealed them to be essential to the plaintiff's case, so that the court had no difficulty in holding that the public interest in the fair administration of justice prevailed.

In this problem, it may well be that the court will find it necessary to inspect the documents to discover whether they are necessary to Brown's case, because, if unnecessary, they need not be disclosed. In *Burmah Oil Co.* v *Bank of England* [1980] AC 1090, where sensitive papers were concerned, the court inspected them before deciding that their evidential value to the plaintiff was so limited as not to outweigh the genuine claim to confidentiality put forward by the Attorney-General. Brown is therefore in the hands of the court, which must perform the difficult task of balancing the two aspects of the public interest.

(c) The Home Office's liability to Green will have to be based on the claim that it has been in some way negligent in permitting Reg to assault him. Similar issues arose in the case of *Dorset Yacht Co. Ltd* v *Home Office* [1970] AC 1004, where the Home Office was held to be vicariously liable for the negligence of prison officers who failed to supervise a party of Borstal boys whom they had taken out on training exercises. The court denied any intention to pass judgment on the policy decision to take the boys out, rather than leaving them safely incarcerated. The liability arose from the negligence of the officers, who had been clearly instructed to supervise the boys carefully at all times. This rationale was further developed in *Anns* v *Merton LBC* [1978] AC 728, where the House of Lords laid down general guidelines on the liability of public authorities. First, the policy decisions made by public authorities would give rise to no tortious liablity unless the decisions were first demonstrated to be ultra vires, and then only if a duty of care could be imposed. Secondly there could be liability if there was negligence at the operational stage of putting the policy into practice.

This distinction was applied in cases like *Rigby* v *Chief Constable of Northants* [1985] 1 WLR 1242. Although the decision in *Anns* v *Merton LBC* was over-ruled in *Murphy* v *Brentwood DC* [1991] 1 AC 398 as far as the general law of tort was concerned, nothing in that decision referred to the distinction between policy and operational stages which therefore remains a valid basis for examining the liability of public authorities.

Applying these principles to Green's case, it will be very difficult for him to prove any liability arising from the policy decision to establish the hostel and send to it prisoners with convictions for crimes of violence. Such policy decisions can hardly be described as irrational and there is no suggestion of illegality or procedural impropriety. If those decisions are intra vires, no liability can ensue. Green would therefore have to demonstrate that liability arose at the operational stage. He could argue that there was negligence in the choice of Reg as an inmate, but Reg's record of impeccable behaviour in custody makes this difficult to sustain. The only possibility seems to be for Green to demonstrate that Reg was supposed to be under supervision at all times, and that the warden and his staff had failed in their duty. If, however, the Home Office had adopted the policy that part of the function of the hostel system was to allow the inmates a degree of freedom from supervision, it would again be necessary to show that this policy was ultra vires before any liability could be imposed.

It would therefore appear that Green may be unable to establish any liability on the part of the Home Office, in which case he will be left only with the right to sue the probably impecunious Reg.

QUESTION 2

How far is it true to say that the Crown, when involved in litigation, is in the same position as any other litigant before the English courts? Are any further reforms to proceedings involving the Crown necessary?

Commentary

This question covers a fairly wide range of issues relating to Crown proceedings and the student will need to be careful to pick up issues which may not all have been covered under that heading. Clearly, the Crown Proceedings Act will form the core of the answer, but there are still areas where common law rules remain applicable. There are further areas where other changes to the law have had an incidental effect upon the Crown, such as Crown service, which has been affected by the development of statutory rights for workers.

Suggested Answer

Until 1947, the Crown enjoyed substantial immunities from liability in English law, and benefited from various procedural advantages in litigation. These derived from historical developments. The impossiblity of subjecting the king to the jurisdiction of his own courts produced the paradoxical saying that 'the king could do no wrong'; because there was no remedy for those wrongs, they did not legally exist. But an immunity which originally attached to the person of the Monarch also applied if he exercised his powers through his servants and ministers. Though the individual servant might be personally liable, the Crown remained immune. When, through the development of parliamentary government, the exercise of the Crown's power was controlled by a government, the immunity remained intact. It was therefore impossible to sue the Crown in tort, and possible to sue in contract and restitution only with the permission of the Crown, if the Attorney-General granted his fiat to a petition of right.

It was, however, possible, in appropriate cases, for the victim of a tort to sue the individual Crown servant responsible. Dicey indeed regarded this as a powerful demonstration of the rule of law, as it forced the individual to accept responsibility for his or her own actions, rather than being able to hide behind some official immunity. But as a means of ensuring adequate compensation for the victim it was seriously defective, until the Crown developed the practice of standing behind its servants and paying any damages awarded against them. Even this did not help in those circumstances where tortious liability attached to the Crown itself, perhaps as employer or landowner, and not to any individual Crown servant. The cases of *Adams* v *Naylor* [1946] AC 543 and *Royster* v *Cavey* [1947] KB 204 showed that the courts were no longer willing to co-operate in evading the effects of Crown immunity by making findings of liability against nominated defendants who were not personally liable. Statutory reform, which had been under discussion for some years, was finally introduced.

The Crown Proceedings Act 1947, s. 2 subjects the Crown to the same liabilities in tort as a person of full age and capacity in the following respects. Most importantly, it is vicariously liable for torts committed by its servants or agents; by s. 6, Crown servants are defined as those directly or indirectly appointed by the Crown and paid out of the Consolidated Fund or other Treasury-controlled moneys. To avoid any suggestion of Crown interference in the judicial system, no such liability exists in respect of those acting in a judicial capacity. The only significant limitation on this form of liability, s. 2(1), gives the Crown the right to plead any defence which the servant could have pleaded. This includes not only the ordinary tort defences but defences like Act of State, which had developed to limit the liability of Crown servants. But as the case of *Nissan* v *Attorney-General* [1970] AC 179 showed, this defence is very limited in scope.

The other forms of tortious liability imposed by s. 2 are employers' liability to employees and liability arising from the ownership or occupation of property.

The Crown is also subjected to liability for breach of statutory duty, but this is subject to two limitations. First, the statutory duty must also be binding on persons other than the Crown. The Crown Proceedings Act is concerned only to extend the ordinary forms of tort liability to the Crown, not to create new forms of liability to which only the Crown could be subject. Secondly, by a common law rule expressly preserved by s. 40(2)(f), the Crown is not bound by statutes unless the statute so provides, expressly or by necessary implication. This rule has been the subject of stringent criticism, as making it far too easy for the Crown to evade liabilities and obligations to which it should be subject. It would be preferable if the presumption were reversed, as it would then be necessary for an express provision to be included in any statute to exempt the Crown from its provisions, thus alerting Parliament to the question.

There remain some specific limitations on the liability of the Crown in tort. Under s. 40(2) the Act only applies to liabilities arising in the UK. No action could therefore be brought, for example, in respect of a nuisance committed by the British Army in Berlin; *Trawnik* v *Lennox* [1985] 1 WLR 532. This seems an undesirable rule as the doctrine of state immunity may well prevent any action being brought in the foreign state either. A major problem arose as a result of s. 10, which exempted the Crown from liability for injuries caused to one member of the armed forces by the negligence of another, if the injury was classed as pensionable. But liability for such 'friendly fire' injuries was accepted by the Crown Proceedings (Armed Forces) Act 1987 and, though the Crown can revive its immunity in case of war or emergency, its failure to do so during the Gulf War may be taken as an encouraging precedent. It has in any case been held in *Mulcahy* v *Ministry of Defence, The Times,* 27 February 1996, that in battle conditions no soldier owes a duty of care to his fellow soldiers, nor does the Crown, as employer, owe any duty of care to military personnel in active combat.

The final issue in relation to tort liability is the provision in s. 40(1) which excludes the possibility of any action in tort against the Monarch in his or her personal capacity. Although this could be criticised, it is perhaps an appropriate way of preserving the Monarch's dignity. It is in any case difficult to imagine any circumstances in which the Monarch would have the opportunity to commit torts in person — perhaps a bite from a royal corgi? In any such case compensation would no doubt be paid ex gratia.

Turning to liability in contract, the Crown Proceedings Act 1947, s. 1 simply states that actions which could formerly have been brought by petition of right can now be brought as of right. Actions in contract against the Crown are now therefore straightforward, with the exception of actions against the Monarch in person which would have to use the old petition of right procedure.

The only area of contractual liability which has given rise to any substantial amount of litigation is the law of Crown service. At common law, Crown servants, both civil and military, were employed at the pleasure of the Crown and could therefore be dismissed at any moment, regardless of any terms in the contract; see *Dunn* v *R* [1896] 1 QB 116. This rule remains in the case of military personnel, whose engagement is not contractual at all; see *Mitchell* v *R* (1890), noted at [1896] 1 QB 121. But for civil servants, the law has been transformed by the extension to them of most of the statutory provisions governing employment. Civil servants are now entitled to redundancy payments, to compensation for unfair dismissal and to protection from racial and sexual discrimination. Although their common law rights remain limited, these are in general insignificant compared with statutory rights. Some categories of Crown servants continue to be governed by special rules, such as prison officers who are subject to strict disciplinary codes. The Crown's treatment of its employees has given rise to some disputes, such as the *GCHQ case* [1985] AC 374, but on the whole its behaviour compares satisfactorily with that of most large employers.

As far as other contractual litigation is concerned, few cases ever come to court. The Crown prefers to settle disputes by negotiation or arbitration, especially where sensitive matters, such as defence procurement, are involved. There have been suggestions in some cases that the Crown may be entitled to certain immunities in contract, but the Crown does not seem to assert these. Most sweeping was the suggestion in *Rederiaktiebolaget Amphitrite* v *R* [1921] 3 KB 500 that the Crown cannot by contract fetter its future freedom of action in matters affecting the welfare of the state. Taken literally, this would entitle the Crown to break any contract it has entered into, but it is doubtful that such a wide proposition can be supported. Indeed, it can be argued that in the case itself there was no actual contract, so the remarks were merely obiter. The Crown has in any case sufficiently wide statutory powers, especially in emergencies, to make such a common law doctrine unnecessary.

Another limitation on the contractual power of the Crown was suggested by the case of *Churchward* v *R* (1865) LR 1 QB 173, where a contract was awarded to Churchward on condition that moneys were voted by Parliament. When Parliament voted against the payment, the contract necessarily fell. It was argued that this made all government contracts dependent on money being voted by Parliament, but this was refuted by the Australian case of

Attorney-General of New South Wales v *Bardolph* (1934) 52 CLR 455, where
the state was held liable even in the absence of a specific vote of money,
provided that the contract was a proper one and was covered by a general vote
of funds. It remains possible, under the doctrine of Parliamentary supremacy,
for Parliament to forbid payments under a contract, and that would be legally
effective. It is not, however, the practice of the Crown to bankrupt its
contractors by refusing to pay its debts.

The Crown Proceedings Act preserves certain procedural immunities. By
s. 25(1) awards of damages against the Crown cannot be enforced by the usual
machinery of execution or attachment but this is no real problem. The Crown
will always be able to pay damages awarded against it and, on the rare
occasions when it does not wish to do so, as in *Burmah Oil* v *Lord Advocate*
[1965] AC 75, it will procure the passage of legislation to reverse the decision.
More serious is the provision in s. 21(1) that the courts cannot grant an
injunction, specific performance or an order for the delivery up of land against
the Crown. It must instead grant a declaration. This is generally satisfactory,
but in *International General Electric Co.* v *Commissioners of Customs and*
Excise [1962] Ch 784, interlocutory proceedings were unsuccessful because no
interim injunction could be granted and there was no such thing as an interim
declaration. This defect in the law was criticised by the Law Commission but
left unreformed. However, in *M* v *Home Office* [1994] 1 AC 377, the House of
Lords held that this did not preclude the granting of an injunction against a
particular Crown servant, even a minister acting in an official capacity. So,
although the Crown is not subject to these coercive remedies, its servants, who
carry out its tasks, are so subject. This demonstrates the willingness of the
courts to restrict the immunities and privileges of the Crown, which is further
illustrated by the historic decision in *Conway* v *Rimmer* [1968] AC 910 which
removed the Crown's absolute right to suppress evidence.

Such immunities as do survive do not seem to cause too many problems for
litigants, particularly as the Crown does not seek to rely on the more extreme
privileges suggested in the cases. But there needs to be continuing vigilance to
ensure that the rule of law is observed and the Crown subjected to the proper
degree of liability.

QUESTION 3

To what extent has English law developed specific rules of tortious liability for
public authorities? Do you consider that the tortious liability of public
authorities should be governed by separate rules?

Commentary

This question raises an issue which has been the subject of considerable debate among academic lawyers. There are great differences of opinion and no 'right' answers. This answer takes one particular perspective, but it would be perfectly possible to adopt a different view and produce an equally satisfactory answer. If the student has studied any comparative material, that would be a valuable addition to the answer. Some students may be studying or have studied tort, and would therefore be in a position to give a more sophisticated analysis of the tort issues involved; this answer does not assume any profound knowledge of tort law in general.

Suggested Answer

The English common law has always applied the same general rules of liability to public and private bodies. There were, particularly before the Crown Proceedings Act 1947, various immunities available to the Crown, though not to other public bodies, and these derived more from the survival of historical rules about remedies than from any theoretical principles about the liability of public bodies. When these immunities were reduced in 1947, the result was to impose on the Crown the ordinary rules of liability, as if it were a private individual.

To enquire why English law made no distinction between the liabilities of public and private bodies is to ask a question whose very existence would not have occurred to most English lawyers over the centuries. Asked about the powers of a corporation, or the rights of an individual, the lawyer would see no need to enquire further about the status of such a person, legal or natural. Provided that a remedy was available, legal redress would be given in accordance with the appropriate precedents, whether they related to public or private bodies. If it is possible to avoid drawing unnecessary distinctions, the law is wise to do so.

In other legal systems, however, the distinction between public and private law is seen as being part of the very fabric of the law, impossible to ignore. This is taken to extreme lengths in France, where a strict separation between the civil and administrative courts promoted the development of distinct principles of public and private liability. Although the administrative courts were happy to apply principles derived from the civil law where no need for special rules appeared, they developed such rules to cover those activities of the administration which have no parallel in the activities of ordinary citizens.

A basic justification for applying the same principles of liability to public and private bodies is that fairness, particularly to the victims of torts, requires that like cases be treated alike. It would clearly be undesirable if public authorities could lay claim to excessive immunities because of their status, and English law tries to prevent this. In *Pride of Derby Angling Association* v *British Celanese* [1953] Ch 149, the plaintiff's fishing rights were injured by discharges of untreated sewage from the Derby Corporation's treatment works. The corporation (the second defendant) argued that, as it was doing its best to provide an adequate sewage system, no injunction should be granted against it, but the court rejected that argument. The fact that it was a public body did not entitle it to commit nuisance.

But it is possible to argue that to impose on public authorities only those forms of liability which can be applied to private citizens is to ignore the extra opportunities available to public bodies to cause loss and suffering to individuals. Perhaps special rules of liability are needed to increase liability, rather than to diminish it. There is considerable pressure on the courts to impose such liability from litigants who see in public authorities potential defendants who are always going to be able to meet any award of damages and who are not going to disappear or go bankrupt. This has caused particular problems in relation to liability in negligence. An early example was the case of *Dorset Yacht Co.* v *Home Office* [1970] AC 1004, where the Home Office was held liable for the negligence of Borstal staff who failed to supervise properly a party of boys on a training exercise. Although primary liability rested with the boys themselves for the damage they had caused, their lack of money led the plaintiffs to sue the Home Office instead, which was held liable on principles deriving from *Donoghue* v *Stevenson* [1932] AC 562.

Subsequent cases, particularly those relating to the negligence of local authorities in the exercise of their discretionary powers, forced the courts to address the issue of the inter-relationship between public and private law in this area. Could public bodies be subjected to tortious liability in respect of decisions which were a lawful exercise of their discretion? This issue was addressed in *Anns* v *Merton LBC* [1978] AC 728, where Lord Wilberforce suggested a double test. For policy decisions, the question to be asked was whether the decision conformed to the public law standard of reasonableness; if it did, no duty of care should be imposed. But when that policy was put into operation, a duty of care could be imposed on normal tort principles, and liability established by private law rules.

The motive for this distinction was to avoid the danger of imposing liability on a public authority for a decision which was intra vires, but caused loss. In the

Dorset Yacht case, the court emphasised that it did not wish the government's penal policy to be determined by the fear of financial liability. It could, however, be argued that the risks involved in adopting an enlightened policy and taking Borstal boys out of confinement should be borne by society at large, not by those unfortunate enough to have their property damaged. The counter argument is that this would impose an open-ended liability on public authorities, though this risk has been reduced. In *Murphy* v *Brentwood DC* [1991] 1 AC 398, the House of Lords overruled *Anns* v *Merton LBC* (1978) as far as the general law of tortious liability for economic loss was concerned, though no comment was made on the distinction between operational and policy decisions, which therefore still appears to be of some value.

Where a public authority has acted ultra vires, there is a possibility of tortious liability, but subject to the ordinary law of tort. In *Cooper* v *Wandsworth Board of Works* (1863) 14 CBNS 180, the plaintiff was awarded damages for a trespass committed as a result of a breach of natural justice. But if only economic loss is caused, no liability will exist. In *Dunlop* v *Woollahra Municipal Council* [1982] AC 158, the plaintiff could not recover damages for the losses he had suffered when the Council had invalidly refused him planning permission. Only in the unusual situation of a decision based on malice will the tort of misfeasance in a public office allow the recovery of damages, as in *Roncarelli* v *Duplessis* [1959] SCR 121.

English law may be forced by European Community law to develop new principles in this area. In the case of *Francovich* v *Italian Republic* C-6/90 [1991] ECR 1-5357, the state was held liable for the losses caused by its failure to implement an EC Directive. The basis for this form of liability will no doubt be developed by the European Court of Justice, and may in time persuade the English courts to develop new principles for domestic liability.

In conclusion, the English courts have generally tried to maintain their basic principle of liability for public authorities, with only a few exceptions. But the continuing pressure from litigants for means of redress is likely to lead to more debate on the proper extent of public liability. On rare occasions, the government may concede a moral obligation to pay compensation even in the absence of legal liability, but more often it will be left to the courts to determine these questions.

QUESTION 4

Consider the following situations in the light of the doctrine of public interest immunity.

(a) Smith was employed by Proton plc in their factory making nuclear warheads for Britain's missile defence system. He was killed in an explosion in the factory. His widow wishes to establish that the defective design of the warheads, or of the system for making them, caused the explosion, and so recover damages from Proton plc.

(b) A charity wishes to seek judicial review of the Home Office's plan to lock up young offenders in secure training centres. It believes that civil servants in the Home Office research department advised the Home Secretary that the scheme would make the offenders more delinquent, not less. The Home Office says all advice to ministers is confidential.

(c) Farmer Giles was shocked to receive a visit from animal welfare inspectors from the RSPCA, who said they had been informed that he was keeping veal calves in illegal crates. This accusation was wholly untrue. When Giles tried to discover the source of the accusation, the RSPCA said that it was their policy never to reveal the identity of their informants, in order to encourage people to inform them of cases of cruelty to animals.

Commentary

As the question makes clear, its principal concern is the doctrine of public interest immunity. It is therefore appropriate to begin with a brief introductory paragraph explaining what public interest immunity is and how it developed, though it would be wrong in such a problem question to write a detailed history. In each part of the question, the student needs to identify briefly the subject matter of the litigation and the parties to it, but the bulk of the answer should be devoted to PII. Because it is a matter for the discretion of the court whether the claim to PII is upheld in any case, the student will be assessed not on the correctness or otherwise of the final conclusion, but on the quality of the arguments deployed, and the depth of knowledge of decided cases.

Suggested Answer

The doctrine of public interest immunity (PII) is intended to ensure that documents are not revealed in the course of litigation if it is not in the public interest that they should be revealed. Originally such a claim could only be made by the Crown and was therefore known as Crown privilege. In *Duncan v Cammell Laird* [1942] AC 624, the House of Lords laid down the unfortunate rule that any claim made by the Crown had to be accepted by the courts, but in

Conway v *Rimmer* [1968] AC 910, this rule was reversed, and the courts themselves took the responsibility of assessing whether or not it would be in the public interest for the documents to be disclosed.

(a)   In this problem, Mrs Smith will be suing her late husband's employers, Proton plc, for negligence in failing to provide him with a safe system of work. She will therefore need the plans of the warheads and of the manufacturing system in order to identify the defects which gave rise to the explosion. But the Ministry of Defence is certainly going to claim that it would be against the public interest for these plans to be disclosed. That claim may be made in spite of the fact that the ministry is not a party to the case. Because of the adversarial nature of Engish legal proceedings, disclosing the documents means revealing them to the parties, their solicitors and barristers as well as to the judge. The possibility of hearing the case in camera does not eliminate the danger of the documents getting into the wrong hands.

In *Conway* v *Rimmer* (1968), the House of Lords laid down that, in deciding whether documents should be disclosed or not, two aspects of the public interest had to be balanced. Firstly, there was a public interest in ensuring that no harm was done to the national interest by disclosing documents which should be kept secret. But secondly, there was a public interest in ensuring that the conduct of litigation was not frustrated. The court distinguished between claims based on the contents of the particular document and those based merely on the class to which the documents belonged. Contents claims would generally be much stronger than class claims. If necessary, the court could inspect the documents to identify the strengths of the arguments for and against disclosure.

Applying these principles to the case of Mrs Smith, it seems very probable that her chances of establishing liability will be almost completely dependent on access to the documents, which, if they do reveal design flaws, will virtually prove her case by themselves. The litigation will be frustrated if she cannot gain access to them. But the arguments against disclosure are particularly powerful. The PII claim will be based on the contents of the documents themselves, and it is hardly possible to dispute an assertion that it would pose a grave threat to national security if the plans of the nuclear deterrent fell into the wrong hands, or if designs indicating how to build a nuclear warhead came into the possession of terrorists. Inspection of the documents is not likely to be necessary to convince the court that these are genuine state secrets. Comparison may be made with *Duncan* v *Cammell Laird* (1942) where the Admiralty was clearly justified in wishing to keep secret the plans of its latest submarine.

There is no doubt that the courts do have the power to order the disclosure even of documents as sensitive as these in the interests of justice, but it is doubtful whether they would do so in this case.

(b) The charity's application for judicial review may be based on the unreasonableness of the Home Office's decision or on the failure to take relevant considerations into account. Under the principle laid down in *Conway* v *Rimmer* (1968) it will be for the court to decide whether the public interest in confidentiality or the public interest in the fair conduct of litigation should prevail.

It appears that the Home Office's objection to the disclosure of documents in this case is based not on the contents of the particular documents, but on the claim that documents containing advice to ministers are a class which need to be kept confidential. The justification for this claim has been explained as the danger that officials might be deterred from being completely candid in their advice to ministers if they knew that such information might one day be revealed to the world through its use in litigation. But the courts have generally been unsympathetic to such assertions. In *Conway* v *Rimmer* (1968) such an argument was advanced in respect of the reports prepared by police officers on the conduct of a probationer, but the court rejected it. They pointed out that any such report would be protected by qualified privilege, so the official would have nothing to fear provided the report was honest. This point was also raised in *Williams* v *Home Office* [1981] 1 All ER 1151, where the court ordered the Home Office to disclose various documents including advice to ministers on the development of penal policy, rejecting the argument that the candour of public servants might be hindered by the remote chance of later disclosure in litigation. It would therefore appear that, unless some other, stronger argument for non-disclosure is presented to the court, the court may feel that the case for secrecy has not been made out.

Turning to the other side of the balance, the court will need to be satisfied that the disclosure of the documents is necessary for the fair conduct of the litigation. In *Air Canada* v *Secretary of State for Trade* [1983] 2 AC 394, this was interpreted as meaning that the applicants must show that it is very likely that the documents sought do contain material supportive of their case; applicants cannot embark on 'fishing' expeditions by demanding any document whether or not they have any grounds for thinking it material evidence. But once the applicants have passed this threshold, it may well be appropriate for the court to inspect the documents, because if they do not in fact assist the applicants' case, there is no need to order disclosure.

In this problem, the applicants seem to have good grounds for suggesting that the documents from the research department will assist their case, by demonstrating that relevant considerations were ignored. The court may feel that this is sufficient to justify an order for disclosure, given the weakness of the opposing case, or may feel it better to inspect the documents before coming to a conclusion. Only if the documents fail to support the applicants' case at all is it likely that disclosure will be refused.

(c) Before *Conway* v *Rimmer*, the term Crown privilege demonstrated clearly that claims for non-disclosure could be made only by the Crown. But in *Rogers* v *Home Secretary* [1973] AC 388, the claim was made by the Gaming Board which, though a public body, was not a government department. The House of Lords stated that claims based on the public interest could be made by any interested party, not just the Crown. This was applied in *D* v *NSPCC* [1978] AC 171, where the defendant, a charitable voluntary organisation, with a recognised status in the protection of children, was held able to claim PII in respect of certain confidential information. It would therefore be open to the RSPCA to raise an issue of PII in this case.

The basis of their claim is the need to offer complete confidentiality to informants who might otherwise be reluctant to contact them. Such claims have been accepted by the courts as being in the public interest. The case of *Rogers* v *Home Secretary* (1973) concerned confidential information supplied to the Gaming Board about an applicant for a gaming licence. The court accepted that, in the sometimes murky world of gaming, informants needed to be given an absolute guarantee of confidentiality. In *D* v *NSPCC* (1978) the charity was held to be justified in claiming that confidentiality served the vital function of encouraging people to report suspected child abuse.

Whether the court would feel that the same justification applied in the case of cruelty to animals is not clear. But such activity can be criminal and the RSPCA is active in prosecution, so it seems that they could assert a public interest in the enforcement of the law. To obtain information about such organised cruelty as cock-fighting or badger-baiting might well require promises of complete confidentiality for informers.

To set against this is the public interest in the fair conduct of litigation. Clearly Giles will be unable to bring proceedings for defamation against the informant if he cannot discover who the informant was, and this may seem unfair, particularly as the defamation may even have been malicious. But the court may feel, as they did in *D* v *NSPCC* (1978) that this is a price worth paying for the better protection of the vulnerable.

Index